D0518396

¡BAJA!

COOKING ON THE EDGE

¡BAJA!

COOKING ON THE EDGE

DEBORAH M. SCHNEIDER

PHOTOGRAPHS BY MAREN CARUSO

RODALE

Notice

Mention of specific companies, organizations, or authorities in this book does not imply endorsement by the publisher,
nor does mention of specific companies, organizations, or authorities imply that they endorse this book.
Internet addresses and telephone numbers given in this book were accurate at the time it went to press.

© 2006 by Deborah M. Schneider
Photographs © 2006 by Maren Caruso

All rights reserved. No part of this publication may be reproduced or transmitted in any form or by any means, electronic or mechanical,
including photocopying, recording, or any other information storage and retrieval system, without the written permission of the publisher.

Printed in the United States of America
Rodale Inc. makes every effort to use acid-free ♾, recycled paper ♲.

Book design by Ellen Nygaard

Permission to use the lyrics for "Mexican Radio," by Stan Ridgway and Wall of Voodoo, on page 1,
has been graciously provided by Stan Ridgway. Check out his other work at www.stanridgway.com.

Library of Congress Cataloging-in-Publication Data

Schneider, Deborah M.
    Baja! cooking on the edge / Deborah M. Schneider; photographs by Maren Caruso.
        p.   cm.
    Includes index.
    ISBN-13 978–1–59486–203–8   hardcover
    ISBN-10 1–59486–203–6   hardcover
    1. Cookery, Mexican.   2. Cookery—Mexico—Baja California (Peninsula)   I. Title.
TX716.M4S36   2006
641.5972'2—dc22   2006005170

Distributed to the book trade by Holtzbrinck Publishers

2 4 6 8 10 9 7 5 3 1   hardcover

We inspire and enable people to improve their lives and the world around them

For more of our products visit **rodalestore.com** or call 800-848-4735

To my stepfather, J. Howard Aitken,
who fed me wild trout, morels he gathered himself,
fiddleheads, and watercress from the streams of Huron County.
His old *Gourmet* magazines and *'Glorious Food'*
started me on my culinary path.
And with endless love and gratitude
to my mother, Margaret Aitken.

CONTENTS

¡GRACIAS!

Writing *¡Baja! Cooking on the Edge* has been by turns enlightening, exciting, and humbling. There is so much more to say than what we managed to get into this book. At every turn, I met generous people whose deep understanding and love of Baja California opened my eyes to the bigger picture and helped me fully appreciate this wonderful place and its people. To all of you, my deepest appreciation.

Thanks to my family, Barry, Anne, and Willy, for selflessly eating their way through the research, testing, and writing of this book. My boundless gratitude to my extraordinary friend and agent, Carole Bidnick, truly a gift from above; also to my Rodale editor, Miriam Backes, for her patience, humor, and keen eye for detail. Thanks also to Rodale designer Ellen Nygaard, Nancy Bailey, Jean Rogers, Wendy Hess, and the entire Rodale team. You all "got" *¡Baja!* right from the start and made it a beautiful reality. Antonia "Toni" Allegra, another gift to my life, encouraged me to write and as a bonus, came up with the title for *¡Baja!* Thanks to Maren Caruso for her gorgeous photography, EK for the food styling, and Arnu for carrying the bag. A very big thank-you to Sherry Lama, who tested the recipes and lived to tell the tale!

Thanks also to my fellow chefs and food lovers who shared their knowledge so generously: Benito Mira-fuentes, the best cook I know; Felipa Ortiz, Denise Roa, and Liliaana Navarette; Manny Lopez Sr. (known to all as "El Presidente"); Melinda Perez and Joe Saldana (*mi amigo chismoso*) and his mother. A very affectionate thank-you goes out to all my kitchen *compadres* over the years, wherever you are now. Thank you for your hard work, your patience, and your humor when things got rough and for showing me the true meaning of dignity in life and work.

Special thanks to Lic. Maria Teresa Matamoros Montes of Baja California's Secretariat of Tourism for her assistance and friendship—see you at McD's! Antonio and Natalia Badan of El Mogor Badan, Dr. Hans Back-hoff, and Leticia Backhoff of Monte Xanic, and Eduardo Liceaga and Dr. Enrique Ferro, of Vinos de Liceaga, graciously shared with me their stories of the Valley. I wish I could have gotten every word of it down in this book. Hugo and Gloria d' Acosta of Casa de Piedra; Chef Jair Tellez, Laja Restaurant; Don and Tru Miller, *patrones* of Adobe Guadalupe, and Chef Martin San Roman, of Rincon San Roman, all took the time to tell me about their experiences in the Valley. Gary Sehnert and Fernando Favela put their educated palates to work to match Baja wines, their passion, with many of the dishes in this book. Special appreciation to Serge Dedina of Wildcoast for his insight on sustainable fisheries and his work to preserve the wild Baja California I love.

Last but certainly not least, I want to recognize all those brave spirits who created the Baja legend over decades of surfing, exploring, fishing, and just hanging out. Your spirit of adventure, your love, and your respect for Baja inspired me to write *¡Baja! Cooking on the Edge*. See you on the beach!

San Diego

Tijuana ● Tecate

Mexicali

U.S.A.

Puerto Nuevo

GUADALUPE VALLEY

Ensenada

San Felipe

Gulf of California
(Sea of Cortés)

Mexico

Pacific Ocean

Loreto

La Paz

BASIC MAP OF

¡BAJA!

CALIFORNIA

Cabo San Lucas

San José del Cabo

INTRODUCTION

Untamed and largely untouched, Baja California still has the wild allure of an uncharted frontier. Thousands of miles of ruggedly beautiful coastline give onto forbidding desert; steep mountains rise from bleak volcanic plains riddled with treacherous, bone-dry canyons. Baja is perhaps the last truly unspoiled region in all of North America. Surely it is no one's idea of paradise, but no one who *really* experiences Baja is ever the same.

You never forget the perfect clarity of the Baja sky and the sharp-edged shadows that lie across the jagged slopes of an unconquered *sierra* while the relentless wind ruffles the ocean and screams up the mountainsides. By night, the Milky Way hangs in three vivid dimensions while falling stars flare across constellations unsullied by city lights and waves crash on a deserted beach. Teeming with life, the restless ocean changes color along the peninsula—cold Pacific green at Ensenada, diamond-dazzling blue at Cabo San Lucas, soft azure in the Gulf of California (the Sea of Cortés) off San Felipe. Baja wins your imagination and never lets you go.

Early explorers, drawn by stories of fabulous pearls, speculated that mysterious Baja California was really an island populated by Amazons and mythical beasts. Buccaneers hid along the hazy coastline, darting out to prey on Spanish treasure ships and other passing traffic. Over the centuries, fortunes were lost and hearts broken as successive waves of trailblazers attempted to conquer and civilize a land so daunting that to this day much of it remains virtually uninhabited.

Here in the extreme southwest corner of North America, life is defined by the ocean, the deserts, and *la frontera*—the border. Separated from mainland Mexico by the Gulf of California, Baja has always felt the influence of *el norte*—the United States. Americans discovered Baja in the early years of the 20th century, when Hollywood stars, gangsters, and gamblers headed across the border to party in Tijuana and Ensenada.

In the period before the Second World War, Baja lured adventurers in the mold of Hemingway to try themselves against massive marlin and swordfish in the waters off Cabo San Lucas. Intrepid "Baja rats" explored the deserted peninsula even before there were roads, creeping into every remote canyon and cove, to camp, fish, and, eventually, surf.

In 1940, John Steinbeck visited the Baja coastline with his friend Ed Ricketts on a biological expedition. The resulting book, *The Log from the Sea of Cortez,* is a remarkable work of memoir, observation, and pure wonder. Here, he evokes the spell that Baja California casts on all who travel there:

> ...*Some quality there is in the whole Gulf that trips a trigger of recognition so that in fantastic and exotic scenery one finds oneself nodding and saying inwardly, 'Yes, I know.' . . . Trying to remember the Gulf is like trying to re-create a dream. This is by no means a sentimental thing, it has little to do with beauty or even conscious liking. But the Gulf does draw one . . . There is always in the backs of our minds the positive drive to go back again. If it were lush and rich, one could understand the pull, but it is fierce and hostile and sullen. The stone mountains pile up to the sky and there is little fresh water. But we know we must go back if we live, and we don't know why.*

> John Steinbeck, *The Log from the Sea of Cortez,* 1940

By the time I first visited Baja California, over 20 years ago, I'd already had my share of adventure. I had left a safe office job as a magazine editor to spend 18 months traveling by motorcycle and camping in western Europe, the Canary Islands, and the rougher parts of North Africa. Along the way, I took my first professional cooking jobs, on charter yachts sailing the Greek Islands. Soon after, through a series of coincidences, I found myself living in San Diego—and it was not long until I discovered Baja nearby.

Well traveled as I was, nothing prepared me for this remarkable place or how it would change my cooking and my whole attitude toward food. First, of course, I encountered wild Baja. Many times, my surfer fiancé and I traveled in caravan (along with other Baja rats), deep into the peninsula, driving south for many hours, finally leaving the paved road to turn toward ocean or gulf. The trail of trucks would creep at single-digit speeds in clouds of dust along red dirt tracks, through a desert landscape completely empty of human settlement. At length, battered and choked with dirt, we would arrive on the coast, set up camp, and live on the beach for days or weeks, surfing and fishing, eating what we brought and what we caught. Many times, these secret Baja places were utterly pristine, free of humans, pollution, and trash—and we left them that way. It was like Eden, like earth before man.

By this time, I was a full-fledged restaurant chef in San Diego, cooking serious California cuisine but hungering for the tastes I found south of the border. My Mexican co-workers began to teach me the basics. We would fill in slow hours at work talking about their *pueblos* and the regional dishes their mothers and grandmothers cooked. I fell in love with *real* Mexican food, fascinated as much by the mix of cultures and cuisines as by the fresh, sprightly flavors.

All the while, at street stands and markets, at backyard barbecues and local *fiestas*, I was tasting and learning the ingenious way that *bajacalifornianos* combined traditional Mexican flavors and local ingredients to make something intriguingly different, inspired by the ocean and influenced by waves of immigration and proximity to the U.S. border. It was unlike anything else I had ever encountered—light, simple, vibrantly fresh and delicious, full of the flavors of the sea and land, and uniquely Baja.

I learned how, despite all odds, determined people have for centuries managed to gain a foothold in Baja's difficult terrain and make a life there. Native Americans feasted on abalone, mussels, deer, and acorn mush. Hungry settlers turned the plentiful abalone into a kind of chorizo sausage and made a form of dried jerky by substituting the wings of bat rays for the usual beef. Spanish missionaries planted and patiently nurtured their groves of grapes, olives, and wheat. Ranchers ran cattle and horses. Subsistence fishermen young and old fearlessly harvested a rain of silver from the chilly Pacific. From Asia came laborers and entrepreneurs, fishermen and traders. All these remarkable people left indelible traces in the culture and foodways of Baja.

My experiences in Baja challenged and inspired me to look at food and cooking technique in a new way. This book is the result: a culinary homage, inspired by the firsthand tastes of Baja and interpreted through my own experiences into delicious recipes emphasizing simple, light flavors, quick and easy techniques, and salsas that dazzle.

Baja's bounty continues to amaze and inspire me. From the coastline come beautiful fish and shellfish. The markets overflow with chiles and perfect vegetables and fruits. Northern Baja is the largest wine-growing region in Mexico, and the wines of Baja are winning international attention. And the cuisine continues to evolve, as well-traveled young *bajacaliforniano* chefs return to their roots, bringing with them their experience cooking in the United States, Europe, and Asia. They are creating a new and exciting modern Baja cuisine that honors the seasons and local products.

Change is as constant as the Baja wind. A second wave of American interest in Baja has begun, this one fueled by wealthy speculators. Remote coastal villages are being eyed for development into luxurious super-resorts along the lines of Cabo San Lucas, Cozumel, and Puerto Vallarta. Instead of a convoy of battered trucks driving for days through miles of desert (and many adventures) to reach a remote surf break, thousands of tourists fly in by the jumbo-jet load.

Will they experience true Baja? Probably not. But development *will* happen. Poorly planned development could destroy estuaries, affect bird migration and whale breeding, deplete water tables, and impact coastal fisheries. And if undertaken without infrastructure and planning for desalinization and sewage, development could result in sprawling slums surrounding a few fortress-like resorts.

The natural treasure that is Baja must be preserved. Well-planned development, with long-term vision, will bring good jobs to the people of Baja California. Global attention focused on sensitive natural sites like the Gulf of California (recently designated a World Heritage site) will help prevent the wrong kind of exploitation. As the world has fewer and fewer truly wild places, ecotourism will become a tremendous source of revenue as well as pride for the people of Baja.

If I were to wish on a Baja star, it would be to ask that for generations to come, people will find still the peace, the beauty, and, yes, the adventure that is Baja California. And that my favorite fish taco stand will always be there, under the brilliant Baja sky.

1
BARBECUED IGUANA
STREET FOOD

I wish I was in Tijuana
Eating barbecued iguana
I'd take requests on the telephone
I'm on a wavelength far from home
I feel a hot wind on my shoulder
I dial it in from south of the border...
From "Mexican Radio," by Stan Ridgway and Wall of Voodoo

On the byways of Baja, there isn't a burrito in sight. Any day, in any town, you can choose from a vast array of made-to-order tacos and salsas, fresh-from-the-ocean seafood *cockteles*, grilled corn, succulent fruits skewered with lime and chili powder, vivid fruit juices, piping hot cinnamon *churros*, neon bright candies that stick in your teeth, and frozen treats with names like Angel's Kiss . . . and that's just the beginning.

Sorry, burger lords, this is the kind of fast food that *everyone* should eat.

Anything that can be grilled, fried, diced, stuck on a stick or in a plastic cup, or wrapped in a tortilla can be had for a few pesos—some is quite imaginative, some just too weird for *los turistas*. (Brains? Got 'em— unless, of course, you'd prefer eyeballs?) Everything is delicious and absolutely fresh.

Street food's allure is immediacy and freshness. The shortest distance from cook to palate is what every chef strives for, and here you have food made before your eyes and handed to you, still sizzling. The salsas were made that day; the tortillas are steaming warm from the *comal* (the griddle). No restaurant can dupli-cate this experience or the sheer pleasure of watching the world go by and eating the same food that, with a few variations, the Mexican people have been eating for thousands of years. Street food and traditional salsas are truly living culinary history.

1

Bajacalifornianos cook what they have, creating a culinary identity all their own. Centuries of near-isolation from mainland Mexico (back in the 16th century, the peninsula was thought to be an island) left Baja to create its own culinary identity, grounded in Mexican tradition but open to outside influences. Cooks take what they like from the rest of Mexico and the world and combine it with the materials at hand to create a special kind of Baja twist.

The obvious example is the Baja fish taco. Legend has it that Asian fishermen long ago inspired the idea of slipping a crisp, deep-fried piece of fish into a taco and topping it with a couple of unusual salsas. Tempura technique plus local ingredients equals an early kind of fusion cooking. The fish taco isn't the only instance of obvious Asian influence: Street stands in Ensenada offer teriyaki tacos and comal-roasted chiles grilled with lime juice and soy sauce. Sashimi-quality raw fish may be dressed with soy sauce, cilantro, and serrano chiles.

Early Baja cooks did not have easy access to meat, so they learned to make local abalone and shrimp into seafood chorizo and put bluefin tuna instead of pork into tamales. *Machaca,* made of dried shredded meat in the rest of Mexico, was made instead with the wings of manta rays. In Puerto Nuevo, they deep-fried spiny lobster and wrapped the succulent tail meat, cowboy style, in large flour tortillas with refried beans, a drizzle of melted butter, and a spurt of sweet-tart *limón*. A fish soup made from cold-water Pacific seafood might be tempered with a habanero salsa drawn from the traditional cuisine of the decidedly tropical Yucatán. A modest *fonda* (café) offers grilled quail for lunch—a gourmet item in the United States but a common snack in northern Baja, where the backcountry fairly teems with these game birds.

Baja cooking continues to evolve, as the inescapable influence of *el norte* creeps across the border in a mingling of ingredients and techniques. In the proud tradition of fusion chefs everywhere, a *taquero* who cooked in American restaurants before opening his own stand back home might grill fish rather than fry it or use chicken rather than pork or beef in tacos, add a touch of soy sauce, basil, or cola in his marinades, or include a modern fruit salsa of his own invention alongside traditional condiments.

The simplicity of street foods makes them a great place for home cooks to start learning the basics: tortilla making, roasting and toasting chiles and aromatics, the many types and uses of salsas, and some fundamental techniques you'll use time and again.

About that iguana? I'm still looking, but I haven't given up. I hear it tastes just like—you guessed it— chicken. Really good, lemon-flavored chicken.

RECIPES

Fish Tacos "La Bufadora"

The fish taco defines the best of Baja, one bite at a time. And like all great street food, the perfect fish taco is very, very simple. Success relies on fresh ingredients, the technique of "double frying" described below, and most of all, speedy service. The fish must be cooked in front of you and eaten within a minute of leaving the fryer. It's hard for a sit-down restaurant to pull off but easy to do in a home kitchen or at a backyard gathering.

This is a very authentic recipe: A *real* fish taco is always on a corn tortilla, never flour. It is always beer-battered and deep-fried, never grilled. And it must have cabbage on it, not lettuce, plus that runny white "secret" sauce (really no secret at all).

The double-frying technique is essential. It speeds up the final cooking (especially for a crowd) and makes for crisper fish. If you don't double-fry, the fish takes a long time to cook and may become soggy instead of brown. Best of all, precooking allows you to do most of the work ahead of time and then at the last minute quickly refry the fish and heat tortillas to order—just like the cooks do at fish taco stands.

Makes 24 tacos, enough for 6 to 8 people

2 cups all-purpose flour

1½ teaspoons baking powder

½ teaspoon granulated garlic

¼ teaspoon cayenne

½ teaspoon dry mustard

½ teaspoon dried whole Mexican oregano, rubbed to a powder

Kosher salt

½ teaspoon freshly ground black pepper

12 ounces (1 bottle) cold beer, plus more to thin the batter if necessary

2 pounds firm, meaty fish (see page 52 for a list of sustainable species)

Freshly squeezed lime juice, preferably from Mexican limones (see page 30)

Vegetable oil, for deep-frying

TO SERVE

Fresh corn tortillas, warmed

Avocado Sauce (see page 34)

Lime wedges, preferably from Mexican limones (see page 30)

Mayonesa Secret Sauce (see page 37)

Salsa de Chiles de Arbol #1 (see page 38)

Pico de Gallo (see page 30)

Finely shredded green cabbage (not lettuce!)

Cilantro leaves (optional)

Chopped white onion (optional)

1. Make the batter: Whisk together the flour, baking powder, garlic, cayenne, mustard, oregano, 1 teaspoon salt, and pepper until well blended. Stir in the beer until there are no lumps. (Batter may be made several hours ahead and refrigerated.)

2. Trim the fish of all blood lines and skin. Cut into pieces the size and shape of your index finger. Sprinkle with a few drops of lime juice and a little salt. (If not using immediately, wrap and refrigerate.)
Pour the oil into a deep, wide pan to a depth of 2 inches and heat over medium-high heat to 350 degrees. (See Safe Frying, page 248. I use a deep-fry thermometer, but I also test the heat by dropping a little of the batter into the oil. It should bounce to the surface almost immediately and be surrounded by little bubbles.)

3. Pat the fish dry with paper towels. Check the thickness of the batter by dipping in one piece of the fish. The batter should be the consistency of medium-thick pancake batter, coating the fish easily but dripping very little. Add a little beer if the batter seems too thick.

4. Add the fish to the batter. Using tongs or chopsticks, swish each piece to make sure it is thoroughly coated, then lift it out of the batter, let it drip once, and lay the fish gently into the hot oil. Cook a few pieces at a time until they float and the batter is set but still very light in color. (Note: If a piece sticks to the bottom, leave it alone—it will release itself.)

5. Remove the fish to a rack to drain; reserve the frying oil. (The fish can be prepared ahead to this point, cooled on a rack, and refrigerated uncovered. Cool the oil and reserve.)

6. When you are ready to serve, reheat the oil to 350 to 360 degrees and refry the fish a few pieces at a time until crisp and golden brown.

7. To serve, hold a tortilla in your hand and add a spoonful of avocado sauce. Top with fish and squeeze lime over the whole thing. Then drizzle on a little secret sauce and a few drops of árbol sauce. Top with pico de gallo and shredded cabbage, and maybe a cilantro leaf or some extra white onions.

Notes: Typically a small shark known as *angelito* is used for fish tacos. Since sharks are thought by some biologists to be threatened, please choose a sustainable fish (see page 52) that is firm and meaty.

I use an ingenious Mexican pan for frying fish tacos. Called a *disca*, it looks suspiciously like a car hubcap with a very wide rim. You fry in the deep well and drain the pieces on the rim, which also keeps everything nice and warm. If you can't find a disca, cook the fish in a large frying pan or sauté pan; drain on a wire rack set on a rimmed cookie sheet.

FOOD ON THE RUN:
PUESTOS, TAQUERÍAS, AND FONDAS

Anyplace you stand up and grab a bite to eat, whether it has wheels or not, is called a *puesto* (Spanish for post or stall). If it has no wheels and there is a seat or two, it becomes a *taquería*. Food here is always cooked to order.

Small sit-down restaurants known as *fondas* serve full meals of what is called *comida corrida* (food on the run), premade food such as *moles*, *birria*, and enchiladas dished up from steam tables and served in a hurry.

Cafeterías and *loncherías* are true restaurants, larger in size, with a long menu of full meals in a diner-like setting with table service.

Grilled Fish Tacos

Some touristy Baja restaurants offer grilled fish tacos, but they are an American invention, never seen at *puestos* or *taquerías*. Nothing will ever replace a true fish taco in my heart, though a grilled fish taco is significantly lighter and tasty—once in a while.

The fish is marinated in a zippy fresh citrus bath and quickly grilled. I like to serve these with, among other things, mango salsa (if you're going to break with tradition, you may as well go all the way). Pico de gallo and the usual rip-roaring bottled hot sauce round things out.

When you shop for fish, please choose a sustainable species (see page 52). I also recommend using a special fish grilling basket to prevent sticking.

Makes 24 tacos, enough for 6 to 8 people

MARINADE

2 tablespoons finely diced white onion
2 tablespoons olive oil
2 tablespoons freshly squeezed lime juice, preferably from a Mexican limón (see page 30)
2 tablespoons freshly squeezed orange juice
1 tablespoon freshly squeezed lemon juice
1 tablespoon chopped cilantro
1 teaspoon minced garlic
$\frac{1}{2}$ teaspoon dried whole Mexican oregano, rubbed to a powder
$\frac{1}{4}$ teaspoon kosher salt

$1\frac{1}{2}$ pounds boneless, skinless white fish fillets

TO SERVE

Fresh corn tortillas, warmed
Diced avocado, Avocado Sauce (see page 34), or Naked Guacamole (see page 34)
Lime wedges, preferably from Mexican limones (see page 30)
Mango Salsa (see page 47)
Salsa de Chiles de Arbol #1 (see page 38) or bottled hot sauce
Pico de Gallo (see page 30), shredded white cabbage, cilantro sprigs, and diced white onion (optional)

1. Combine all marinade ingredients. Cut the fish into several large pieces and add to the marinade.

2. Refrigerate for 1 to 3 hours (no longer or you'll have ceviche). Drain the fish and discard the marinade.

3. Half an hour before cooking, clean the grill thoroughly with a brush and wipe it down with an oil-dampened rag. Preheat the grill on high. Grill the fish until it is barely firm to the touch and opaque through the center. Do not overcook.

4. Remove to a platter and break into chunks to serve. Keep loosely covered.

5. To serve, hold a tortilla in your hand and add a spoonful of avocado. Add a few pieces of fish, a squeeze of lime, mango salsa, and árbol salsa; finish with the optional toppings.

Note: The fish may also be baked or sautéed.

Variations: Substitute Man Bites Shark marinade (see page 73) or Achiote Marinade (see page 142).

Shrimp Tacos

The only thing that comes close to being as good as a fish taco is a shrimp taco, and most stands sell both. The batter for shrimp tacos is spicier and thicker, and it fries up crunchier. Salsas and condiments are much the same, but some prefer shredded lettuce to cabbage and add chopped red onion. It's your taco, so do what you want.

Before frying the shrimp, make sure everything is ready to serve: The salsas and condiments are on the table, and the tortillas are warm.

Makes 24 tacos, enough for 6 to 8 people

2 pounds best-quality large shrimp, preferably Mexican, peeled and deveined
$\frac{1}{2}$ lime, preferably Mexican limón (see page 000)

BATTER

Scant 1$\frac{1}{2}$ cups all-purpose flour
$\frac{1}{2}$ cup rice flour (available at Latin markets)
1$\frac{1}{2}$ teaspoons baking powder
$\frac{3}{4}$ teaspoon granulated garlic
$\frac{3}{4}$ teaspoon cayenne
$\frac{1}{2}$ teaspoon dried whole Mexican oregano, rubbed to a powder
1$\frac{1}{2}$ teaspoons kosher salt
$\frac{1}{2}$ teaspoon freshly ground black pepper
12 ounces (1 bottle) cold beer, plus more to thin the batter if necessary

Vegetable oil

TO SERVE

Fresh corn tortillas, warmed
Avocado Sauce (see page 34)
Mayonesa Secret Sauce (see page 47)
Salsa de Chiles de Arbol #1 (see page 38) or bottled hot sauce
Shredded iceberg lettuce or green cabbage
Pico de Gallo (see page 30)
Diced red onion mixed with chopped cilantro (optional)
Lime wedges, preferably from Mexican limones (see page 30)

1. Cut each shrimp into two or three pieces. Spritz a little lime over the shrimp to moisten—don't overdo it—and refrigerate.
2. Make the batter: Combine the flour and seasonings in a bowl and mix thoroughly with a whisk. Add the beer all at once, whisk until smooth, and set aside at room temperature for 30 minutes.
3. Pour the oil into a deep, wide pan to a depth of 2 inches and heat over medium-high heat to 365 degrees (see Safe Frying, page 248).
4. Check the batter; it should be a thick coating consistency. If it seems too thick, add beer, water, or milk, 1 teaspoon at a time, until the right consistency is achieved. It's better to be slightly too thick than too thin!
5. Pat the shrimp dry and add to the batter. Fish out a few pieces at a time (I use chopsticks) and fry until golden brown. Drain the shrimp on paper towels.
6. To prepare hold a tortilla in your hand and add a spoonful of avocado sauce. Add the shrimp, a squeeze of secret sauce, and a healthy shot of árbol salsa. Top with lettuce, pico de gallo, and onion and cilantro. Squeeze lime over the whole thing.

Note: Save the shrimp shells to make Seven Seas Broth (see page 103).

THE BURRITO MYTH

● ● ●

In most of Mexico, a *burrito* is a small draft animal with long ears and a sweetly stubborn disposition, used to haul heavy loads. A friend's mother, who owned a tortilla factory, used to take a warm tortilla, squish it into a rope-like roll that she called a burrito (remember doing this with soft white bread?), roll it in sugar, and give it to him for a snack after school.

What we call a burrito probably originated in Texas and New Mexico, along the Sonoran border. Sonoran cooks make enormous flour tortillas to eat alongside the grilled meats that are local specialties. It wouldn't take too many cowboys to figure out how to fill one of these huge tortillas with beans, meat, and salsa, tuck in the ends, and roll it up to create a portable meal.

So, do burritos really exist in Baja? Tourist restaurants usually offer burritos. American-style "wraps" are appearing on menus as *tacones*, filled with anything from salad to turkey *mole*. Neighborhood *puestos* and *fondas* will give you a blank look if you order one. But there's nothing to stop you from making your own, as in the Puerto Nuevo–style lobster burrito (see page 59).

Cocktel de Mariscos
(SEAFOOD COCKTAIL)

Refreshing and light, *cockteles* are immensely popular at street stands and puestos everywhere in Baja. Cocktel (not to be confused with ceviche) is something like a chunky gazpacho combined with lots of fresh, lightly cooked seafood: Shrimp, octopus, calamari, clams, crab, oysters, and periwinkle are the most popular, singly or *campechana*—some of everything.

　　The seafood is mixed with its own chilled cooking broth, a splash of tomato juice, and a heaping spoonful of diced cucumbers, red onions, and tomatoes, all topped with perfect avocado, lots of fresh-squeezed lime juice, and a few dashes of fiery hot sauce. On the side, *gamesa* crackers (Mexican saltines).

　　For some reason, cart cockteles tend to taste better than the ones I've had in restaurants. My advice: Eat early in the day—the better carts sell out and close up before the day gets hot.

Makes 8 servings as a light appetizer

About 4 cups Seven Seas Broth (see page 103) or water

Total of 4 cups prepared seafood (choose four of the following items to combine; more than four gets confusing.)

8 ounces small squid, cleaned and cut into rings

8 ounces best-quality small shrimp, preferably Mexican (peel after cooking)

1 cup cooked octopus cut into slices

3 large scallops, cut into quarters

8 ounces snow, stone, or Dungeness crab legs, shelled

8 ounces fish, free of skin and bone, cut into 1-inch pieces (see page 52 for a list of sustainable species)

8 ounces periwinkle, cleaned and cut into small pieces

8 ounces farmed abalone, cleaned and cut into small pieces

8 raw or cooked oysters

8 raw or cooked cherrystone clams

2 cups Pico de Gallo (see page 30)

1 cup peeled, diced cucumber

1/2 teaspoon kosher salt

1 cup freshly squeezed lime juice (about 6 large limes, preferably Mexican limones; see page 30)

About 2 cups Clamato, tomato, or Snappy Tom juice

1/2 cup ketchup

TO SERVE

2 avocados, pitted, peeled, and cut into 3/4-inch dice

Lime wedges, preferably from Mexican limones (see page 30)

Salsa de Chiles de Arbol #1 (see page 38) or bottled hot sauce

Saltine crackers or Tostaditas (see page 248)

1. Bring the broth to a fast simmer in a large pot. Add the seafood and cook at a bare simmer for 3 to 5 minutes, or until just barely opaque. Remove from the heat and cool the seafood in the cooking liquid. Chill.

2. Drain the seafood, reserving the cooking liquid, and mix with the pico de gallo and cucumber. Add the salt, lime juice, Clamato juice, ketchup, and reserved cooking liquid. (Can be made ahead to this point and chilled.)

3. To serve, spoon into small glass bowls, footed sundae glasses, or martini glasses (if poolside, use clear plastic cups). Add lots of the juice.

4. Top with avocado. Serve immediately, with lime wedges, árbol sauce, and crisp, salty crackers.

Note: If using clams or oysters be sure to reserve their juices and add to your cocktail.

Variation: To make Cabo Coconut Cocktel, omit the Clamato juice and substitute a 12-ounce can of coconut milk. Add 3 large serrano chiles (minced), 2 more tablespoons lime juice, and twice as much cilantro. Taste for salt; this variation needs to be spicy and well seasoned.

Ceviche, Ensenada Style

Ensenada-style *ceviche* is a celebration of absolute freshness and immediacy. It's made with raw, fresh-ground (not diced) fish combined with diced tomatoes, onion, cilantro, and chiles and then quickly tossed with freshly squeezed lime juice, creating something like a very substantial, fresh-tasting salsa. It should be eaten within several hours, scooped onto thick, crunchy tostadas, liberally seasoned with hot sauce and limes. At most cocktel stands, you can snack on fresh ceviche for free while you wait your turn.

Ensenadans make delicious ceviche with fresh tuna or generic white fish that has been put through a meat grinder; pans of the pink ground fish are offered for sale at fish markets. On the gulf side and in Cabo, fresh mackerel is often used. Stateside, sustainable fish choices for homemade ceviche include wild salmon, Alaskan halibut, pole-caught yellowfin tuna, and mackerel.

Whatever fish you use, pristine freshness is a must. Buy whatever saltwater fish is freshest from a reputable fish dealer. (Note that freshwater fish should never be eaten raw!) Keep the fish ice cold at all times and use it that day. Marinating in lime does not preserve or sterilize food.

When making ceviche, you don't want the fish to soak in lime juice until it turns white and rubbery—the true tender flavor of the fish is utterly lost amid a barrage of acid, spice, and onion.

If you prefer not to eat raw fish, the fish can be quickly cooked in lightly salted water or fish stock and chilled before proceeding with the recipe.

Makes 4 cups, enough for 36 tostadas, serving 6 to 8 people

12 ounces very fresh saltwater fish, with all skin, bones, and fat lines removed
6–8 limes, preferably Mexican limones (see page 30)
1–1½ teaspoons kosher salt
2 cups Pico de Gallo (see page 30)
3 or more fresh serrano chiles, quartered lengthwise and minced (wear rubber gloves)

TO SERVE
Round tostadas or thick home-style tostada chips
A variety of bottled Mexican hot sauces
Lime wedges, preferably from Mexican limones (see page 30)

1. Wash your hands, cutting board, knives, and bowls very thoroughly. Either grind the fish through the coarse plate of a very clean meat grinder, chop it finely by hand, or cut it into tiny dice, ¼ inch or less. Squeeze the limes over the fish, add the salt, and stir well. Refrigerate for 2 hours.

2. Just before serving, add the pico de gallo and chiles. Adjust the seasoning with lime juice or salt, if necessary, bearing in mind that you will be adding hot sauce to the mix. Stir thoroughly and refrigerate until ready to serve, ideally within 1 hour.

3. Serve in a bowl set on ice. Serve the tostadas on the side with an assortment of hot sauces and the limes.

Variations: Fresh scallops, shrimp, abalone, and calamari all make excellent ceviche. And finely diced raw beef is nothing short of phenomenal prepared in this style! Lean filet or sirloin is excellent, but so is flap meat, which is very finely shot through with bits of fat—deliciously, terribly *macho*.

Carne Asada Tacos

To find a good *carne asada* taco, look for clouds of fragrant, meaty smoke swirling down the street and follow your nose to a cart or *puesto* with a grill (*parrilla*) covered with swathes of grilling meat and *cebollitas* (green onions) over leaping flames. The busy *taquero* swiftly dices the meat with a great rattle of his knife, loads it onto corn tortillas with a smear of avocado sauce, and wraps each in a little square of absorbent gray paper that acts as both plate and napkin. On the cart will be quartered limes, chopped white onions and cilantro, pickled jalapeños and red onions, pico de gallo, radishes, and at least one hot sauce, such as chipotle salsa or salsa de chiles de árbol.

Carne asada is just as quick and simple to make at home, on the outdoor grill or in a grill pan. If you cook it indoors, turn on the fan—it will be smoky.

Makes 24 tacos, enough for 6 to 8 people

CARNE ASADA

½ teaspoon freshly ground black pepper
2 garlic cloves, minced
3 tablespoons minced onion
1½ tablespoons best-quality Japanese soy sauce
3 tablespoons olive oil
2 tablespoons freshly squeezed lime juice, preferably from a Mexican limón (see page 30)
2½ pounds flap meat or skirt steak

TO SERVE

Fresh corn tortillas, warmed
Avocado Sauce (see page 34)
Cebollitas (see page 178)
Whole roasted jalapeño chiles or Pickled Jalapeño Peppers (see page 180)
Pico de Gallo (see page 30)
Chipotle Salsa (see page 40)
Diced white onion
Pickled Red Onions (see page 180)
Radishes
Lime wedges, preferably from Mexican limones (see page 30)
Cilantro sprigs

1. Make the carne asada: In a nonreactive bowl, combine the pepper, garlic, onion, soy sauce, oil, and lime juice.
2. Cut the meat into pieces about 4 inches across, add to the bowl, and mix well to coat. Marinate in the refrigerator for 4 to 6 hours.
3. Half an hour before cooking, clean the grill thoroughly with a brush and wipe it down with an oil-dampened rag. Preheat the grill on high. Grill the meat on one side until it is well browned and nicely marked—even slightly charred on the thin edges—about 5 minutes. Turn and cook briefly on the other side until the meat is done to your liking. (Tested with an instant-read thermometer, medium-rare will be 125 degrees, medium at 140 degrees, and well-done when it flaps like shoe leather.)
4. Remove the meat to a platter and let rest for 5 minutes or so, then slice across the grain. Cut the slices into small cubes.
5. Serve immediately on the tortillas with your choice of accompaniments.

Note: The best cut for carne asada is a wide, thin, well-marbled cut known as flap meat. Second best would be skirt steak. Both cuts are flavorful and juicy and have enough fat to withstand the high heat of the grill without drying out. Flank steak, which looks similar, is too lean and dry for this kind of full-bore cooking. Substitute a sirloin tip instead.

HOW TO TACO

■ ● ■

On every main street in every town, outside factory gates, at bus stops, and tucked into odd corners, *puestos* and *taquerías* dish up the quickest and most delicious tastes in all Baja: tacos—fresh tortillas, quickly made to order or reheated on the grill in front of you, folded around an infinite variety of fillings, and served with fresh salsas that complement your choice. Restaurants try to serve tacos, but it isn't the same. A truly great taco is fresh and immediate, made when you order and eaten in the wink of an eye.

Most taquerías specialize in a few items, done right. A long-time favorite of mine is Tacos la Pura Vida (The Good Life), a well-worn storefront with board shutters at the north end of the main drag in Rosarito Beach, before you get to the main tourist strip. You can get tacos to go from the sidewalk; inside are four small tables with rough benches made from splintery wood, painted the same azure blue used on many fishing boats.

Front and center, right on the street, the taquero rules in his white apron, tending a vertical spit of pork meat *al pastor* roasting a deep ochre before a gas flame, topped with the traditional pineapple crown and an onion, dripping fragrant juices onto a small grill and an iron *plancha* (griddle).

The *patrona* regales us with the menu: *tacos al pastor*, of course, but also diced *carnitas* pork, grilled beef *carne asada*, *tripas* (tripe), crumbly, succulent chorizo sausage, and fatty, soft *cabeza* (meat boiled from the cow's head).

Sadly, we are too late, she says, for *lengua* (tongue), *sesos* (brains), and her personal favorite: *ojos*, or eyeballs. These all sell out very fast. She sets little bowls of radishes, diced onions, and cilantro on the table and returns with three more small bowls of salsas: pale green tomatillo salsa with specks of cilantro, a fiery salsa made purely of crushed red chiles, and another salsa of guajillo chile, tomato, garlic, and onion.

We order and watch the taquero as he wields a long curved knife, first shaving long shards off the spit of roasting pork for our tacos al pastor and then dicing the meat and spreading it onto the plancha to reheat and crisp. Carne asada goes onto a corner of the grill, while the tripas, chorizo, and carnitas are cut into small pieces and made piping hot on the plancha alongside tortillas. Cabeza is scooped out of a metal pot on the corner of the grill. Everything cooks for a minute or two, and then he assembles the tacos, wrapping one end of each in a twist of grayish paper to absorb the juices.

The tacos arrive on small, very fresh corn tortillas, folded around generous portions of crisp-edged carnitas; soft, fatty cabeza; crumbly, richly flavored chorizo. The tripas are chewy and a little gamey and take nicely to a sprinkle of onion and a dash of the very hot salsa. The tacos al pastor are dripping with golden juice, redolent of achiote and spices, bite after glorious bite; these hardly need a sauce. We eat the carnitas with tomatillo sauce and onions and lots of cilantro and then lick our fingers.

"*¿Está bien*?" asks the patrona, but she knows it is wonderful.

"More?"

More, of course!

Tacos al Pastor

Pork tacos prepared *al pastor* (shepherd style) are found all over Mexico. Thin slices of boneless pork are marinated with a chile paste, the recipe to which is jealously guarded by each stand. The slices are stacked onto a tall vertical spit, like a Greek gyro. The spit is topped with half an onion and a good-size chunk of pineapple, then set before a flame and reflector, where it turns and cooks all day long, sending wonderful wafts of chile and pork on the breeze. When a customer places an order, the *taquero* slices the outside off the pork with a huge curved knife, dices it up, and quickly crisps the edges on a hot griddle before folding the meat into a warm corn tortilla. The meat isn't spicy, but the taste of roasted chiles combined with a little onion and cilantro (and some of the roasted pineapple, if he likes you) is hard to beat.

This easy version goes from an overnight marinade to grill to taco in 15 minutes and includes a treat—thick slices of grilled *piña* (pineapple). If you aren't using the grill, an oven-friendly version follows the main recipe. For more information on working with dried chiles, see page 36.

Makes 24 tacos, enough for 6 to 8 people

MARINADE

5 dried guajillo chiles
5 dried chiles negros or ancho chiles (see note on the opposite page)
3 large garlic cloves, minced
½ cup white vinegar, preferably Heinz, plus more to thin the marinade if necessary
2 tablespoons achiote paste (available at Latin markets)
1 teaspoon kosher salt
¼ teaspoon ground cumin
⅛ teaspoon ground cloves
1 tablespoon vegetable oil
2 tablespoons finely minced white onion
¼ cup water

4 pounds boneless country-style pork ribs or pork shoulder
1 ripe pineapple

TO SERVE

Fresh corn tortillas, warmed
Diced white onion
Sliced radishes
Cilantro sprigs
Tomatillo Salsa (see page 44)
Salsa de Chiles de Arbol #1 (page 38)

1. At least 6 hours before cooking, make the marinade: Heat a heavy griddle or frying pan over medium heat and gently toast the chiles, pressing them down quickly with a spatula. Turn and repeat on the other side. Be very careful not to scorch the chiles or they will have an off taste. Cool and then remove the stems, seeds, and stringy ribs.
2. Tear the chiles into small pieces and pulse in a spice grinder until they are as finely ground as possible.
3. In a blender, combine the garlic, vinegar, achiote, salt, cumin, and cloves. Puree until well combined. Add the ground chiles and blend for several minutes, or until the sauce is very smooth; if necessary, add a tablespoon or so of vinegar to make a thick paste.
4. Heat the oil over medium heat in a frying pan. Add the onion and cook, stirring, for 1 minute. Add the chile paste; use the water to swish out the blender and add to the pan. Cook, stirring, for 3 minutes, or until thickened. Scrape onto a plate and cool completely.

5. Cut the pork into lengthwise slices about ¾ inch thick and smear a layer of the chile paste on each side (thick enough to draw a line in). Stack the slices in a shallow container, cover, and refrigerate for 6 to 12 hours.
6. Cut the crown off the pineapple and cut a slice off the bottom. Carve off the prickly skin, slicing from top to bottom, then cut the flesh into slices ½ thick; set aside.

Grill method: Half an hour before cooking, clean the grill thoroughly with a brush and wipe it down with an oil-dampened rag. Preheat the grill on high. Remove any thick blobs of chile paste from the meat, as these will burn. Grill the meat and pineapple for 7 minutes on each side, directly over the flame (if your grill is as hot as a blast furnace, medium is okay). Watch carefully to make sure the chile paste is not burning; if needed, turn down the heat or move the meat to a cooler part of the grill. The pineapple should be given a half-turn partway through cooking to make nice crosshatch marks. When the meat is cooked to an internal temperature of 145 degrees (don't overcook!), remove to a warm plate.

Oven method: Preheat the oven to 375 degrees. Spread the meat out in one layer in a shallow, lightly oiled baking dish or on a rimmed cookie sheet. There should be some open space between the pieces; it's better to use several baking dishes than crowd the meat. Cut half of the pineapple slices into quarters and scatter over the top. Reserve the rest for another use, like piña colada or agua fresca de piña (see page 226). Roast the meat and pineapple for 30 to 40 minutes, or until well browned and crisp; there should be some caramelized juices in the bottom of the dish. Remove from the oven, cover the cooked meat and pineapple loosely with foil, and let stand 5 minutes while you heat the tortillas.

To serve: Heat the tortillas; keep them warm in a cloth napkin or tortilla warmer. Dice the meat into small bits, mix with the juices on the plate or in the baking dish, and fill the tortillas. The pineapple can be chopped up or cut into quarters. Serve with the onion, radishes, cilantro, and your choice of salsa or hot sauce.

Note: True pasillas or chiles negros are long, thin dried chiles with shiny skin. Anchos are wide and roughly triangular, as wrinkly as raisins. Pasillas are more authentic for al pastor, but anchos are acceptable.

ABOUT TORTILLAS

Corn tortillas are the daily "bread" of Mexico. Authentic street tacos are always served on fresh, warm, *corn* tortillas, about 4 or 5 inches in diameter. Small corn tortillas, only a few inches across, are sold as *chicanitas*. They may be used for small appetizer tacos or as a base for *antojitos*. Corn tortilla directions are found on page 238.

Flour tortillas are considered more refined and are served with sit-down meals. Soft, thick, handmade tortillas, 6 to 8 inches in diameter, are known as *gorditas*. These are rolled out and cooked fresh as diners are seated and are served hot from the griddle.

Very large flour tortillas, what we call wraps, are traditional in the north central border regions of Mexico, where they accompany grilled meat. Flour tortillas are easy to make from scratch (see page 242).

Carnitas Tacos

Pork is the most beloved meat in Mexico, and the results are deliciously varied: huge sheets of the skin, fried in lard to make melt-in-your-mouth cracklings called *chicharrones*; tubs of rendered lard for use in tamales and tortillas; skeins of spicy, flavorful chorizo sausage redolent of garlic and chiles.

For me, a pig's finest hour is when hours of slow simmering transform it into *carnitas*, with its mouthwatering smell and moist texture. Carnitas is easy to make, even if you don't have a whole pig to cook.

Makes 24 tacos, enough for 6 to 8 people

2 tablespoons lard or vegetable oil
3 pounds boneless pork shoulder
    or country-style pork ribs
½ teaspoon kosher salt
About 4 cups water
½ orange

TO SERVE

Fresh corn tortillas, warmed
Frijoles Refritos (see page 245)
Raw Tomatillo Salsa (see page 44)
Salsa de Chiles de Arbol #2 (see page 39)
Naked Guacamole (see page 34)
Lime wedges, preferably from Mexican limones
Sliced radishes
Diced white onion
Chopped cilantro

1. Melt the lard in a deep, narrow pot. Cut the pork into 2-inch chunks and brown well on all sides. Pour off and discard excess fat (or strain it and reserve for frying or to make flour tortillas). Add the salt and enough water to barely cover the meat.
2. Set over medium heat until the water begins to bubble, then reduce the heat to low and cook at a bare simmer for 1½ hours. Add the orange and cook for another hour, or until the meat shreds easily.
3. Discard the orange, turn the heat to high, and boil all the water off to make a thick glaze. Break the meat into shreds and serve right away with your choice of accompaniments.

GRACIAS, SEÑOR PIG

At the rough end of Rosarito Beach, there's a *puesto* specializing in carnitas. Its wooden shutters open right onto the street. Inside is a massive cauldron, 5 feet wide, used for simmering the meat, with a wooden spoon as big as an oar. Heat lamps hang over a long oval wooden trough filled with heaps of succulent meat. Different parts of carnitas go by different names: *Macisa* is firm and usually cut into cubes; *buche* is soft, fatty, and full of flavor; *surtida* is a mixture of *macisa* and *buche*; *costilla* is the rib meat; and *cueritos* is the cooked skin.

Two cooks hustle around behind the long, L-shaped counter, crisping up carnitas on long flat griddles while they warm tortillas, fill them with the rich meat, and serve them to a wall of serious diners at the counter who don't even look up between tacos.

If you stand to watch, odds are the *cocinero* will offer you a taste of the meat. It was here that an ex-vegetarian of my acquaintance sampled the carnitas and then said, "I can't believe I just ate meat in the street, right out of a man's hand."

Fresh Chorizo Tacos

Mexican chorizo is fresh pork or beef sausage, highly flavored with garlic and chiles but not usually *picante* spicy. It is very different from Spanish or Philippine-style chorizo, which is hard, dried sausage.

Chorizo is fried until crumbly and browned and then it's wrapped in soft tacos, sprinkled on beans, or served on a crisp tostada with crema, onions, and cilantro. You'll often see *huevos con chorizo* (scrambled eggs with chorizo) featured on Mexican breakfast menus.

Good pork chorizo is readily found in Latin markets, but you can easily make your own—homemade is deliciously superior to store bought. Not only do you control what part of Mr. Pig your sausage is made from, but you can season everything to your liking and even develop flavorful twists of your own. You can use beef, turkey, or chicken thigh meat instead of pork.

Makes about 3 cups sausage, enough for 24 tacos, serving 6 to 8 people

HOMEMADE CHORIZO

1 pound boneless pork shoulder or butt, with plenty of fat

4 garlic cloves

3 tablespoons chopped white onion

2 teaspoons kosher salt

1 teaspoon freshly ground black pepper

2 tablespoons ground guajillo or New Mexico chile (see page 37)

1 tablespoon ground cumin

1 teaspoon dried whole Mexican oregano, rubbed to a powder

1 teaspoon crushed hot chile

3 tablespoons white vinegar, preferably Heinz

TO SERVE

2 tablespoons canola oil

Fresh corn tortillas, warmed

Mexican crema, crème fraîche, or sour cream

Diced white onion

Chopped cilantro

Shredded iceberg lettuce or green cabbage

1. Make the chorizo: Set up a meat grinder with the finest disk. Cut the meat into cubes and grind once; then pass through again. For a very fine, almost pasty texture, grind the meat a third time. (If you don't have a grinder, ask your butcher to do this for you.)

2. In a mini food chopper or food processor, pulse together the garlic, onion, and salt to a paste. Blend in the pepper, ground chile, cumin, oregano, and crushed chile. Blend in the vinegar. Scrape into a bowl. Add the pork and mix well. Knead until the meat and seasonings are well mixed. The sausage may be used right away, but it tastes better after a night in the refrigerator.

3. To serve, heat the oil in a medium frying pan and fry the chorizo until browned and crumbled into small pieces. Top each tortilla with a dollop of crema and sprinkle with the chorizo, onion, cilantro, and lettuce.

Pollo Lucas Tacos

Lucas spice (see the opposite page) is used on all manner of treats in Baja. Although grilled chicken is not generally one of them (since that's not a traditional choice at puestos or fondas), it occurred to me that it would be a wonderful vehicle for this crazy sweet-and-sour seasoning. And it is. This recipe combines the bright flavor of a fresh lemon marinade and is seasoned with the Lucas spice just before it comes off the grill. Great with guacamole, corn tortillas, and beans.

Makes 6 servings

12 boneless, skinless chicken thighs or 4 boneless, skinless chicken breasts
$\frac{1}{3}$ cup freshly squeezed lemon juice
1 teaspoon kosher salt
1 teaspoon dried whole Mexican oregano, rubbed to a powder
3 garlic cloves, finely minced
1 tablespoon olive oil

LUCAS SPICE

1 tablespoon ground guajillo chile (see page 37)
3 tablespoons sugar
$\frac{1}{4}$ teaspoon kosher salt

TO SERVE

Frijoles Refritos (see page 245)
Fresh corn tortillas, warmed
Naked Guacamole (see page 34)
Pico de Gallo (see page 30)

1. In a nonreactive bowl, combine the chicken, lemon juice, salt, oregano, garlic, and oil; mix thoroughly. Refrigerate for up to 4 hours.

2. To make the Lucas spice: Stir together the ground chile, sugar, and salt in a small bowl. Set aside.

3. Half an hour before cooking, clean the grill thoroughly with a brush and wipe it down with an oil-dampened rag. Preheat the grill on high. Grill the chicken on both sides and then dust lightly with the spice mix. Grill 2 minutes more on each side.

4. Remove to a platter. Cut into thin strips or dice.

5. To serve, smear some beans inside a tortilla. Stud with the chicken and top with a small amount of guacamole and pico de gallo.

Note: The chicken may be roasted instead of grilled.

PUCKER UP

■ ■ ■

Nuclear-strength flavor combinations of sour and salty are very popular Baja street treats, especially when combined with ground chile powder or hot chiles.

LIMÓN AGRIA
Translated literally: a sour lime, but that ain't the half of it. The top is cut off a lime, holes are poked in the flesh, and a hot chile de árbol is stuck into each hole. The top is sprinkled with salt, and you walk down the street sucking the acid, salty, hot juice and making faces.

LUCAS SPICE
Lucas is slang for "crazy," and it is aptly applied to the seasoning called lucas spice: a combination of ground chiles, ascorbic acid, and salt that is extremely sour, salty, and chile-savory (though not spicy) all at once. It's shaken on fruit, jícama, and grilled corn. Children dip candy into lucas spice or lick it off their fingers (many ultrasweet Mexican candies come already coated with a layer of lucas). Adults drink ice-cold beer out of frozen glasses whose rims have been dipped in lucas. The stuff is wild, and it's easy to develop the habit.

CHAMOYA
One might expect a neon pink sauce to be sweet, but *chamoya* sauce is extremely sour and salty, with a vinegar finish and a hint of garlic. Some versions are spicy. In fact, chamoya is best compared to Chinese salted plums or the American candy known as the "nuclear warhead." (Don't say I didn't warn you.) Chamoya is dripped onto tostadas or *duros* (fried crispies), drizzled onto fruit and candy, and even rolled into the Mexican version of sushi. Squeezed over shaved ice (*raspado*), it becomes a *chamoyada*. Some enterprising bartenders make margaritas with it. It's been spotted on popcorn and, lately, in frozen fruit bars.

TAMARINDO
Tart-sweet tamarind tastes even sweeter after sampling any of the preceding pucker-makers. It comes in blocks of pulp, laden with seeds, and must be soaked and strained before use. Tamarind is a popular flavor for *agua fresca*, a drink made with fruit, water, and sugar (see page 225). And you can buy tamarind-flavored sodas, ice creams, and frozen fruit bars. Tamarind candy rolled in chile powder is a remarkable taste sensation.

Traditional Quesadillas

Quesadillas, a popular street snack predating the Spanish, are turnovers made from raw corn *masa* dough stuffed with savory fillings and either toasted on a comal or fried in shallow oil. Empanadas (see page 120) are somewhat the same; the names seem to be used interchangeably.

A quesadilla does not need cheese, but it helps to stick the filling together. See the chart below for some common fillings or use whatever fairly dry filling you like.

Makes about 24 small quesadillas, enough for 6 to 8 people

Corn Masa (see page 238)
Your choice of filling

1. Follow the directions on page 238 for making corn tortillas. Form the dough into balls. Press into circles about 5 inches wide in a tortilla press, but don't make them too thin. Place a spoonful of filling just below the center line of each circle. Fold the dough over and gently pinch closed to seal.
2. Flatten each quesadilla lightly and toast on a hot, dry comal or griddle until firm or fry on both sides in a small amount of oil until golden brown.
3. Cool for 1 minute before eating. Quesadillas should be eaten right away.

BUILD YOUR OWN STREET TREAT!

Stuff a taco, roll and fry a *taquito*, or fill a quesadilla or empanada.

FILLINGS	GARNISHES	SALSAS
Frijoles Refritos (see page 245)	*crema*	Salsa de Chiles de Arbol (see page 38)
shredded beef or chicken	shredded lettuce/cabbage	Pico de Gallo (see page 30)
Carnitas or shredded pork	diced white onion	Tomatillo Salsa (see page 44)
Carne Asada (see page 13)	cilantro	Naked Guacamole (see page 34)
Asadero or Cotixa cheese	pickled red onion	Avocado Sauce (see page 34)
grilled or smoked fish	cotixa/añejo cheese	Chipotle Salsa (see page 40)
cooked lobster, shrimp, or crab	shredded epazote leaf	Salsa al Comal (see page 32)
sautéed mushrooms	roasted jalapeños	Roasted Jalapeño Salsa (see page 41)
grilled turkey	sliced radishes	Mango Salsa (see page 47)
Rajas con Crema (see page 179)	sliced green onions	Red Onion–Habanero Salsa (see page 118)
Nopales (see page 173)	Cebollitas (page 178)	
zucchini flowers	diced avocado	
epazote or other greens	marinated tomatoes	
roasted pineapple	pitted olives	
pickled jalapeño (see page 180)	toasted nuts	
cooked potatoes and chorizo	ground chile	
roasted peppers	limes	

Ancho Chile Quesadillas

The addition of ancho chile powder creates a lovely adobe-colored *masa* dough with more flavor than your usual corn tortilla, here presented with a filling of roasted chiles and cheese.

The dough tends to be a little more delicate and sticky than regular tortillas; don't press the dough too thinly and handle it carefully. Wipe the plastic liner clean with a paper towel between squishes. If you mess one up, just scrape it off the plastic and do it again.

Makes about 24 small quesadillas, enough for 6 to 8 people

2 cups masa harina (dry tortilla flour)
2 tablespoons ground ancho or California chile
  (see page 37)
½ teaspoon kosher salt
½ teaspoon granulated garlic
1½–2 cups warm water

2 fresh Anaheim or poblano chiles
6 ounces asadero or Oaxacan cheese, grated
Kosher salt or sea salt

TO SERVE
Sliced avocado
Limes, preferably Mexican limones (see page 30)
Mango Salsa (see page 47) or other salsa

1. Make the masa: In a bowl, combine the masa harina, ground chile, salt, and garlic. Stir with a whisk or sift together until well mixed. Add 1½ cups of water and stir with a fork until combined, adding more water as needed to make a damp dough that does not crack around the edges. Form into a ball, wrap in plastic, and let stand at room temperature for 1 hour. (Masa can be made ahead to this point and refrigerated. Use within 48 hours.)

2. Roast the chiles over a flame until the skin is blistered and the flesh is cooked. Wrap in a paper towel until cool. Remove the stem, seeds, and charred skin. Cut into small dice.

3. Heat a dry comal or griddle. Following the directions on page 241, press the masa into disks 4 inches in diameter and a little thicker than a regular tortilla.

4. Carefully peel the tortilla off the plastic onto a cutting board. Place a small amount of cheese and a few morsels of green chile in the center; then fold in half, pinch the edges together to seal, and toast on both sides until the masa is cooked and the cheese is melted.

5. Sprinkle with salt and serve warm with any of the accompaniments suggested above.

Achiote Pork Torta

With Baja so close to the United States, it's a given that sandwiches—called *tortas* south of the border—would be popular there. Soft, football-shaped white rolls known as *teleras* or *bolillos* (see the opposite page) are piled high with meat, guacamole, lettuce, tomatoes, and often pickled jalapeños.

In this recipe, the pork marinade is flavored with *achiote,* a paste made of ground annatto seeds, vinegar, and other seasonings. It can be found in any Latin market in small, dark-red bricks.

This super-quick recipe can go from marinade to grill to torta in 15 minutes. Feel free to substitute chicken for pork.

Makes 6 sandwiches

3 large garlic cloves, minced
2 tablespoons white vinegar, preferably Heinz, plus more
    to thin the marinade if necessary
2 tablespoons freshly squeezed orange juice
2 tablespoons freshly squeezed lime juice, preferably
    from a Mexican limón (see page 30), or lemon juice
½ teaspoon kosher salt
½ teaspoon ground cumin
1 package (4 ounces) achiote paste (available at
    Latin markets)
10 cilantro sprigs, stemmed and chopped
2 pounds boneless pork butt or shoulder

TO SERVE

6 large soft white sandwich rolls or a baguette
Sliced asadero or Chihuahua cheese (optional)
Shredded lettuce
Sliced ripe Roma tomatoes
Naked Guacamole (see page 34)
Sliced red onion
Pickled jalapeño slices and hot salsa or other salsa
    (optional)

1. In a blender or food processor, combine the garlic, vinegar, juices, salt, and cumin. Pulse until well combined. Crumble in the achiote and pulse to combine into a very soft paste; add more vinegar by the tablespoon to loosen it up if necessary. Blend in the cilantro.

2. Cut the meat into lengthwise slices ½ to ¾ inch thick. Lay the meat between two sheets of plastic wrap and pound to an even thickness of ¼ inch. Coat the slices generously with the paste and refrigerate for at least 6 hours and no more than 12 hours.

3. Half an hour before cooking, clean the grill thoroughly with a brush and wipe it down with an oil-dampened rag. Preheat the grill on high.

4. Remove the meat from the marinade and shake off as much of the paste as possible. Place the meat on the grill, close the lid, and grill for 5 to 7 minutes on each side, checking often to make sure the meat doesn't burn or cook too quickly; if it does, move it to a cooler part of the grill. The meat is done perfectly when it has an internal temperature of 145 degrees. Do not overcook or the meat will dry out. Set the meat aside, loosely covered with foil.

5. To serve, split the rolls and toast on the grill, then layer from the bottom up: cheese, meat, lettuce, tomatoes, guacamole, onion, jalapeños, and salsa. Skewer with a couple of toothpicks and cut in half.

Variation: Here are some torta filling options, to name just a few—all to be layered with guacamole, lettuce, tomato, onions, and, if you wish, pickled jalapeños: cheese, pork, *jamón* (ham), Carne Asada (see page 13), grilled chicken, Pollo Lucas (see page 20), shrimp sautéed with garlic and butter, grilled fish fillet with Thousand Island dressing.

MEXICAN BREADS

●●●

Yes, it is the land of tortillas, but Mexican bakers also create terrific breads and pastries. Mexico, like the United States, is a nation of immigrants, and those immigrants brought their food traditions with them. In every town, you will find excellent *panaderías* turning out bread, baguettes, and rolls, and *pastelerías* turning out sumptuous European-style cakes, pastries, and cookies. The small city of Tecate, east of Tijuana, is famous for its French-style sweet bread.

Teleras are football-shaped, soft white rolls that make fabulous sandwiches, or *tortas*. Breakfast is often a sweet roll or crusty white roll called a *bolillo* or *birote*, which might be stuffed with a banana or a pickled jalapeño and dipped in the jalapeño juice. (Makes your toasted oats seem awfully tame.)

Sweet rolls are often very sweet, in fanciful shapes like rings or hearts or crescents or shells, dyed impossible pastel colors of pink and yellow, and coated with thick layers of cinnamon sugar or icing. More and more *panaderías* offer an array of delicious whole-wheat (*integral*) pastries, less sweet but just as good.

Mexican bakeries are fun to visit. The baked goods are stacked on trays in the front of the shop. You pick up a basket and a pair of tongs and choose exactly what you want. I always buy too much, but somehow, it always gets eaten.

Tamales with Shrimp "Chorizo" and Fresh Corn

Tamales are a common street item, sold warm from insulated coolers on street corners, in stores, and from the trunks of cars at the border. Most tamales are filled with the usual pork or chicken. I first heard about this uncommon seafood *tamal* in Ensenada and had to include it here.

Seafood chorizo is a Baja tradition. Chorizo made from abalone originated in Baja on Isla Cedros, south on the peninsula, whose early residents had little to eat but abalone. Restaurant Haliotis (the Latin name for abalone) in Ensenada serves delicious abalone chorizo.

I have opted for a shrimp version, since shrimp is easier to find. You may make it with abalone if you like, but please be sure to buy farmed baby abalone (sometimes available from Baja), not wild-harvested or imported abalone, since poaching is a major problem.

This is a big recipe, but if you're going to spend the time it takes to make tamales, you may as well make a lot of them and freeze any extras after steaming. Tamales reheat perfectly in the microwave.

Makes 25 medium tamales, enough for 10 to 12 people

SHRIMP CHORIZO

1 pound best-quality shrimp, preferably Mexican, peeled and deveined
1 tablespoon freshly squeezed lime juice, preferably from a Mexican limón (see page 30)
¼ cup finely minced white onion
1 tablespoon ground guajillo chile (see page 37)
1½ teaspoons kosher salt
1 teaspoon ground cumin
1 teaspoon crushed hot chile
½ teaspoon freshly ground black pepper
½ teaspoon dried whole Mexican oregano, rubbed to a powder
2 large garlic cloves, very finely minced
2 tablespoons white vinegar, preferably Heinz

MASA DOUGH

3 cups Maseca brand masa for tamales (dry masa)
1½ teaspoons baking powder
1 teaspoon kosher salt
3 cups warm water
1 cup lard or shortening

CORN

2 ears sweet white corn
2 tablespoons olive oil
¼ cup chopped cilantro

Dried corn husks for wrapping tamales (hojas)

TO SERVE

Lime wedges, preferably from Mexican limones (see page 30)
Salsa de Chiles de Arbol #1 (see page 38)
Cooked Tomatillo Salsa (see page 45)

1. Make the shrimp chorizo: Cut the shrimp into ⅛-inch pieces and chop roughly a few times. Place the shrimp in a small bowl, squeeze on the lime juice, and set aside.
2. In a mini chopper or food processor, combine the onion, ground chile, salt, cumin, crushed chile, pepper, oregano, and garlic; pulse to a smooth paste. Add the vinegar and combine well. Scrape into a bowl, add the shrimp, and combine well. Refrigerate for 1 hour while you prepare the corn and masa.

3. Make the masa dough: Sift the masa, baking powder, and salt into a bowl. Add the water and beat well.

4. In the bowl of a standing mixer fitted with a whip attachment, beat the lard until it is light and fluffy. Add the masa a little at a time and beat on medium speed until the mixture is fluffy (it will resemble cake frosting and a small piece will float in water). Set aside.

5. Make the corn: Shuck the corn and cut off the kernels. Heat the oil and cook the corn over medium heat, stirring, until cooked through. Remove from the pan. Cool and add to the shrimp. Stir in the cilantro.

6. Soak the dried corn husks in warm water for 15 minutes, or until pliable. Rinse under cold running water to remove any grit and stack neatly.

7. Set a corn husk with the pointed end facing away from you. Take a heaping tablespoon of masa and spread a layer about ¼ inch thick over a 2 by 2-inch area in the center of the corn husk, leaving 1 inch on each side and 2 inches top and bottom. (If the husks are too narrow, overlap two side by side.)

8. Place a tablespoon of shrimp filling in the middle of the masa. Fold the two sides to the center, overlapping, and then fold the top down and the bottom up to overlap. (The packets should be about 3½ inches long by 2½ inches wide.) Tie with a strip of corn husk, if you like; it isn't essential. Repeat until all the masa and filling are used up.

9. In a deep stockpot with a lid, position a round cake rack on ramekins, so there is at least 3 inches of clearance between the rack and pot bottom. Add water so there is an inch of air below the rack. Drop several pennies in the bottom of the pot. (The pennies will rattle as the water boils. When you can't hear them, you need to add more water.)

10. Set the finished tamales on the rack; place them on end, packed closely together, or shingled. Lay a damp towel over the tamales, cover the pot, bring to a boil, and steam on medium-high heat for 1½ hours. When done, the tamales will still feel a bit soft. Wrap in foil to keep warm if not serving immediately.

11. Serve with lime juice and the salsas.

SALSAS

Salsas are much more than mere condiments. They are the ancient stars of the Mexican table, the authentic bearers of culinary tradition, always equal in importance to more elaborate dishes. Whether playing a supporting role on a main dish or enjoyed by themselves, bright salsas make the meal, layering bursts of color, intense flavor, and texture onto what is, basically, very simple food.

Most salsas are quick and easy to make from readily available fresh or dried ingredients. Sparkling flavor comes from using really flavorful ingredients, like fresh limes and ripe tomatoes. And serve them fresh: Salsas should be made within an hour of mealtime.

Salsas are good for you, too—all those fantastic flavors come packed with vitamins and phytochemicals (such as lycopene) from fresh tomatoes, chiles, citrus, and fruit. Most salsas contain little or no fat and give nutritional wallop to every bite. It's rare enough to find great-tasting food that's good for you—make the most of it!

TACOS AL GUSTO

The Mexican people prize their individualism and revel in the quirky traits that set them apart from one another and the world. The bewildering array of salsas and garnishes found on every cart and *puesto* illustrates this perfectly. No Mexican would allow someone else to fix his taco; it's an interactive affair, preparing the taco *al gusto* (to your taste) with a smear of this and a dab of that, layered in a fashion unique to the individual. No cook, no matter how skilled, can duplicate the way you make your taco.

Opposite page, clockwise from top left:
Mango salsa (see page 47), Salsa al Comal (see page 32),
Raw Tomatillo Salsa (see page 44),
Salsa de Chiles de Arbol #3 (see page 39),
Pico de Gallo (see page 30)

Pico de Gallo

This fresh tomato salsa is the classic table salsa and goes with almost everything fried or grilled.

The texture of the sauce is important. You can chop everything by hand with a large sharp knife. Chopping in a food processor is fine, as long as the salsa is used right away, before it becomes watery. Because this is really a ratio recipe ($^2/_3$ tomatoes to $^1/_3$ onions), you can adjust any of the amounts to your taste. I like it made with lots of onions, salt, lime, and chile. Don't be afraid to season boldly.

Makes 2½ cups

5 large ripe Roma tomatoes
6 cilantro sprigs, stemmed
1 small white onion
2 fresh serrano chiles (optional)
2 teaspoons kosher salt, or to taste
Juice of 1 lime, preferably Mexican limón (see below)

1. On a large cutting board, core the tomatoes and slice thinly. Push to one side. Roughly chop the cilantro and push it beside the tomatoes. Cut the onion into the smallest dice you can manage and push aside. Chop the chiles.
2. Use the side of your knife to push the onion and chiles back into the middle of the board. Chop by holding the tip of your knife down with one hand and pivoting the blade back and forth, occasionally sweeping the pile back into the center with the edge of your knife. Chop until the onions are a little more finely diced.
3. Scoop up the tomatoes and cilantro, put them on top of the onions, and keep chopping back and forth—sweeping into a pile—until all the ingredients are finely chopped and blended together.
4. When the salsa is a rosy, juicy heap, scoop everything, including the juices, into a serving bowl. Season with the salt and lime juice. Let the flavors mellow for at least 30 minutes before serving.

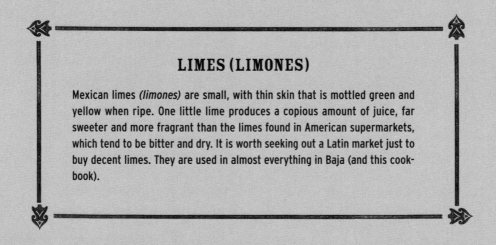

LIMES (LIMONES)

Mexican limes *(limones)* are small, with thin skin that is mottled green and yellow when ripe. One little lime produces a copious amount of juice, far sweeter and more fragrant than the limes found in American supermarkets, which tend to be bitter and dry. It is worth seeking out a Latin market just to buy decent limes. They are used in almost everything in Baja (and this cookbook).

HOT, HOTTER, HOTTEST

●●●

It should come as no surprise that powdered hot chiles were used as a weapon and torture device by pre-Hispanic peoples—to this day, hot-pepper spray is a common self-defense implement.

Why do people eat food that causes pain? The sensation of pain causes the body to release natural painkillers known as endorphins, feel-good chemicals that cause the body to relax and, in high enough amounts, cause a feeling of disassociation or floating. Chile-heads call it "the rush."

A chile's "heat" is a chemical burn. It comes from a compound called capsaicin and can actually be measured. The Scoville scale was invented in the early 20th century by chemist Arthur Scoville, who must have had a bad experience at some point to precisely gauge the concentration of capsaicin in a chile.

There is no upper limit to the Scoville scale. The common sweet bell pepper has zero Scovilles, which means it has no measurable heat. Pure capsaicin registers 16 *million* Scovilles. By contrast, the habanero, one of the hottest chiles on earth, rings in at a mere 250,000 Scovilles. Jalapeños are the mildest of the hot peppers, with a reasonably demure 2,500 Scoville score.

I have developed my own, completely subjective scale:

CHILE	REACTION
Jalapeño	Tickle
Serrano	Burn
Chile de árbol	Cough
Chile piquín	Sweat
Cayenne (fresh)	Cry
Thai "bird" chile	Gasp for breath, gulp beer
Habanero	Burn, cry, gasp, gulp beer, run from room

Anyone's first instinct is to grab a drink—beer or otherwise—but liquids do not diminish heat. In fact, drinking can make things worse. Better ways of putting out the fire in your mouth: Eat something creamy (like yogurt), suck on a lime, or down a spoonful of sugar.

Salsa al Comal
(ROASTED TOMATO SALSA)

This sauce would traditionally be made and served in a *molcajete*, a shallow bowl carved out of rough volcanic rock. The rough stone grinds the vegetables to a thick, velvety texture that cannot be matched with any other cooking tool. But I have had very good results chopping the sauce by hand with a large knife on a cutting board, continually sweeping the salsa into a pile and chopping it down until a fine texture is achieved. The salsa can also be pulsed in a food processor, but this tends to make it watery.

Makes 1 ½ cups

3 ripe Roma tomatoes
1 unpeeled garlic clove
1 fresh serrano chile
¼ small white onion, chopped

4 cilantro sprigs, stemmed and roughly chopped
Pinch of kosher salt
Freshly squeezed lime juice or vinegar
Water

1. Lay a sheet of foil in a heavy cast-iron frying pan or comal. Over medium-high heat in a well-ventilated area, dry-roast the tomatoes, garlic, and chile, turning often, until the skins are blackened in places and the vegetables are soft.
2. Peel the garlic and chop together with the chile. Add the onion and continue chopping until the onion is very fine. Use the edge of the knife to sweep the ingredients back into a heap.
3. Core the tomatoes and add to the pile. Chop a few times to break them down and keep chopping until all the ingredients are fine and blended together and the salsa is quite smooth.
4. Place in a bowl and stir in the cilantro, salt, and lime juice to taste. Thin to the desired consistency with a little water. Let stand for 30 minutes before serving.

ROASTING VEGETABLES FOR SALSAS

A particular roasting method is used for fresh chiles, tomatoes, onions, and garlic that will be used in salsa. Roasting blisters and blackens the skin of the vegetable, but the long, slow cooking also concentrates and evolves complex flavors.

Garlic must be separated into cloves but not peeled; it is roasted in the papery skin, which protects it, and then peeled. Tomatoes, onions, and chiles should be washed and well dried. Don't remove stems or seeds at this point; you want the juices to be kept inside the vegetables.

Cook in a well-ventilated area, since some smoke may be produced. Heat a *comal* or sturdy frying pan over moderately high heat. (I like to use my old cast-iron frying pan, but I get equally good results with a thin, blue-steel comal.) Because of the high heat, don't use a nonstick pan. Lay a sheet of aluminum foil in the bottom of the pan and set your washed and dried vegetables on it. Let the vegetables sit in one place until well blackened in spots, then turn them to another side. Continue roasting and turning until the vegetables are soft with some black spots where they have touched the hot surface. This can take as little as 5 minutes for serranos and garlic or as long as 20 minutes for jalapeños and tomatoes. Lift the foil right out of the pan and let the vegetables cool before proceeding with the recipe. Any juices that run out should be used in the recipe as well.

Naked Guacamole

Buttery-rich guacamole is the perfect foil for spicy salsas, salted *tostaditas*, or highly seasoned meats. This recipe highlights the wonderfully subtle flavor of ripe avocado with a little crunchy onion, ripe tomato, salt, lime, and cilantro—nothing else.

Guacamole is tastier and more attractive when it has a little texture, even chunks of avocado, so please make it by hand and not in a food processor or, heaven forbid, a blender. If you have a *molcajete*, use it to make and serve guacamole, as is traditionally done in Mexico.

Guacamole is only as good as your ingredients. Use ripe Hass avocados (see the opposite page) and fresh tomatoes, never canned. Though it's tempting to add other herbs and spices (and plenty of other guacamole recipes do), simple really is best.

Makes 4 servings

2 perfectly ripe Hass avocados
¾ teaspoon kosher salt, or to taste
1½ teaspoons freshly squeezed lime juice, preferably from a Mexican limón (see page 30)

1 ripe Roma tomato or 6 to 8 sweet cherry tomatoes, seeded and finely chopped
¼ white onion, finely chopped
12 large cilantro sprigs, stemmed and roughly chopped

1. Remove the seed and peel from the avocados (see the opposite page) and place in a bowl or molcajete.
2. Sprinkle with the salt and lime juice and crush with a fork, potato masher, or tejolote. When the consistency is that of a chunky puree, stir in the tomato, onion, and cilantro.
3. Taste for seasoning. If the guacamole is to be eaten with tostadas as a snack, it should be more highly seasoned. Served alongside carnitas or carne asada, I prefer it less seasoned, so it balances the other flavors.

Avocado Sauce

This is not guacamole but a creamy, thin sauce used at many street stands to lend a little moisture and flavor to fish tacos or carne asada tacos. The sauce is best made in a blender or food processor.

Makes ½ cup

¼ ripe avocado, peeled
Pinch of kosher salt
A few drops of freshly squeezed lime juice, preferably from a Mexican limón (see page 30)
1–2 tablespoons water or milk
2 cilantro sprigs, stemmed and chopped (optional)

1. Place the avocado, salt, and lime juice in a blender or small food processor. Add 1 tablespoon water and pulse. Add more liquid as necessary to make a sauce the consistency of thick cream.
2. Add the cilantro and pulse again just to blend. Taste for seasoning; it should be a little bland.

AVOCADOS

■ ■ ■

The avocado is a fruit—a sumptuous, fat-laden, silky-textured fruit. Although originally descended from a small, wild variety native to the subtropical Americas, different cultivated species are now available. Depending on where you live, they seem to be divided into California/Mexican types—such as Hass and Fuerte, with their dark, pebbly-rough skin and high oil content—and the Florida species—which are larger and have smooth, shiny green skin.

The best avocado, to my mind, is the Hass, which has firm buttery flesh, a lush 30 percent oil content, and heavenly flavor. A Hass will cost you more, but it's worth it. The Fuerte is also acceptable. Other avocados have a stringy, watery texture, a lower oil content, and less taste, but they are appreciably lower in calories.

Test an avocado for ripeness by gently pressing the fruit in the palm of your hand; it should yield slightly. Gentle pressure at the stem end should also reveal a flesh-like softness. If all the avocados for sale are rock-hard, they will ripen perfectly on their own at room temperature. No matter how badly you want guacamole, wait until they're ripe; underripe avocados tend to be bitter, hard, and flavorless. Have patience.

It is sometimes suggested that the pit be returned to the guacamole to prevent browning. In my experience, this makes absolutely no difference. The only way to prevent browning (oxidization) is to press a piece of plastic wrap firmly onto the surface, forcing out all air.

PITTING, PEELING, AND STORING AVOCADOS

Cut the avocado in half lengthwise, from pointed top to round bottom. Twist gently to separate the halves. Hold the half with the pit flat in the palm of one hand and tap the pit with the edge of a chef's knife. The knife will bite into the pit; twist and remove the pit, still pinned to the knife. Tap the flat of the knife sharply on the edge of a trash can to dislodge the pit.

To remove the skin, take a large spoon and run the edge of it between the skin and the flesh of the avocado. Then work the spoon in and scoop the green "meat" out in one perfect piece. Or cut the halves lengthwise into quarters. Hold each quarter cut side down and peel the skin away from the flesh (this only works on ripe avocados!).

Scrape away any bruised spots. The avocado can now be sliced into a "fan," mashed, or chopped.

Note: Avocados should be used within an hour after peeling. If you wish to hold them longer, generously brush all exposed surfaces, inside and out, with fresh lime or lemon juice. Drizzle more juice on a plate and set the avocado halves, flat side down, on the juice. Fit the empty skin back on top. Refrigerate until ready to use, up to 24 hours. There will be a small amount of discoloration but no change in flavor.

CHILES 101

While many Americans see a chile and think "hot," chiles have a wide range of distinct flavors and heat levels and very specific uses—not always for heat. Most Mexican food is not spicy hot at all but relies on chiles and fresh vegetables for its subtlety and rich savor. In fact, Mexican cooks are horrified to see the uninitiated ladling hot sauce on their food indiscriminately. It's like putting ketchup on *foie gras*.

Every chile, dried and fresh, has its own personality, along with very specific culinary uses. To further confuse the matter, the same fresh chile may have a different name when dried and have another half-dozen names in different parts of Mexico.

Fresh and dried chiles are used differently. Fresh chiles are roasted to bring out their flavors and are often served stuffed. Dried chiles are used exclusively in the pantheon of complex sauces and flavorings (*adobos*) that are the pride of Mexican cookery.

The heat in chiles comes from the chemical capsaicin and lingers mostly in the seeds and white ribs inside the chile. The thinner the chile and the more seeds it contains, the hotter it will be.

The flesh between the ribs, even in a fiery habanero chile, is never unbearably hot. Sampling this flesh (carefully) is a good way to introduce your palate to the flavors of different chiles, and this will help you cook with them creatively. As you sample many kinds of chiles, you will also notice that they affect your taste buds in different ways. Some register in the back of your throat, some on the tip of your tongue, and some down the sides of your tongue.

Even among hot chiles, the heat level can vary dramatically from pepper to pepper, so never assume that the next chile of any type will be as bland as the one you just tasted.

Dried chiles should always be very clean as well as flexible rather than stiff and crumbly. They should be whole, with stem intact—try not to buy broken pieces. If you are buying chiles in a package, make sure there are no signs of bug infestation.

Dried chiles often look similar but are different colors when ground and have different tastes. There are three main types: long, dark red, and smooth (guajillo, New Mexico, California); wide, dark brown to black, and wrinkled (ancho, mulato, and pasilla or negro); and small, bright red, and narrow (chile de árbol, piquín or tepín, and puya or Japonés).

All chiles should be treated with caution. Use gloves when you handle them and be careful when toasting dry chiles; the fumes can be extremely irritating.

Poblano   California   Jalapeño   Serrano   Habanero   Güero   Chilaca   Guajillo

Below, from left, beginning on opposite page:

FRESH CHILES

POBLANO Wide and short, shiny, very dark green to almost black. Poblanos are charred and peeled to bring out their wonderful flavor. Used in salsas, *rajas* (page 179), or stuffed to make authentic chile relleno. Sometimes moderately spicy.

CALIFORNIA OR ANAHEIM Slender and 6 to 8 inches long. Usually mild but may have some heat in the ribs. Used for salsas, *rajas*, stuffing.

JALAPEÑO Rounded, dark green, shiny, 3 to 4 inches in length. Pleasantly hot, fresh-tasting. Used raw in salsas, charred, pickled, sliced into rings, or stuffed.

SERRANO The preferred chile for salsas. Slender, bullet shaped, 2 to 3 inches long. Used raw in salsas, charred, sliced. Usually hotter than jalapeños.

HABANERO OR SCOTCH BONNET Small, round with ridges, lovely orange-gold color. Always extremely hot and should be handled and eaten with caution.

GÜERO Pale yellow chile about 2 to 3 inches in length, rounded, with a waxy skin. Has a gentle, lingering heat. May be grilled, pickled, or roasted and eaten whole.

CHILACA Long and slender, twisting, chocolate brown. Most often used in the traditional cooking of central Mexico. Seldom found fresh north of the border. When dried, it becomes the true *pasilla* or *negro* chile.

DRIED CHILES

GUAJILLO The most commonly used, in red chile salsa or on enchiladas. Dark red to almost black, shiny, 6 to 8 inches in length. Guajillos have a full, rounded chile flavor and cook/grind to dark red.

NEW MEXICO Look similar to guajillos, but cook/grind to a darker color and have a different, deeper flavor.

CALIFORNIA Sometimes lighter colored. Cook/grind to a lovely bright red, with a light, almost sweet taste.

ANCHO Dried poblano chile that looks like a large flat raisin on a stem. The deeply wrinkled flesh has a rich, fruity flavor. Often called, incorrectly, a pasilla.

MULATO A different variety of dried poblano that looks very similar to the true ancho but has a different flavor.

CHIPOTLE A ripe jalapeño that has been dried over wood smoke, with a hot, smoky flavor. Sold dried or canned in adobo—cooked until soft with tomatoes, vinegar, salt, and spices.

CHILE DE ÁRBOL Long, thin, full of seeds. Has a quick, sharp heat. Used whole for flavor or ground with water, garlic, vinegar, and salt for hot sauce.

PIQUÍN OR TEPÍN Tiny, very hot. Ground chiles have an orange tinge. Used whole or ground into a very hot salsa.

PUYA OR JAPONÉS Medium heat and fruity flavor.

| New Mexico | California | Ancho | Mulato | Chipotle | Chile de árbol | Piquín | Puya or japoné |

Three Hot Salsas with Chiles de Arbol

Chiles de árbol are thin and red and about 3 inches long. Resembling pointed spears, árbols have a sharp, fierce, piercing heat. Tempered with vinegar and salt, árbol salsas are especially good with any kind of seafood. Dispense small droplets into soups; onto *aguachiles*, seafood *cockteles*, or tostadas; or alongside the creamy sauce on fish tacos. Arbol salsas are at their hottest within an hour after being made, and then the heat diminishes. Slightly.

Salsa de Chiles de Arbol #1: Red Hot with a Little Vinegar and Salt

Excellent in seafood soups and on anything fish or shellfish. Little drops, please.

Makes ½ cup

1 large garlic clove, unpeeled
1 cup dried chiles de árbol (about 30 chiles), stemmed
⅓ cup water
½ teaspoon kosher salt
1 teaspoon vinegar, preferably Heinz

1. Lay a sheet of foil in a heavy cast-iron frying pan or comal. Over medium-high heat in a well-ventilated area, dry-roast the garlic until the skin is blackened in places and the garlic is soft (about 7 minutes). Remove the peel.
2. Wearing gloves, seed the chiles and place in a blender. Process until well pulverized. Add the garlic, water, and salt and puree until as smooth as possible. Scrape into a bowl and add the vinegar. Let stand 30 minutes. Taste for seasoning. The sauce should be hot and highly seasoned; add more vinegar and salt if necessary. If desired, the salsa may be thinned with a little water.

Note: This sauce may be strained before serving, but I don't bother. If you want it hotter, leave the seeds in.

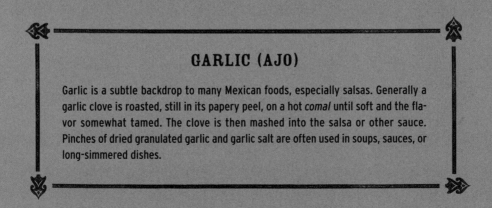

GARLIC (AJO)

Garlic is a subtle backdrop to many Mexican foods, especially salsas. Generally a garlic clove is roasted, still in its papery peel, on a hot *comal* until soft and the flavor somewhat tamed. The clove is then mashed into the salsa or other sauce. Pinches of dried granulated garlic and garlic salt are often used in soups, sauces, or long-simmered dishes.

Salsa de Chiles de Arbol #2:
Smoky, Blackened, and Chunky

Good with pork or anything fatty or rich. Has a smoky, slightly bitter taste and is often paired with a bowl of diced raw onions.

Makes ⅔ cup

1 large garlic clove, unpeeled
1 cup dried chiles de árbol (about 30 chiles), stemmed
½ cup water
½ teaspoon kosher salt

1. Lay a sheet of foil in a heavy cast-iron frying pan or comal. Over medium-high heat in a well-ventilated area, dry-roast the garlic until the skin is blackened in places and the garlic is quite soft (about 7 minutes). Remove the peel.
2. Quickly toss the chiles into the hot pan and press down with a spatula for a few seconds; the chiles will blacken on one side in a flash. Remove to a bowl and allow to cool completely. Wearing gloves, crumble the chiles into small pieces. Put into a blender and process until finely ground. Add the garlic, water, and salt and pulse until well blended. Add a little more water if necessary but don't water it down.

Salsa de Chiles de Arbol #3:
with Roasted Tomato

The most sophisticated of the three—but it still packs quite a wallop. This salsa should be used fresh. (Halve the recipe if you don't need the full amount.)

Makes 2 cups

2 large garlic cloves, unpeeled
1 cup dried chiles de árbol (about 30), stemmed
½ cup hot water
2 ripe Roma tomatoes
½ teaspoon kosher salt

1. Lay a sheet of foil in a heavy cast-iron frying pan or comal. Over medium-high heat in a well-ventilated area, dry-roast the garlic until the skin is blackened in places and the garlic is quite soft (about 7 minutes). Remove the peel.
2. Wearing gloves, remove most of the seeds from the chiles and break the flesh into small pieces; soak in the water for about 30 minutes, covered. Transfer to a blender and puree until as smooth as possible. Add the garlic, tomatoes, and salt and pulse until fairly smooth, adding cold water by the tablespoon as needed. Scrape into a bowl and let stand for 30 minutes. Add a little more water, if necessary; taste for seasoning.

Chipotle Salsa

Chipotles are wood-smoked, dried jalapeños. They are most often found canned and reconstituted *en adobo* with tomato, vinegar, and garlic. Add roasted tomatoes and garlic to tame their fire and chipotles make an excellent salsa, good on everything from tostadas (with a dab of crema) to shrimp to roast chicken and rice. I even like a spoonful of chipotle salsa swirled into soup to liven things up. I love this salsa on carne asada, too.

Makes 1 cup

2 ripe Roma tomatoes
1 garlic clove, unpeeled
3 canned chipotle chiles, about half of a 4-ounce can
3 tablespoons finely chopped white onion
3 tablespoons water
¼ teaspoon kosher salt
Juice of ½ lime, preferably a Mexican limón (see page 30)

1. Lay a sheet of foil in a heavy cast-iron frying pan or comal. Over medium-high heat in a well-ventilated area, dry-roast the tomatoes and garlic until the skins are blackened in places and the vegetables are soft. Peel the garlic.
2. In a food processor, pulse the garlic until finely chopped. Add the chiles and pulse until fine. Place in a serving bowl.
3. Put the onion in the food processor and pulse until quite fine. Core the tomatoes and chop into chunks; add to the processor and pulse until finely chopped. Transfer to the serving bowl and stir well. Thin with water and add the salt and lime juice. Let stand for 30 minutes before serving.

Note: The proportions of tomatoes and chipotles can be adjusted to suit your taste.

CRYING TIME: BOTTLED HOT SAUCE

Every place you eat in Mexico will have at least one brand of bottled hot sauce available for adding heat *al gusto*.

For Mexican food, imported Mexican hot sauces are the best: Huichol, Salsa Amor, Tapatío, and La Chula are some popular brands, but there are dozens to choose from. They tend to be thick and reliably hot. Standard American hot sauces are too thin and vinegary to have the desired effect, and Asian hot sauces taste—well, Asian.

You can make your own powerful hot sauce from dried chiles de árbol or chiles piquín (see page 38).

Roasted Jalapeño Salsa

I found this salsa at a *puesto* by the fish market in Ensenada. Olive green flecked with bits of charred chile skin, it is very attractive served with an array of other salsas (just make sure your guests don't confuse it with the much milder tomatillo salsa).

Believe it or not, this is one of the milder salsas in this section, despite being made purely from roasted jalapeños. The long, slow cooking seems to sweeten and mellow the heat just a tad. But don't be fooled—this is not for the fainthearted. It's meant to be served as a condiment with food—excellent with grilled meats, fish tacos, or anything fried—not scooped up with tostadas, though that might be fun to watch. The salsa keeps for several days, refrigerated.

Makes 1½ cups

10 large firm jalapeño chiles
3 large garlic cloves, unpeeled
1 teaspoon kosher salt
$\frac{1}{3}$–$\frac{1}{2}$ cup water

1. Lay a sheet of foil in a heavy cast-iron frying pan or comal. Over high heat in a well-ventilated area, dry-roast the chiles and garlic until the skins are blackened in places and the vegetables are soft (about 20 to 25 minutes; remove the garlic after 7 minutes).

2. Alternatively, if the grill is on, you can wrap the chiles and garlic in two layers of foil and grill the packet over medium heat for 15 to 20 minutes, turning often.

3. Cool the chiles. Peel the garlic and place in a blender with the salt and $\frac{1}{3}$ cup water; pulse several times to chop the garlic. Wearing gloves, remove the stems from the chiles and tear the flesh into strips; add to the blender. Pulse several more times, until the chiles are coarsely chopped; if necessary add water a tablespoon at a time. Don't overthin the sauce and don't puree until smooth—a little texture is nice. Scrape into a bowl and allow to rest for 30 minutes. Taste for seasoning. Zowie!

Note: You can also make the sauce in a *molcajete*: Grind the garlic and salt to a paste. Add the stemmed jalapeños and grind to a textured puree, adding small amounts of water as necessary. Thin with more water, adjust salt (if necessary), and serve right in the molcajete.

Sweet and Hot Ancho Chile Salsa

The dark green, spade-shaped fresh chile known as poblano is, when dried, called ancho, which means "wide" or "broad." (Note: This chile is sometimes incorrectly labeled pasilla or even mulato.) It has an acid-sweet taste that blends well in salsas with tomatoes, fresh or dried chiles, or dried fruit, as in this simple salsa. This is spectacular daubed on grilled turkey or dark-meat chicken.

Makes about 2 cups

1 ripe Roma tomato
1 garlic clove, unpeeled
3 dried ancho chiles
2 dried chiles de árbol
½ cup seedless black raisins
1¼ cups boiling water
2 tablespoons vegetable oil
¼ cup finely minced white onion
1 teaspoon kosher salt

1. Lay a sheet of foil in a heavy cast-iron frying pan or comal. Over high heat in a well-ventilated area, dry-roast the tomato and garlic until the skins are blackened in places and the vegetables are soft (about 20 minutes for the tomato; remove the garlic after 5 minutes). Remove from the pan.
2. Set the anchos in the hot pan, pressing quickly on both sides with a spatula and removing immediately from the pan. Be careful not to scorch the chiles. Allow to cool.
3. Wearing gloves, remove the stems and seeds from both the anchos and árbols; tear the chiles into pieces and put them in a blender. Add the raisins and water. Cover and let stand for 30 minutes. Peel the garlic and add to the blender, along with the tomato. Puree on high speed for several minutes, or until completely smooth.
4. In a large frying pan, heat the oil over medium heat and fry the onion until softened and sweet but not brown. Add the chile puree and cook the sauce, stirring, for about 5 minutes, or until thickened. Add the salt and taste for seasoning.

Grilled Chile and Tomato Salsa

I had a salsa like this at El Taco de la Ermita in Tijuana, the famous "gourmet taco stand" and one of the most remarkable places to eat in all of Baja. *Chef-patrón* Javier Campos spoons a little thin, flavorful salsa onto a tortilla before layering on the other ingredients, adding an underlying zip. This is my version of his unique salsa. Add to a taco or serve on the side with any grilled meat or fish. The salsa ingredients should be grilled until well blackened, and the salsa should be thin.

Makes 1½ cups

3 large fresh Anaheim chiles
1 fresh serrano chile
3 ripe Roma tomatoes
2 garlic cloves, unpeeled

About ½ cup water
1 teaspoon white vinegar, preferably Heinz (optional)
¾ teaspoon kosher salt, or to taste

1. Lay a sheet of foil in a heavy cast-iron frying pan or comal. Over high heat in a well-ventilated area, dry-roast the chiles, tomatoes, and garlic. Roast the Anaheims and tomatoes until well blackened on all sides; roast the garlic and serrano until just softened.

2. Cool the chiles. Core the tomatoes and drop into a food processor. Stem the serrano, peel the garlic, and add them to the processor.

3. Stem and seed the Anaheims; do not peel. Add to the processor and pulse until smooth. Scrape into a bowl and add the water, vinegar, and salt. The sauce should be fairly thin.

CHARRING

Charring is a technique used to remove the skin from a chile and add a little smoky flavor, without overcooking it. It's a quick process that is best done through direct contact with a flame, such as a gas burner flame or a grill on high, but it can be done successfully under a very hot broiler. All surfaces of the chile must be quickly and completely blackened, as opposed to pan-roasting, where only the parts of the vegetable in direct contact with the hot pan will blacken.

Charred chiles are often those that will be further cooked, such as the fresh poblano chiles used in *rajas* or chiles rellenos. Fresh chiles have an unpalatable thick skin that must be removed. Tomatoes or other vegetables are sometimes charred in specific recipes.

To char, wash and dry the vegetables. Set directly in the flame on the burner or over the hottest part of the grill. Char quickly, watching constantly and turning often, for a minute or two—no longer. (Caution: Chiles will puff up and have been known to explode. Poke a hole in them to prevent this.)

If you char chiles over an indoor burner, work in a well-ventilated area. Remove the stems from the chiles. I sometimes thread vegetables onto metal skewers, which hold them in place over the burner. If you are using a broiler, preheat on high and set the vegetables as close as possible to the heat source. Watch carefully and turn often.

Raw Tomatillo Salsa

You'll wonder how you ever got along without tomatillo salsa—crunchy, acidic, full of flavor, just the right complement to rich food like grilled beef, pork *carnitas*, or shrimp.

Tomatillos look like hard little green tomatoes, 2 to 3 inches in diameter and wrapped in papery brownish husks. They are unrelated to tomatoes, belonging instead to the ground-cherry family and native to North America.

To prepare tomatillos, strip off the husks and wash well under warm water to remove the sticky film from the skin.

Makes 1½ cups

6 medium tomatillos, husked and washed
½ cup diced white onion
1 large fresh serrano chile, stemmed
12 cilantro sprigs, stemmed
½ teaspoon kosher salt, or to taste

1. In a food processor, pulse the tomatillos until chunky. Add the onion, chile, cilantro, and salt and pulse to make a chunky, thick puree.
2. Taste for salt and add more as needed.

Cooked Tomatillo Salsa

Smoother, sweeter, and more sophisticated.

Makes 1½ cups

6 medium tomatillos, husked and washed
1 garlic clove
¾ cup white onion cut into 1-inch chunks
1 large fresh jalapeño or serrano chile, stemmed and cut into 1-inch pieces
1 teaspoon kosher salt
12 cilantro sprigs, stemmed

1. Cut the tomatillos into quarters and place in a 1½-quart saucepan. Add the garlic, onion, chile, and salt.

2. Add just enough water to barely cover the tomatillos and quickly bring to a boil over high heat. Boil the vegetables until the tomatillos have just begun to soften and the tip of a knife can be inserted, about 5 minutes; do not overcook.

3. Drain off the cooking water and transfer the vegetables to a blender. Add the cilantro leaves. Pulse until a thick, textured sauce forms. A little chunky texture is nice in this salsa, though you may prefer to puree it completely.

MOLCAJETE

This odd, ingenious little tool was North America's first food processor. It's used to mash, grind, and puree and also acts as a serving dish. The stubby little bowl, traditionally carved from black lava rock, stands on three short, sturdy legs (more stable than four). A cone-shaped tool called a *tejolote*, also made of lava rock, is used to grind, stir, and mash. There's even a special brush made of natural fibers for cleaning the *molcajete* and *tejolote*.

In pre-Conquest times the *molcajete* was used to grind nuts, seeds, chiles, and soft vegetables into seasoning pastes and salsas, such as *mole* and guacamole. Most salsas made in the *molcajete* are served in the stone bowl.

The *molcajete* is still a fixture in the Mexican kitchen. Salsas made with a *molcajete* and *tejolote* have a velvety, airy texture that's impossible to duplicate with knife, blender, or food processor.

Molcajetes may be presoaked in water to keep food cool through evaporation or heated in an oven and used to serve bubbling hot dishes like fajitas and *fundido* (melted cheese with strips of roasted pepper).

Learning to use the *molcajete* requires some patience and practice. Tip: Choose very soft vegetables and very dry, crumbly (toasted) ingredients. Use more of a stirring motion, rather than pounding or smashing, which will cause splattering.

Mango Salsa

Versions of this salsa are wildly popular on both sides of the border, even though it is probably an American invention. If you can't get great mangoes, try orange-fleshed Mexican papayas, peaches, apricots, or nectarines—whatever is in season and flagrantly ripe.

I like this salsa best made with a flaming habanero, the chile that takes no prisoners, but it's equally good with serrano chiles or even the faintest hiss of heat. Whatever you use, make sure to season the salsa assertively with lime juice and salt.

Mango salsa goes wonderfully with any kind of seafood—sautéed, grilled, or roasted—such as seared scallops, crab cakes, grilled shrimp, or pan-roasted sea bass or salmon. Or try it atop creamy goat cheese on toasted bread.

Makes about 1⅓ cups

1 large mango, peeled, pitted, and cut into ⅛ inch dice
⅓ cup finely diced red onion
1 teaspoon kosher salt
2 teaspoons sugar
1 teaspoon white vinegar, preferably Heinz
1 tablespoon freshly squeezed lime juice, preferably from a Mexican limón (see page 30)
½ teaspoon minced fresh habanero chile or 2 tablespoons minced fresh serrano chile
1½ tablespoons finely chopped cilantro
1 teaspoon finely chopped mint
2 tablespoons finely diced red bell pepper (optional)

Combine all ingredients in the order given. Let stand at room temperature for at least 30 minutes before serving. It should be used the same day it is made.

Mayonesa Secret Sauce

Simply essential for fish tacos. Just a little bit is all you need.

Makes ½ cup

½ cup mayonnaise or lime-flavored mayonnaise
1–2 teaspoons white vinegar, preferably Heinz
1½ tablespoons water or milk

Place the mayonnaise in a bowl and use a fork to slowly stir in vinegar to taste. Add water to loosen to the consistency of thick cream.

2
SILVER RAIN
COOKING FROM THE COAST

El que hambre tiene, en pescado piensa.
(When you're hungry, you can only think of fish.)
—Mexican folk saying

Separating the Gulf of California in the east from the Pacific Ocean to the west, the Baja peninsula is edged with almost 2,000 miles of unspoiled, steep rocky coastline that, even today, is mostly empty of human settlement.

In contrast, the waters offshore teem with life. The Gulf of California (also known as the Sea of Cortés), with its mangrove swamps, islets, and underwater seamounts, is unique—and one of the most ecologically diverse and important sites on the planet. On the Pacific side, huge forests of underwater kelp sway in the mingling of cold and warm currents over offshore canyons. Surrounding the entire peninsula are some of the richest fishing waters in the world.

Sardines and anchovies were once so numerous here that passing schools looked like a silver rain streaming beneath the water. With the little fish came their valuable predators: huge schools of yellowfin and bluefin tuna, albacore, and jack. It was the fishing industry built on sardines and tuna that brought settlement and prosperity to the Baja coast in the early years of the 20th century.

The waters of Baja California still yield abundantly.

By eight o'clock in the morning, Ensenada's fish market, the old Mercado Negro, has been in full swing for hours, two long rows of busy stalls, back to back, staffed by fishermen in white rubber boots and bright yellow aprons. Chill air creeps from the nearby harbor, where fishing boats, trawlers, and *pangas* rock in the swell from the Pacific.

The gleaming catch from hundreds of miles of coastline lies neatly stacked on huge wooden tables, species and prices scrawled on soggy pieces of cardboard. Fish is piled on large blocks of cloudy gray ice that melts with a listless drip onto the wet concrete floor. The air is dense with cold and moisture. Smaller fish are stacked like cords of wood: corvina, surf perch, rock cod, calico bass, gulf snapper, lingcod, mackerel, even some small barracuda, still wearing a malicious glare in their cold black eyes. By the door two shovelnose sharks, each as long as a man, flop out of a wheelbarrow. Their odd thick skin is dry and gray-blue.

Smaller fish, like corvina and red snapper, are ready to fry, with deep slashes cut down the sides. Every table has a plastic dishpan full of rosy pink fresh tuna, ground like hamburger, ready to be turned into Ensenada-style *ceviche*.

One fisherman tosses onto his table a gleaming, bright-pink-speckled lingcod that's clearly just off one of the boats at the wharf. He stops to pluck a tiny octopus out of the gaping mouth of one of the fish and says, "See? He's still eating his breakfast!"

There's a white sea bass from the Sea of Cortés, a yard long and weighing at least 50 pounds. There are massive center-cut chunks of swordfish, more than a foot in diameter and 3 feet long. Whole yellowfin tuna loins cut in cross section show the quadrilateral muscle partitions. The flesh is a deep brownish color, not the luminous clear red of the sashimi grade favored by sushi chefs; that goes immediately to Japanese buyers at a premium.

Another table is stacked with white-bellied halibut, close to 3 feet in length, wide and flat, mouths agape with wicked, crooked teeth. Tucked among bullet-shaped yellowtails and the gleaming mackerel at one table are a dozen or so bright orange garibaldi—the state fish of California, but legal to sell in Mexico. "I guess that's why you call it El Mercado Negro [the Black Market]", says a passerby.

Huge flying squid, usually strangers to these waters, are a bonus this year from the *El Niño* current; there are heaps of these eerie tentacled visitors, along with fresh octopus, legs hanging limply over the edge of the tray. More plastic pans are piled with fillets of bat ray, *cazón* (shark), and smaller bass and rockfish. Buckets of huge pismo clams sit on the floor: the chocolate and the gray, also some deeply ridged clams from the bay at San Quentín. In tubs there are orange abalone, out of the shell; dark-gray periwinkles; black *choros*, or mussels, as long as your hand; heaps of mahogany-colored smoked tuna, marlin, and swordfish.

One fisherman has an iced basin of fresh sweet shrimp (*ebi*) to sell, an occasional catch from an offshore deep-water canyon. Another table holds fans of beautifully arranged shrimp in all sizes, from little-finger size to huge, fat San Felipe "blue" shrimp that instantly bring to mind the better uses of garlic and butter. Crates of blue crab, fresh sardines, and more clams sit helter-skelter on the ground.

Outside the fish market entrance, rows of busy fish taco stands are now doing a booming mid-morning business. The smell of frying fish and hot oil, toasting corn tortillas, and wet pavement permeates the air. One *puesto* has the tail of an enormous basking shark, as tall as a man, mounted on the wall. Another keeps a hunched, ratty crow in a cage, as beady-eyed as the fish in the market. Otherwise, the stands are nearly identical—brightly painted open-air *puestos* with wooden benches and shelves and rows of giant goblets holding an array of colorful salsas: *pico de gallo, chile de árbol*, creamy *mayonesa* sauce, roasted jalapeño salsa, bright green tomatillo salsa, lime wedges, and pickled jalapeños and carrots.

Bajacalifornianos love seafood of all kinds. Their cuisine is rich in quick, often ingenious preparations that enhance the simple pleasure of eating perfectly fresh seafood, and they often use less common fish and shellfish, such as sea snails or smaller fish. With its seafood *cockteles* and campfire-grilled spiny lobsters, its abalone chorizo and piquantly sauced fish steaks, its sumptuous shrimp and fat, sweet shellfish, Baja inspires you to regard—and cook—the sea's abundance in a whole new way.

RECIPES

SUSTAINABLE BAJA

To me, Baja California *is* its coastline, rugged and clean, primal and untouched. Or so I thought. While researching this book, I discovered that some of the common fish and shellfish species caught in the Pacific and the Sea of Cortés are threatened, some to the verge of extinction, due to overfishing, environmental degradation from pollution, and destruction of "nursery" habitats, such as estuaries. The same scene is being played out all over the world. Mexico, along with other responsible nations, is taking steps to regulate and conserve its fisheries, but much remains to be done worldwide—and you, the consumer, are the key.

Serge Dedina, Ph.D., executive director of the conservation group Wildcoast, puts it this way: "What is good for consumers to purchase commercially and what is okay to eat at a fisherman's house are two different issues."

Each of the seafood recipes in this book notes the species commonly used in Baja, then suggests an alternative, *sustainable* fish choice.

Certified and sustainable fisheries aim to maintain sizable fish populations and assure the livelihood of fishermen and their families for generations to come. These fisheries work within set catch limits and seasons. Biologists monitor the fish populations. Fishermen use methods that reduce bycatch (accidental killing and waste of other species), avoiding gillnetting, long-line fishing, and drift netting, which are very destructive to all sea life.

The Alaskan halibut and American Dungeness crab fisheries are two successful examples of managed sustainable fisheries. Australia and New Zealand have announced long-term plans to make their export fisheries 100 percent sustainable.

How can you help? Make informed, sustainable choices. Educate yourself at one of the Web sites listed below about which fish are sustainable choices and about fishing methods. Know where your seafood comes from and how it was caught. Don't buy, cook, or eat threatened species. Whenever possible in markets or in restaurants, choose fish from certified sustainable fisheries in the United States and worldwide that use responsible fishing methods. It's urgent that we change our ways. Educate yourself—and vote with your dollars.

MONTEREY BAY AQUARIUM (www.mbayaq.org), through their Seafood Watch, maintains a handy printable consumer guide for shoppers and restaurateurs. This is the gold standard to use when shopping.

MARINE STEWARDSHIP COUNCIL (www.msc.org) monitors fisheries worldwide and certifies sustainable species and fisheries.

WILDCOAST (www.wildcoast.net) is an international organization dedicated to the preservation of the coastal Californias and works extensively in Baja California.

PASSIONFISH (www.passionfish.org) fosters education and dialogue among fishermen, distributors, chefs, and consumers.

CHEFS COLLABORATIVE (www.chefscollaborative.org) provides a forum for chefs and consumers to learn about sustainable seafood and agriculture.

SEAFOOD CHOICES ALLIANCE (www.seafoodchoices.com) was founded by the seafood industry to reach out directly to consumers. There is not always full agreement between the industry and conservation groups about what constitutes sustainable fisheries, but informed consumers look at all sides of an issue.

Manuela's Roast Tuna Loin
with Chipotles

Ensenada has always been home to a large tuna fleet, so tuna is an important part of the area's culinary heritage. When you have tons of tuna, imaginative preparations are always appreciated! A third-generation Ensenadan told me about this tuna "roast"—the kind of thing you'd serve for Sunday dinner, if you had a 200-pound tuna handy. Try to buy the fish in one large piece; the narrow part toward the tail works well, but don't use the very end—it can be sinewy and tough.

Sustainable choices for preparing this at home include pole- or troll-caught bigeye or yellowfin tuna, albacore, farmed sturgeon, or Alaskan halibut in season.

Oven-roasted potatoes are the perfect side dish.

Makes 6 servings

2½ pounds tuna in a large, thick piece
1 tablespoon kosher salt
3 tablespoons vegetable oil
8 garlic cloves, cut in half lengthwise
½ large white onion, cut into thin strips from root end to stem end
3 large fresh green Anaheim chiles, seeded and cut into thin 2-inch strips

¼ teaspoon dried thyme
2 bay leaves
1½ tablespoons finely chopped chipotles in adobo
3 ripe Roma tomatoes, cut into eighths
¾ cup white wine
Lime wedges, preferably from Mexican limones (see page 30)

1. Preheat the oven to 350 degrees. Season the tuna well with the salt and place it in a baking dish just large enough to hold it.

2. In a medium frying pan, heat the oil over medium heat and sauté the garlic until golden. Add the onion and Anaheims and cook until the vegetables just start to wilt. Add the thyme, bay leaves, chipotles, and tomatoes and cook for 2 minutes.

3. Spoon the vegetables over the tuna, pour the wine over, and cover with foil. Bake for 25 to 30 minutes (until the fish registers 140 degrees on an instant-read thermometer). Let stand about 10 minutes under the foil before serving. Serve with the lime wedges.

Fresh Tuna Salad

We eat so much fashionably seared-raw tuna that we forget how delicious fully cooked, moist tuna can taste. And for tuna salad, you may never go back to canned once you taste how fabulous it is with fresh fish.

This salad is terrific as an *antojito* (appetizer), on crackers or *tostadas*, in sandwiches, stuffed into long fingers of endive, or packed into a hollowed-out ripe tomato or avocado for a light lunch.

The sustainable choice: troll- or pole-caught bigeye, yellowfin, or albacore. Avoid bluefin tuna.

Makes 3 cups, enough for 36 tostadas

2 cups (about 1 pound) cooked tuna or albacore pieces (see below)

1/3 cup finely chopped red or white onion, rinsed in cold water

2 large ripe Roma tomatoes, seeded and finely diced

1 medium fresh serrano chile, minced (optional)

10 cilantro sprigs, stemmed and chopped

1 tablespoon freshly squeezed lime juice, preferably from a Mexican limón (see page 30), or lemon juice

2 teaspoons red wine vinegar

2 tablespoons olive oil

1/2 teaspoon kosher salt, or to taste

1/4–1/3 cup mayonnaise, to taste

Hass avocado, pitted, peeled, and diced (optional)

1. Prepare the tuna and set aside.

2. In a bowl, combine the onion, tomatoes, chile, and cilantro. Toss with the lime juice, vinegar, oil, salt, and mayonnaise.

3. Break up the tuna and add to the bowl; it will flake naturally into chunks. Stir to combine. Chill for 30 minutes and taste for seasoning. You may want to add more lime juice, salt, or even chiles—I like it spicy.

4. Even more delicious topped with diced avocado.

Variation: Leave out chiles and cilantro; add 1/4 cup pitted and chopped green olives or capers.

Tuna Roasted in Foil

A rewarding way to use up small pieces or tails.

Makes 2 cups

2 tablespoons olive oil

1 teaspoon kosher salt

Juice of 1 lime, preferably a Mexican limón (see page 30)

1 pound tuna or albacore (not sashimi grade)

1. Preheat the oven to 375 degrees. Lay out a double thickness of foil, about 18 inches long. Spread the oil, salt, and lime juice in the center of the foil.

2. Roll the tuna around to coat, then wrap the tuna in the foil, sealing the ends tightly.

3. Roast the packet for 30 minutes, or until the internal temperature is 140 degrees when tested with an instant-read thermometer. Remove from the oven, poke a 1-inch hole in the foil, and cool for 15 minutes.

4. Refrigerate, still in the foil, until completely cold.

TUNA—CALIFORNIA'S SECOND GOLD RUSH

Tuna fishery has a long, proud history in the San Diego—Baja California region. In the past, tuna (which can weigh hundreds of pounds apiece) were caught by the three-pole method: three men, three poles hooked to one line and one huge hook. It was hard, bloody, dangerous work. Teams of fishermen stood in low troughs along the side of the boat. When the frenzied fish bit down on the hook, three men together would flip the fish out of the water and over their heads onto the deck of the boat, jerk the hook out of the fish, and throw the hook back into the water.

When the boat was full to the gunwales, the catch was brought ashore and sent directly to small local canneries, where the tuna was cleaned, packed in olive oil, and canned for sale across the country. (The vast olive groves outside Ensenada were planted to supply their local canneries.)

Tuna hunting today has gone high-tech. Huge ships use helicopters, satellite tracking, and sonar to pursue ever-dwindling schools of tuna all over the world. The industry has moved offshore, mostly to the South Pacific, to evade American regulation of catches and fishing methods. The huge tuna that fishermen once risked their lives to take have nearly vanished from the sea, victim to unregulated overfishing and insatiable worldwide demand. The tuna bycatch (marine animals and other fish killed and discarded by fishermen) is also a cause for worry. With these great fish dies a way of life that we will never see again.

Sustainable choice: Buy pole-caught or troll-caught tuna from a regulated American fishery and avoid bluefin tuna.

Fisherman's Sashimi

Slices of velvety fresh fish—raw and sweet—are dressed in an intriguing blend of Mexican and Asian flavors, meant to be eaten quickly and appreciatively. Whether you call it sashimi, ceviche, or carpaccio is up to you. As long as the fish is ultra-fresh (buy from a reliable fish market) and the knife very sharp, it's hard to go wrong.

Tuna from the "corrals" off the coast of Ensenada would be the fish of choice in Baja, but other fish are equally exquisite raw, such as fresh Alaskan halibut, wild troll-caught salmon, or very fresh mackerel or yellowtail. And these are all sustainable choices. A combination of different colored fish is lovely.

Makes 6 to 8 servings

1 pound extremely fresh, sashimi-grade saltwater fish (see note above)
1/4 cup best-quality Japanese soy sauce
1 tablespoon freshly squeezed lime juice, preferably from a Mexican limón (see page 30)

1/4 small bunch cilantro, stemmed
3 Italian parsley sprigs, stemmed
3 green onions, thinly sliced
1–2 fresh serrano chiles, sliced crosswise into paper-thin circles

1. Chill a large serving platter. With a very sharp, thin knife, cut the fish into slices roughly 2 inches long, 1 inch wide, and 1/4 inch thick. Arrange the slices in an attractive pattern on the platter, wrap, and chill the fish until you are ready to serve.
2. Combine the soy sauce and lime juice.
3. Just before serving, roughly chop the cilantro and parsley. Pour the soy over the fish. Scatter the herbs and green onions over the fish. Serve the chiles in a small dish on the side.

SUSHI ON THE EDGE

South-of-the-border sushi makers sometimes incorporate salty/sour *chamoya* sauce as well as their traditional salsas into their sushi. Avocado, tomato, and tomatillo are favorite ingredients as well as grilled steak or chicken, corn, and cilantro along with the usual Japanese accompaniments of soy and wasabi.

Sashimi (thinly sliced raw fish) is also very popular, but in Baja they like to load on the chiles and cilantro and then dip it into soy sauce.

How does it all taste? Fantastic—neither Japanese nor Mexican, a delicious meeting of cuisines.

ENSENADA

■ ■ ■

To eat in Ensenada is to celebrate the best of land and sea. Long-established farms and ranches as well as a busy fishing port have fueled the economy for over 120 years. Local cooking centers on beef, chicken, vegetables, and fish. Wines from the Guadalupe Valley, just inland, are good and getting better.

Restaurant food is mostly home-style, though many local chefs cook with verve and originality. Seafood, even in the humblest establishments, is uniformly fresh, simple, and excellent. *Puestos* sell fish tacos, chicken *sopes*, grilled quail, seafood *cuockteles*, *chirimoya* ice pops, spicy goat soup, and teriyaki tacos.

This last vividly exemplifies the culinary legacy of Ensenada's Asian heritage. Chinese and Japanese fishermen and itinerant workers settled here generations ago. Today their descendants are proudly Mexican, and Asian ingredients have been in common use since long before fusion cooking became popular. Soy sauce, for example, is a frequent ingredient in local specialties, from grilled chiles to *ceviche*. And the town is full of good Chinese restaurants.

This is a real working town, not a tourist construct. Any traveler venturing a few steps beyond the curio shops that fill the streets closest to the cruise-ship dock finds the real Ensenada: neat neighborhoods, schools and colleges, bustling shops, cafés, museums, and cultural centers. The old adobe Santo Tomás winery has been turned into an atmospheric dining room, with tables set among the enormous wine barrels. Across the street is the original bottling plant, which is built around a huge copper brandy still (*alambre*) from the 1930s and features work by local artists and artisans. This is the only place many of the rare vintages from local wineries are sold (outside of the wineries themselves).

On the road out of town is one of Ensenada's oldest street stands, built decades ago when the paved road ended here and travel southward was a *real* adventure. Batches of tamales steam all day long in enormous old kettles built into a platform of handmade adobe brick. In addition to the tamales—filled with cheese and green chiles, fresh corn, pineapple, spiced chicken, or succulent shredded pork—the puesto sells cool, syrupy coconut milk, right out of the green shell, made to order (the *patrón* whacks the top off the coconut with an ancient machete). The *puesto* also sells cured green olives and olive oil from local olive groves, giving travelers a taste of old Ensenada to take with them.

PUERTO NUEVO:
UP TO YOUR KNEES IN LOBSTER

● ● ●

Around the beginning of the 20th century, Puerto Nuevo—now a short drive south of Tijuana—was a remote fishing village. Back then, the kelp beds along the coast were so laden with spiny lobsters that they were considered a garbage catch, fit only for bait or fertilizer. Being subsistence fishermen, the villagers sold their valuable fish and ate the unwanted lobster.

In time, a couple of small shacks began serving home-style food to the traffic between Ensenada and Tijuana, and the legend of lobster Puerto Nuevo style was born: deep-fried split lobsters served with beans, salsa, and large flour tortillas.

The town and its restaurants grew slowly. On treacherous roads, Puerto Nuevo seemed a long way from the border. For years, the only people who drove this far south were locals, a trickle of tourists headed for the beaches and casino of Ensenada, and other intrepid Americans coming to fish, surf, and camp further down the peninsula.

When I first saw it in the early 1980s, Puerto Nuevo was still a muddy cluster of potholed dirt roads tumbling down a steep drop-off to a little cove. A few very basic restaurants served the local specialty. We ate in one—a rough shell of cinder block without windows or a door. Or even a kitchen—in a corner of the room, an elderly woman fished split, fried lobsters from a cutoff 55-gallon drum full of boiling lard, while simultaneously rolling and cooking fresh flour tortillas on a griddle. Customers at the few battered tables rolled the deep-fried lobster tails in the warm tortillas along with beans, salsa, lime juice, and drizzles of margarine and drank beer from the bottle. Nine musicians in spangled suits blasted the room with *mariachi* music as my sister, who had discovered margaritas at several stops on the way south, laid her head on the table and went to sleep. As the last echoes of "Rancho Grande" faded down the pitch-black street, I ate my lobster, then hers.

As the food of the poor has become the food of the wealthy, the sleepy little town has been gentrified, with paid parking, public restrooms, and menu-waving touts clustering thick as seagulls in front of the dozens of restaurants that pack the newly cobblestoned streets. The funky shacks of yore have been replaced by curio shops and three- and four-story lobster *palacios* catering to busloads of tourists and a partying crowd from Southern California too young to remember when just getting here was an adventure.

Still, when done right, lobster Puerto Nuevo style is a trip back to old Baja. For those willing to deep-fry a lobster in lard, the recipe is on the following page. For everyone else, a less authentic, equally delicious no-lard lobster taco recipe follows below it.

Lobster, Puerto Nuevo Style

This is a faithfully authentic recipe, lard and all (see page 58). Have the salsas made, the tortillas warmed, and beans ready before cooking the lobsters. See below for a lard-free alternative.

Makes 6 servings

About 2 pounds good-quality lard, for deep-frying
6 spiny lobsters (1½ pounds each; see page 60)

TO SERVE

Fresh large flour tortillas, warmed
8 tablespoons (1 stick) margarine, melted (not butter!)

Lime wedges, preferably from Mexican limones
   (see page 30)
Frijoles Refritos (see page 245)
Pico de Gallo (see page 30)
Salsa de Chiles de Arbol #1 (see page 38)

1. In a large, deep, heavy pot, melt the lard over medium heat to 350 degrees on a deep-fry thermometer. *Important:* Do not fill the pot more than halfway with lard; see Safe Frying, page 248.
2. With a sharp knife, kill the lobsters by inserting the knife between the head and tail, to sever the spinal cord. Split the lobsters in half lengthwise. Scoop out the contents of the head with a spoon and discard. Rinse and pat dry thoroughly; the lobsters must be clean and dry before frying.
3. Carefully slip the lobster halves into the hot lard a few at a time. (*Important:* The level of the hot lard must remain well below the top of the pot.) Cook for about 5 minutes, or until the tails are curled and pink. Drain well.
4. The usual method of eating is to pull the tail meat from the shell and lay it in the middle of a tortilla. Spoon on some margarine and a squirt of lime juice. Add some beans and pico de gallo. Top with salsa. Fold the two sides in toward the middle and then roll snugly from the bottom up. Repeat as needed.

Much Easier Lobster Tacos

Makes 6 servings

6 spiny lobsters (1½ pounds each; see page 60)
4 tablespoons (½ stick) butter
1 garlic clove, minced

TO SERVE

Fresh corn or flour tortillas
Lime wedges, preferably Mexican limones (see page 30)
Frijoles Refritos (see page 245)
Pico de Gallo (see page 30)
Salsa de Chiles de Arbol #1 (see page 38)

1. As close as possible to serving time, kill the lobsters according to the directions above. Cook the lobsters by either boiling in salted water, splitting and grilling, or splitting and broiling.
2. In a small saucepan over low heat, melt the butter and stir in the garlic. Remove from the heat and reserve.
3. Warm the tortillas on a comal or griddle and keep hot in a tortilla warmer or wrapped in foil.
4. Remove the meat from the lobster tails (reserve the shells for stock, see page 103). Cut the tail meat into small cubes, no larger than ½ inch. Toss with the garlic butter and keep warm.
5. To serve on a tortilla, layer beans, lobster, lime juice, and salsas.

Campfire-Grilled Lobster
with Orange-Chipotle Glaze

When camping in Baja during lobster season, you sometimes catch so many of the doggone things that you get a little tired of lobster, lobster, lobster! The easiest way to cook them is on a grill rigged over the evening campfire—no pots to wash. And the smoky flavor is exceptionally good.

This recipe was inspired by those campfire lobsters. The smoky taste now comes from chipotles, and the cooking method is revised for the backyard grill.

Makes 6 servings

4 tablespoons (½ stick) butter
1 large shallot, minced (about 2 tablespoons)
1 medium garlic clove, chopped
3 tablespoons minced fresh ginger
2 teaspoons cornstarch

1 cup freshly squeezed orange juice (juice of about 3 oranges)
½ teaspoon kosher salt
3–4 tablespoons canned chipotles in adobo, finely chopped
3 spiny lobsters (about 2 pounds each; see below)

1. Make the glaze: In a saucepan over medium heat, melt 2 tablespoons of the butter and cook the shallot, garlic, and ginger until just softened; do not brown. Mix the cornstarch with the orange juice until dissolved. Pour into the garlic mixture and cook, stirring, until thickened. Add the salt. Turn off the heat and set the glaze aside for 15 minutes. Then strain the glaze and stir in the chipotles to taste. Keep warm.

2. Preheat the grill. Kill the lobsters according to the directions on page 59. Split the lobsters in half lengthwise and remove the dark vein and the green material in the head (we're here for the tail).

3. Melt the remaining 2 tablespoons butter and brush over the lobster meat. Pour half of the glaze into a small bowl and use a basting brush to coat the lobsters generously with the glaze. Place the lobsters on the grill over medium-low heat, cut side up (do not turn over at any time), and close the lid.

4. Every 2 minutes, brush with more glaze. The lobsters are cooked when the meat is firm and the juices bubble in the shell; total cooking time is about 5 to 7 minutes. Discard the basting glaze.

5. Serve the lobsters with the reserved glaze on the side for dipping.

Note: The lobsters can also be cooked successfully under a broiler. Baste the lobsters frequently with a little butter and sauce as they cook.

SPINY LOBSTER

Nothing says "leave me alone" quite like the formidably armored carapace of the California spiny lobster (*Panulirus interruptus*). What it lacks in claws it makes up for in spikes and speed. California spiny lobsters can live to be 50 years old and may grow to more than 2 feet in length. The tail meat has a slightly coarser texture than its Maine cousins, but it is sweet and delicious and tastes best grilled, sautéed, or fried rather than steamed. Good news: Baja-caught spiny lobsters (as well as the California and Australia varieties) are now certified sustainable. So eat up!

LIVING ON BAJA TIME:
SAN FELIPE

● ● ●

San Felipe is a colorful little town built on white-sugar sands, lapped by warm turquoise waters. Flip-flops and big straw hats are necessities, and nobody ever dresses up, for anything, no matter what. There are no big hotels (yet), no golf, no shopping—nothing but beach and sky and water, dunes to play on, fish to catch, and shrimp to eat. Exquisitely fresh, huge, lavender blue, crunchy sweet shrimp.

Fishermen pull their boats right up on the sand across from the *malecón* (boardwalk), which is lined with dozens of open-air restaurants. Out of the boats and into the restaurants go coolers loaded with the famous fish of the Gulf of California—*corvina, huachinango, sierra* (mackerel), *liza* (mullet), *pargo, cabrilla, pompano*—and plenty of those gorgeous shrimp.

Each *puesto* takes pains to stand out from the others with colorful hand-painted signs—a quirky kind of fishy folk art—but the menus all offer the same dishes: *cocktels de mariscos* (seafood cocktails, see page 10) featuring your choice of octopus, shucked oysters and clams, calamari, *pata de mula* (a kind of scallop), *caracol* (sea snail), and of course shrimp. If you can't pick one thing, there is always a *campechana*—a little of everything.

That's for starters, along with tostadas loaded with ceviche of fish or shrimp. Clams, dug that day, might be steamed with butter or topped with garlic and cheese and baked. Soups are made with shrimp, fish, or a bit of everything, like Caldo de Siete Mares (Seven Seas Soup, see page 102).

This is all a buildup to the main event, which in San Felipe is going to involve shrimp. Order it lightly crumbed and fried (*empanizada*); sautéed with butter, garlic, and a squirt of lime (*al mojo de ajo,* see mussel recipe on page 78); or roasted with salt and garlic in the shell (*a la plancha*; see page 65). More elaborate presentations include large shrimp *costa azul* (stuffed with cheese, wrapped in thinly sliced bacon, then grilled) or *diabla* (sautéed with chipotle chiles and fresh tomatoes; see page 68). Shrimp are skewered in brochettes with onions and green chiles and then grilled, or they're battered and deep-fried for tacos. Thin patties of chopped shrimp flecked with bits of cilantro are lightly coated with bread crumbs, browned in butter, and served with an assortment of sauces (see page 66).

The finest shrimp are served *en aguachile*—raw, split, and basted with fresh lime juice and ground chiles just before being served with strips of onion and cucumber, crisp tostadas, and drops of hot sauce.

In the fancy restaurants, huge butterflied shrimp are breaded with coconut and orange, sautéed, and served with a *crema*-laced huitlacoche sauce or an orange sauce with cascabel and mora chiles. Enormous poblano chiles are stuffed with shrimp and served with a pistachio sauce. And shrimp are plated with salsa de cilantro or sautéed with achiote.

You don't have to eat shrimp, or even fish; there's plenty of great food in town. Groups of fishermen chat on the *malecón* as the first stars appear, heading home at the end of the long day. One carries a hatful of little clams for his wife to cook.

And so goes another day in San Felipe, where the old-school Baja experience lives on.

Aguachiles
(SHRIMP MARINATED IN LIME JUICE)

In Baja, *aguachiles* is often made with shrimp just minutes out of the ocean and served in a *molcajete* (a bowl/mortar carved from porous volcanic stone). The molcajete is soaked in water before use, and the stone retains moisture and keeps the shrimp cool. Ingenious!

Try to find fresh, never-frozen shrimp for this recipe. Best-quality frozen shrimp will also work well—even strips of very fresh white fish are delicious in this preparation. Don't marinate too long or the delicacy of the seafood will be lost.

I first tasted this dish along with *rattlesnake mezcal*, which made a big impression, as you can imagine. Good tequila is easier to find and makes an excellent accompaniment, as does ice-cold Mexican beer.

Makes 4 servings as an appetizer

1 pound best-quality large shrimp, preferably Mexican
6–8 limes, preferably Mexican limones (see page 30)
¼ teaspoon kosher salt
1 small cucumber, peeled and thinly sliced
½ small white onion, thinly sliced
1–2 teaspoons ground California chile (see page 37)

TO SERVE

Salsa de Chiles de Arbol #1 (see page 38) or bottled picante sauce
Tostadas (see page 248) or purchased tortilla chips

1. Peel the shrimp, devein carefully, and wash under cold running water. (Save the shells in the freezer for stock.) Pat dry with paper towels.
2. Squeeze the limes over the shrimp and sprinkle with the salt. The shrimp should be thoroughly coated with lime juice but not swimming in it.
3. Stir in the cucumber and onion and let marinate in the refrigerator for 45 minutes to 1 hour, stirring twice. Stir again just before serving and sprinkle with a little of the chile powder.
4. Serve in a soaked molcajete or other chilled dish. Shake salsa on the tostadas and alternate bites with the shrimp, cucumber, and onion.

Variation: Taquería Rossy in Cabo San Lucas serves aguachiles with a bright green salsa of raw jalapeños pureed with lime juice. Stem and seed 4 large jalapeños, cut into pieces, and place in a blender along with a pinch of salt and the juice of 2 limes. Puree, thin with water, and apply judiciously.

Cucarachas
(GARLIC SHRIMP IN THE SHELL)

Warning: These are messy and addictive! For maximum flavor and shock value, be sure to leave the heads and shells on, though it is just as tasty without. To eat, tear off the head and suck the fatty head meat, then peel and eat the rest of the shrimp. The whole idea is to eat with your hands and lick the succulent sauce and seasonings from your fingers, so this preparation is not for the fastidious. Nor is the name, which is wry Mexican humor at its best.

Makes 6 servings as an appetizer or 4 as an entrée

2 pounds best-quality large, shell-on, head-on shrimp, preferably Mexican
⅓ cup vegetable oil
2½ tablespoons garlic salt, or to taste

¼ cup finely ground or powdered Romano or Parmesan cheese
Thinly sliced green onions
Salsa de Chiles de Arbol #1 (see page 38)

1. Rinse and drain the shrimp. With a pair of sharp kitchen scissors, make a shallow cut up the back of the shrimp shells. (If there is a large vein, cut just deeply enough to remove it.) Leave the shells on.
2. In a wok or heavy frying pan, heat the oil over medium-high heat. Stir-fry the shrimp in two batches, turning constantly, for about 2 minutes, or just until pink, curled up, and firm to the touch. Scoop the cooked shrimp into a large mixing bowl and keep warm under a lid or foil tent. Do not drain the shrimp or remove any oil clinging to them. Do not discard the cooking oil in the pan.
3. When all the shrimp are cooked, toss them with the garlic salt and cheese.
4. Turn the shrimp and any juices onto a serving dish, sprinkle with the green onions, and drizzle on the reserved cooking oil. Serve with the salsa on the side and lots of paper napkins.

Note: Head-on frozen shrimp are commonly sold at Asian markets.

SHRIMP SIZING
(or Just What Is a Jumbo Shrimp, anyway?)

Shrimp are sorted by size, grade, and processing.

SIZE The larger the number, the smaller the shrimp size. *Small:* 30–60 per pound; *Medium:* 20–30 per pound; *Large:* 10–20 per pound; *Extra large:* less than 10 per pound

GRADE Shrimp vary wildly in quality. Best-quality wild shrimp are graded as whites, 1 and 2 grade. Other wild shrimp may be sold as pinks. Most farmed shrimp are so-called tiger shrimp, which are marketed as brown or black. They may taste like mud or be quite good; you will have to find a reliable brand. Shrimp farming, especially in Asia and Mexico, has had a bad environmental track record in the past.

PROCESSING Shrimp may be bought: whole, with heads and shells intact; heads removed, shell on; peeled and deveined raw, with or without tail; and peeled and deveined cooked, with or without tail. Remember the count per pound reflects processing.

Camarones a la Plancha
(SALT-SEARED SHRIMP)

Shrimp cooked *a la plancha* in their shells are absolutely delicious: juicy, scattered with salt, spritzed with lime, and eaten so piping hot they burn your fingers. Yes, they're messy, but so what?

Makes 6 servings

**3 pounds (or more) best-quality very large, shell-on shrimp,
preferably Mexican**
Kosher salt
Lime wedges, preferably from Mexican limones (see page 30)

1. Rinse and drain the shrimp. With a pair of sharp kitchen scissors, make a shallow cut up the back of the shrimp shells. (If there is a large vein, cut just deeply enough to remove it.) Leave the shells on.
2. Heat a large heavy griddle or frying pan over medium-high heat until a drop of water "dances" on the surface. Wipe the griddle with a paper towel barely dampened with vegetable oil.
3. Pat the shrimp dry. Add to the hot pan in one layer (do not overcrowd the pan; cook in batches if necessary) and cook, stirring and turning with a spatula, just until the shrimp are pink, curled up, and firm to the touch, about 3 minutes.
4. Turn onto a platter, sprinkle with salt, and serve immediately with the limes and lots of napkins.

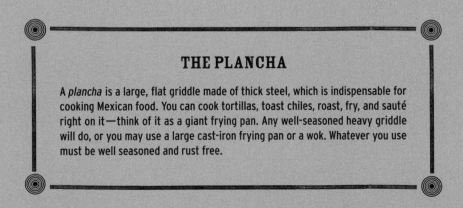

THE PLANCHA

A *plancha* is a large, flat griddle made of thick steel, which is indispensable for cooking Mexican food. You can cook tortillas, toast chiles, roast, fry, and sauté right on it—think of it as a giant frying pan. Any well-seasoned heavy griddle will do, or you may use a large cast-iron frying pan or a wok. Whatever you use must be well seasoned and rust free.

Shrimp Cakes

This is a good way to use odd-size shrimp pieces or small shrimp such as rock shrimp. Made *milanesa* style—breaded with fresh bread crumbs and fried in oil and butter until golden—the cakes are crispy-crusted and succulent. They may be made in cocktail, appetizer, or entrée size. These are delicious with any of the sauces or salsas in this book. I particularly like them with Raw Tomatillo Salsa (see page 44), Mango Salsa (see page 47), or Roasted Poblano Chile Sauce (see page 92).

Makes 10 entrée, 20 appetizer, or 32 cocktail cakes

1 pound best-quality shrimp, preferably Mexican, peeled and deveined
1 celery rib, finely sliced crosswise
¼ medium white onion, roughly chopped
1 tablespoon mayonnaise
½ teaspoon kosher salt
¼ teaspoon freshly ground white pepper

Juice of 1 lime, preferably a Mexican limón (see page 30)
1 egg, beaten
1 cup fresh bread crumbs (divided use)
20 cilantro sprigs, stemmed and chopped
2 tablespoons vegetable oil
1 tablespoon butter

TO SERVE
Lime wedges, preferably from Mexican limones (see page 30)

1. In the bowl of a food processor, pulse the shrimp until finely chopped but stop before it turns to a paste. Scrape into a bowl. Mince the celery and onion by hand or in the food processor and add to the shrimp.
2. Stir in the mayonnaise, salt, pepper, and lime juice; combine thoroughly. Add the egg and stir well.
3. Fold in ¼ cup of the bread crumbs and the cilantro and test the consistency; the mixture should just hold together when formed into a patty. Add more bread crumbs if needed.
4. When the correct consistency is reached, spread the remaining ¾ cup of bread crumbs on a plate. Form the shrimp mixture into balls, using a ¼-cup measure or a tablespoon (¼ cup per ball makes 10 entrée cakes; 2 tablespoons per ball makes 20 appetizer cakes; 1 tablespoon per ball makes 32 mini cocktail cakes). Drop the balls into the bread crumbs and flatten gently into thick patties. Turn the patties to coat all sides with crumbs.
5. Heat a 12-inch skillet over medium heat. Add the oil. When the oil is hot, add the butter. Shake off excess crumbs and cook the cakes on both sides until golden brown. Allow 2 cakes per person. Serve right away with lime wedges.

Shrimp in Salsa Verde

Salsa Verde is a favorite in many Baja California restaurants. The bright acidity of tomatillos sparks against the rich taste of shrimp (or other seafood)—with a little tequila thrown in for good measure! A small amount of butter brings all the flavors together.

Makes 6 to 8 servings

8 medium tomatillos, husked, washed, and quartered (about 2 cups)
2 garlic cloves, peeled
½ medium white onion, chopped
1 fresh serrano chile, or more to taste
2 tablespoons vegetable oil (divided use)
¾ cup water or Seven Seas Broth (see page 103)

2 pounds best-quality shrimp, preferably Mexican, peeled and deveined
⅓ cup 100 percent agave tequila
2 tablespoons butter, cut into small pieces
¼ cup chopped cilantro leaves
Kosher salt

TO SERVE
Lime wedges, preferably from Mexican limones (see page 30)

1. In a food processor, puree the tomatillos until they are as smooth as possible. Add the garlic, onion, and chile and pulse until the vegetables are very smooth.
2. Heat a nonstick 10-inch frying pan over medium heat. Add 1 tablespoon of the oil. When it is hot, add the tomatillos and cook the sauce, stirring often, for several minutes, or until it thickens. Add the water, increase the heat, and cook for 5 minutes, stirring often. Set aside, covered.
3. In a large skillet or wok, heat the remaining 1 tablespoon oil over medium-high heat. Pat the shrimp dry and add, all at once, to the skillet. Cook, stirring constantly, until the shrimp are barely pink.
4. Remove the pan from the heat (so the tequila will not ignite) and pour on the tequila all at once. Swirl the pan and then return to the heat. Add the tomatillo sauce and bring to a boil.
5. Remove from the heat and whisk in the butter. Stir in the cilantro and adjust the seasoning with salt. Serve right away with limes on the side.

Shrimp a la Diabla

Don't be fooled by the name: This recipe tastes of fresh tomatoes and garlic, with only a little hint of smoky heat at the end. The sauce may be made ahead of time, which makes the cooking even faster.

Makes 6 servings

4 ripe Roma tomatoes, seeded and cut into quarters
½ medium white onion, chopped
2 garlic cloves, peeled
2 tablespoons vegetable oil (divided use)
¾ cup water or chicken stock
¼ teaspoon kosher salt

1 can (7 ounces) chipotles in adobo, finely chopped or pureed
2½ pounds best-quality shrimp, preferably Mexican, peeled and deveined
½ cup white wine
2 green onions, finely sliced

1. In a food processor, pulse the tomatoes until they are very finely chopped. Add the onion and garlic and process until the mixture forms a smooth puree.
2. In a 10-inch skillet, heat 1 tablespoon of the oil over medium heat. Pour in the tomato mixture and fry the sauce, stirring often, until thickened—about 5 minutes.
3. Add the water, stir well, and cook for 5 minutes, stirring often until the sauce thickens again. Remove from the heat and stir in the salt and half of the chipotle puree. (For a spicier sauce, add more chipotle, a tablespoon at a time, until the desired heat is achieved.) Set aside and keep warm.
4. In a 12-inch skillet over medium-high heat, heat the remaining oil. When it is hot, pat the shrimp dry and add all at once. Cook and stir for a minute, until the shrimp are barely pink.
5. Remove the pan from the heat and add the wine. Swirl the pan to deglaze. Return to the heat and pour the chipotle sauce over the shrimp. Heat through and serve immediately, with the green onions scattered on top.

Note: Diabla sauce can also be served cold with cooked peeled shrimp or mixed cooked seafood topped with diced avocado.

Shrimp Ranchero

El Rosario, 250 miles south of San Diego, is a remote place even now, with a few homes clinging to an arid valley rimmed by jagged white mountains. It's tough country, even by *bajacaliforniano* standards.

Doña Anita Espinoza is the village matriarch. For most of her life, which has spanned the era from horse-drawn carts to computers, there were no real roads beyond El Rosario—just a treacherous dirt track that washed out with the infrequent rains. In the very early days, she says, it was a big deal if two cars came by in a *year*. La Doña is famous with Baja travelers for coining the ultimate Baja truth: "Bad roads—good people. Good roads, all kinds of people."

She is also renowned for her work with charities such as the Flying Samaritans, and her family's restaurant, Mamá Espinoza's, is famous for La Doña's home-style cooking, especially her *camarones rancheros;* this recipe is a variation.

Makes 6 servings

6 ripe Roma tomatoes
3 tablespoons butter
1 tablespoon vegetable oil
1 cup finely diced green bell pepper
1/4 medium white onion, finely diced
4 garlic cloves, minced

1 pound best-quality medium shrimp, preferably
  Mexican, peeled and deveined
2 teaspoons tomato paste
1 teaspoon kosher salt
1/4 cup crumbled cotixa, queso fresco,
  or feta cheese

1. Core, seed, and finely dice 3 of the tomatoes. Core, seed, and puree the remaining 3 tomatoes in a blender or food processor; you should have between 3/4 and 1 cup of puree.
2. In a large skillet, melt the butter with the oil over medium-high heat. When it is foaming, add the pepper and cook, stirring, for 1 minute. Add the onion and garlic; cook and stir until the vegetables are barely softened.
3. Turn the heat to high, add the shrimp and cook for 1 minute, stirring, until the shrimp are barely pink. Add the diced tomatoes, tomato puree, and tomato paste.
4. Season with salt, turn the heat to medium, and cook, stirring occasionally, until the sauce has thickened.
5. Divide among heated plates and sprinkle each with a little of the cheese. Serve immediately.

Seared Shrimp with Tangerine, Cilantro, and Pasilla Chile

In Cabo San Lucas, it seems that every ambitious restaurant serves a version of this sauce, usually made with orange juice. I prefer the tang and brilliant color of tangerines. It's important to use freshly squeezed juice; don't let it boil or it will lose its delicate flavor.

Makes 6 servings

2 tablespoons butter
1½ tablespoons minced shallot
1 teaspoon chopped garlic
3 tablespoons minced fresh ginger
2 teaspoons cornstarch
2 cups freshly squeezed tangerine juice
1 tablespoon olive oil
2½ pounds best-quality large shrimp, preferably Mexican, peeled and deveined (tails may be left on)

12 grape tomatoes or cherry tomatoes, cut in half
½ teaspoon crushed red chile
Pinch of kosher salt
¼ cup chopped cilantro leaves
½ lemon
1 dried pasilla, ancho, or guajillo chile, seeded, toasted, and ground (see page 37)

1. Make the sauce: In a saucepan over medium heat, melt the butter and sauté the shallot, garlic, and ginger until just softened; do not brown.
2. Mix the cornstarch with 1 cup of the tangerine juice until dissolved. Add to the pan and cook, stirring, until thickened. Add the remaining 1 cup of juice.
3. Turn off the heat and set the sauce aside for 15 minutes, then strain through a fine sieve and keep warm over very low heat while you cook the shrimp.
4. In a large frying pan or well-seasoned wok, heat the oil over high heat until it shimmers.
5. Pat the shrimp dry with a paper towel and add to the pan all at once. After about 5 minutes, when the shrimp are half-cooked (curled and pink but slightly soft), add the tomatoes, crushed chile, and salt. Cook and stir just until the shrimp are firm; do not overcook.
6. Remove the pan from the heat and stir in ¼ cup of the strained sauce and half of the cilantro. Squeeze the lemon over the shrimp.
7. Heap the shrimp and tomatoes onto heated serving plates. Drizzle each serving with some of the remaining sauce, sprinkle with some cilantro and ground chile, and serve.

Ginger Shrimp with Mango-Jalapeño Coulis

This is a thoroughly modern recipe inspired by Cabo San Lucas, where the cooking leans toward the tropical and an infusion of American money and culinary influence has brought a strong Asian-fusion edge to many restaurant menus. This simple recipe is sure to please as an hors d'oeuvre, appetizer, or entrée.

Makes 6 servings as an entrée

½ cup very thinly sliced fresh ginger
2 tablespoons chopped white onion or the white parts of
   4 green onions
2 fresh serrano or Thai chiles, stems removed
3 tablespoons freshly squeezed lime juice, preferably
   from Mexican limones (see page 30)
2 tablespoons brown sugar
1 teaspoon kosher salt
1½ pounds best-quality medium shrimp, preferably
   Mexican, peeled and deveined

1 tablespoon vegetable oil
½ white onion, julienned
½ red bell pepper, julienned
½ zucchini, julienned

TO SERVE

Cilantro leaves
Mango-Jalapeño Coulis (see below)

1. In a food processor or powerful blender, process the ginger, chopped onion, chiles, lime juice, brown sugar, and salt to a smooth paste. Combine the paste and shrimp and refrigerate for 1 to 3 hours.
2. Shake off as much of the marinade from the shrimp as possible. Press the marinade through a sieve and reserve only the juice.
3. Heat a 12-inch skillet or a wok over medium-high heat and add the oil. When it is hot, add the shrimp and julienned onion; toss and cook for a moment. Then add the bell pepper and finally the zucchini. Cook just until the shrimp are pink and firm and the vegetables are barely wilted but still a bit crunchy—about 1 minute.
4. Add the reserved juice from the marinade and cook, stirring occasionally, for a minute or more, until the sauce thickens and coats the shrimp and vegetables. Scatter the cilantro leaves over the shrimp and serve with dabs of the coulis.

Mango-Jalapeño Coulis

A coulis is a thick puree made from fresh fruit or vegetables. Adjust the heat to suit your taste, but this should be potent—fruity, sweet, hot, and vinegary in equal measure.

Makes ¾ cup

1 small fresh jalapeño chile, seeded and coarsely chopped (leave the seeds in for more heat)
1 very ripe, sweet mango, peeled, seeded, and chopped
1½ tablespoons freshly squeezed lime juice, preferably from a Mexican limón (see page 30)
1 teaspoon rice vinegar, or to taste
¼ teaspoon kosher salt, or to taste
1 teaspoon brown sugar

Put all the ingredients into a small food processor or a powerful blender and puree until completely smooth. Taste for seasoning and heat; add more chile, lime juice, or vinegar to your taste.

Man Bites Shark
(FISH TACOS IN ADOBO)

Now that I have your attention: Don't eat shark! (See below.) Sustainable choices include other very firm fish such as yellowtail, farmed sturgeon, wahoo, or ono. All will yield great results.

This is a home-style recipe, not something you would find at a taco stand. You could serve the fish in fillets as an entrée, instead of tacos, but it's so delicious with the condiments it's a shame not to go native!

Makes 6 servings

2 pounds firm fish (see note above)
2 tablespoons ground cumin
2 tablespoons ground guajillo chile (see page 37)
2 teaspoons dried whole Mexican oregano
2 teaspoons kosher salt
$\frac{1}{2}$ teaspoon freshly ground black pepper
$1\frac{1}{2}$ tablespoons vegetable oil
1 tablespoon freshly squeezed lime juice, preferably from a Mexican limón (see page 30)
$1\frac{1}{2}$ tablespoons white vinegar, preferably Heinz
2 teaspoons best-quality Japanese soy sauce
1 tablespoon finely chopped garlic

2 tablespoons finely chopped white onion
6 fresh jalapeño chiles

TO SERVE
Fresh corn or flour tortillas, warmed
Basic Black Beans (see page 247)
Lime wedges, preferably from Mexican limones (see page 30)
Diced white onion
Shredded white cabbage
Salsa al Comal (see page 32)
Salsa de Chiles de Arbol #1 or #2 (see pages 38–39)

1. Cut the fish into 8 pieces of equal size and place in a glass bowl or 1-quart resealable bag.
2. Mix together the cumin, ground chile, oregano, salt, pepper, oil, lime juice, vinegar, soy sauce, garlic, and onion to form a thick paste; taste for seasoning (should be well seasoned). Spread the spice paste over the fish and refrigerate for 2 to 4 hours.
3. Preheat the oven to 375 degrees. Set the fish in an oiled baking dish and spread a layer of the marinade on top. Bake until the fish is firm to the touch and cooked through, about 10 minutes per inch of thickness.
4. While the fish is in the oven, roast the chiles in a foil-lined comal or heavy cast-iron frying pan, turning often, until slightly softened and blackened in places (see page 43 for information on roasting chiles). Use a fork to shred the fish into bite-size pieces. Serve with the tortillas, black beans, and condiments.

SHARK

In spite of their fearsome reputation, sharks rarely attack, and most are harmless to humans. The reverse is not true.

Shark goes by many names: *cazón, tiburón,* and, when small, *angelito* (little angel). It is a staple of the Baja diet. Most fish tacos in northern Baja are made with shark, and many fishermen rely on the shark catch for their livelihood. Unfortunately, shark populations may be threatened, and so little is known about them that biologists cannot assess their future. Until we know more about their prospects, shark is not a sustainable choice, so please substitute one of the other meaty fish recommended with the recipes in this book.

Crab and Roasted Corn Chowder with Chile

Here is a real special-occasion soup that easily makes a meal. Smoky charred poblanos and roasted corn combine with sweet, sumptuous crab and cream, a little heat from serranos, and the final fresh addition of tomatoes and cilantro. It's not the simplest of recipes, but much of the work can be done a day or two ahead.

In Baja, such a soup would feature small blue crabs harvested from shallow inshore waters on the Pacific side of the peninsula. But American Dungeness crab is a great, sustainable alternative.

Makes 8 generous servings

Kernels from 2 ears fresh white sweet corn
6 tablespoons canola oil (divided use)
2 large fresh poblano chiles
1 fresh nopal, about 8 ounces (see page 173)
1 pound Dungeness crabmeat, picked over
4 garlic cloves, minced
1 small onion, finely diced
1 fresh serrano chile, sliced (optional)
½ teaspoon ground coriander
2 thyme sprigs or ½ teaspoon dried thyme
5 cups Seven Seas Broth (see page 103) or chicken broth
2 cups heavy cream
2 cups milk
1 large Yukon gold potato, peeled and diced

1 tablespoon kosher salt
Freshly ground black pepper
¼ cup cornstarch
½ cup sherry

TO SERVE
1 tablespoon butter
5 cilantro sprigs, stemmed and chopped
3 large ripe Roma tomatoes, seeded and neatly diced
Kosher salt
2 teaspoons ground guajillo chile (see page 37)
Green part of 2 green onions, finely sliced
Sliced serrano chiles (optional)

1. Roast the corn: Heat a heavy (preferably cast-iron) pan until very hot. In a bowl, toss the corn with 2 tablespoons of the oil. Sear the corn in the hot pan, stirring only once, until the corn is colored.
2. Char the poblanos: Turn the poblanos over a gas flame or under a hot broiler until the skins are blackened and charred all over. Wrap in a paper towel and set aside to cool; use a paper towel to rub off the skin. Remove the stems, seeds, and ribs. Cut into ½-inch dice.
3. Prepare the cactus paddle following directions on page 173. Cut into ½-inch dice.
4. Divide the crab into two roughly equal portions, reserving the larger pieces for garnish. Chill until needed.
5. Heat the remaining 4 tablespoons oil in a large pot with a heavy bottom. Over medium-high heat, sauté the garlic, onion, serrano, the smaller pieces of crabmeat, and the cactus until just softened. Add the corn and poblanos and cook for 1 minute. Add the coriander, thyme, broth, cream, and milk. Bring to a bare simmer over medium heat and reduce the heat to low to keep the soup simmering gently. Add the potato to the soup. Season with salt and pepper. Simmer for 30 minutes, or until the potatoes are tender.
6. Dissolve the cornstarch in the sherry. Bring the soup to a boil and stir in the sherry. Adjust the seasonings and keep warm over low heat.
7. To serve, melt the butter in a small nonstick frying pan. Sauté the remaining crab. Combine the cilantro and tomatoes in a small bowl and season with a pinch of salt. Divide the warm crab evenly among warmed soup plates, mounding it up. Ladle the soup around the crab. Top the crab with a spoonful of the tomatoes and cilantro and scatter a pinch of ground chiles and green onions on the soup. Serve very hot, with the serranos.

Crab Quesadillas

The crab quesadilla is simple and unforgettable, elevated to greatness by the use of fresh crab, picked from the shell, along with generous amounts of Oaxacan cheese and sharp green onions. Using homemade *masa* takes it right over the top, but feel free to substitute good-quality fresh corn tortillas.

   Dungeness crab is a sustainable choice. One cooked Dungeness crab will yield over a cup of sweet, delicious meat—enough for six quesadillas. A good second choice would be 2 pounds of American-caught fresh Alaskan king crab legs.

Makes 6 servings

Fresh Corn Masa (see page 238) or 18 fresh corn tortillas
Melted butter
8 ounces Oaxacan or Jack cheese, shredded
1 pound Dungeness or king crabmeat, picked over
2 large green onions, sliced

TO SERVE
1 avocado, pitted, peeled, and thinly sliced
Salsa de Chiles de Arbol #1 or #2 (see page 38–39)

1. Form the masa into golf ball—size portions and line a tortilla press with heavy plastic. Form tortillas according to the directions on page 241.
2. For each quesadilla: Heat a comal or heavy griddle and brush with a little melted butter. Lay a tortilla on the hot pan. Quickly scatter several tablespoons of cheese evenly over the tortilla, followed by 2 tablespoons of crab and ½ tablespoon of green onions.
3. When the cheese has begun to melt, fold the tortilla in half and flip over.
4. Lay a slice of avocado on top and serve immediately with the salsa.

Chipotle Crab Cakes with Tamarind Sauce

Serve these as an appetizer topped with the tart-sweet tamarind sauce and buttery-rich avocado—or the salsa of your choice. Bite-size versions are great with cocktails. Dungeness crab is a sustainable choice.

Makes about 20 appetizer or 30 cocktail crab cakes

1 pound Dungeness crabmeat, picked over
$\frac{1}{4}$ white onion, minced
1 celery stalk, finely minced
$\frac{1}{4}$ medium red bell pepper, minced
$\frac{1}{4}$ cup packed cilantro leaves, finely chopped
Juice of 1 lemon
2 teaspoons kosher salt
$\frac{1}{4}$ cup mayonnaise
2 eggs, beaten

2 tablespoons pureed chipotle chiles
1–1$\frac{1}{2}$ cups homemade bread crumbs, dried out
Panko bread crumbs (available in Asian markets)
Oil, for shallow frying

TO SERVE
Tamarind Sauce (see below)
Diced avocado

1. In a bowl, combine the crab, onion, celery, bell pepper, cilantro, lemon juice, and salt.
2. Place the mixture in a colander or sieve set inside a bowl. Set a small plate on the crab, weight with a soup can, cover, and refrigerate for 12 to 24 hours to drain.
3. Transfer the crab to a bowl and stir in the mayonnaise, eggs, and chipotles. Add $\frac{3}{4}$ cup of the bread crumbs and toss to combine. The mixture should look moist (not gummy) and should stick together without crumbling. You may need to add more bread crumbs, little by little, to achieve the desired texture.
4. Spread a generous layer of panko on a plate. Scoop out balls of the crab mixture, using $\frac{1}{4}$ cup for appetizers or 1$\frac{1}{2}$ tablespoons for cocktail servings. Drop the balls into the panko. Roll around to coat and press gently into thick patties. Shake off excess crumbs. (The crab cakes may be made to this point and refrigerated.)
5. Heat a 12-inch nonstick skillet over medium-low heat. Add enough oil to generously cover the bottom of the pan $\frac{1}{8}$ inch deep (about $\frac{1}{4}$ cup). Cook the crab cakes until crisp and golden brown on both sides and firm. Drain and keep warm. Serve with a little tamarind sauce on the plate and some diced avocado.

Tamarind Sauce

Makes 1$\frac{1}{2}$ cups

$\frac{1}{2}$ cup tamarind paste
$\frac{3}{4}$ cup boiling water
2–3 tablespoons cold water
2 teaspoons brown sugar

$\frac{1}{2}$ teaspoon freshly squeezed lime juice, preferably from a Mexican limón (see page 30)
$\frac{1}{4}$ teaspoon kosher salt
1 tablespoon butter

1. Break the tamarind paste into pieces in a small heatproof bowl. Pour on the boiling water, stir to combine, and soak for 30 minutes. Rub the paste through a coarse sieve to remove the seeds and fibrous strands. You should have about $\frac{1}{4}$ cup of tamarind puree.
2. In a small saucepan, combine the tamarind puree, cold water, brown sugar, lime juice, and salt. Warm over gentle heat; do not boil. Whisk in the butter and keep the sauce warm until needed.

Note: Tamarind paste may be purchased at Asian and Latin markets.

Choros al Mojo de Ajo
(MUSSELS WITH GARLIC AND BUTTER)

One of the classic (and simplest) Mexican preparations of fish and shellfish, *al mojo de ajo* is a pungent, buttery, wine-touched, lime-spiked, over-the-top garlic feast. It may seem like too much of everything, but trust me: It's just enough! A friend standing downwind from an al mojo de ajo preparation once said, "I'll probably have to burn my clothes after this, but it's worth it."

Good-quality garlic is essential. The stuff in the jar just will not cut it. Choose fresh, firm heads of whole garlic (not "elephant") and peel and chop immediately before use. The same sauce recipe can be used on abalone, shrimp, lobster, or fish fillets (see variation below).

Makes 8 servings

2¹⁄₂ pounds black mussels
15 large garlic cloves
16 tablespoons (2 sticks) butter
2 tablespoons olive oil

1 cup dry white wine
1 teaspoon chopped Italian parsley
Lime wedges, preferably from Mexican limones
   (see page 30), or lemon wedges

1. Scrub the mussels well with cold water and a stiff brush. Discard any that do not close when tapped. Keep covered with a damp cloth in the refrigerator. Just before cooking, remove the fibrous beards by cutting them off close to the shell.

2. Chop the garlic in a mini food processor or by hand; you should have between ¹⁄₄ and ¹⁄₃ cup. Place in a small saucepan and add the butter. Melt over very low heat. (The smell will make you swoon!) When it's just melted, turn off the heat and leave the pan on the warm burner.

3. In a large Dutch oven with a lid, large enough to hold all the mussels, heat the oil over medium-high heat. Add the mussels and wine. Shake the pot a couple of times to even the mussels out and cover. Cook for 5 to 7 minutes, shaking the pot once or twice, until the mussels are opened. Discard any that do not open.

4. Uncover and pour the butter and garlic into the pot, heat for 30 seconds, and stir. The sauce must be very hot, but do not allow the garlic to brown.

5. Sprinkle with parsley and serve with lime wedges on the side.

Variation: To make a classic al mojo de ajo sauce for fish, scallops, calamari steaks, shrimp, lobster, or farmed abalone, lightly flour and sauté the seafood until cooked. Remove from the pan and pour the butter and garlic into the pan. Shake the pan until the butter is heated through and pour over the seafood. Serve with lemon.

Mussels in Melted Tomato with Ginger

This recipe relies for its impact on the best-flavored tomatoes available, with a good balance of sweetness and acidity; I like the full flavor and tartness of the organic "Sweet 100" cherry tomatoes raised by the Del Cabo co-op in Cabo San Lucas. This variety is now widely available in the United States.

Makes 6 servings

2½ pounds black mussels
1 pint cherry tomatoes (see note above)
2 tablespoons olive oil
1 tablespoon chopped garlic

2 tablespoons minced fresh ginger
¼ cup water
½ teaspoon kosher salt
½ bunch cilantro, chopped

1. Scrub the mussels well with cold water and a stiff brush. Discard any that do not close when tapped. Keep covered with a damp cloth in the refrigerator. Just before cooking, remove the fibrous beards by cutting them off close to the shell.

2. In a food processor, puree the tomatoes until smooth. You should have about 2 cups of puree.

3. In a large Dutch oven with lid, large enough to hold all the mussels, heat the oil over medium heat. Add the garlic and ginger and cook, stirring, for 1 minute. Add the water and salt and bring to a boil; stir in the tomato puree.

4. Add the mussels to the pot. Shake the pot a couple of times to even them out, reduce the heat to medium-low, and cover. Cook for 5 to 7 minutes, shaking the pot once or twice, until the mussels are opened. Discard any that do not open.

5. Stir in the cilantro and serve in wide soup bowls with the cooking broth ladled over the top.

MUSSELS (CHOROS)

Gleaming black mussels grow on every rocky area down the Pacific coast of Baja California, clinging together in vast colonies against tides, icy water, winter storms, hurricanes, and smashing waves. Undisturbed, mussels may grow to enormous size, over 6 inches in length.

Wild mussels make terrific bait, but for cooking buy cultivated black mussels raised in cold-water nurseries. Mussels are easy to grow, and mussel farms can actually have a beneficial effect on the environment by cleaning the water around them.

Mussels may be eaten steamed, roasted, or smoked and are essential elements in soups and Ensenada's famed paellas.

Mussels should be as fresh as possible, as they lose size and flavor with every day out of the water. They should never, *ever* stink or drip smelly fluid. Greenshell mussels are impressively large but don't taste like much. Use them as a last resort.

Pismo Clams Stuffed with Garlic and Cheese

The Baja shoreline is a serried rank of rocky points, sweeping beaches, and river estuaries, where huge pismo clams, 4 or 5 inches across, are harvested for use in *cockteles* and many other recipes, including this succulent preparation packed with garlic and stringy Oaxacan cheese.

   Pismo clams are seldom exported, but any large clams such as cherrystones are a good substitute, as are large mussels. Oaxacan cheese is a stringy, creamy melting cheese similar to mozzarella.

Makes 4 servings as an appetizer

4 very large pismo clams or 8 cherrystone clams
Splash of white wine
2 tablespoons vegetable oil
8 large garlic cloves, minced
½ cup minced white onion
½ teaspoon freshly ground black pepper

¼ teaspoon dried whole Mexican oregano, rubbed to a powder
1 tablespoon butter (optional)
6 ounces Oaxacan, asadero, or mozzarella cheese, cut into small cubes
1 tablespoon chopped Italian parsley

1. Preheat the oven to 375 degrees. Scrub the clam shells thoroughly with cold water and a stiff brush, especially along the hinge area and lip of the shell; do not soak the clams in water.

2. Put the clams in a heavy pot along with ½ inch of water and the wine. Put a lid on the pot and cook over medium heat until the clams have just barely opened but are still slightly undercooked—3 to 5 minutes. Remove the lid and let the clams cool for a few minutes. Reserve the cooking liquid.

3. Work on a plate to catch all the delicious clam juices. Pop the clams open and separate the shells. Remove the cooked clam meat from the shells, reserving the shells. Carefully remove the sandy "stomachs" with a sharp knife and discard. Chop the clams into small pieces. Pour all the juices from the clams back into the pot with the cooking liquid, then strain the reserved liquid through a fine sieve to remove any sand or bits of shell.

4. Heat the oil over medium heat in a frying pan and add the garlic and onion. Cook until the onion is translucent and then add the chopped clams, pepper, oregano, and the strained cooking liquid. Cook until most of the liquid has evaporated, leaving just enough for the mixture to slide easily in the pan.

5. Add the butter and stir until it is incorporated into the clam mixture, making it creamy. Reduce the heat to low. Stir in the cheese until it melts and forms long strings. Spoon the clam mixture into the reserved clam shells and bake briefly, about 4 minutes, just to heat the shells. Serve very hot, dusted with the parsley.

Note: You will probably not need to add salt to the recipe, but taste for yourself and season to your liking.

Stuffed Clams Roasted in the Coals

In the little town of El Sauzal, a simple cart sells this delicious variation on the stuffed clam. Owner Elizeo Benítez Arellano (who says he picked up the idea for the recipe at a local cooking competition) shucks, cleans, and stuffs an *almeja chocolate* (brown pismo clam), closes it up, and wraps it in foil. Then he buries the clam in the coals of a wood-burning fire pit. After a few minutes, when it is bubbling hot, he opens it up and squeezes fresh lime into the shell. It's fabulous. This recipe is designed "per clam," so it is easily adaptable.

Makes 1 serving

1 large pismo clam or 2 large cherrystone clams
1 tablespoon Pico de Gallo (page 30)
1–2 teaspoons white wine

1 teaspoon Chinese oyster sauce
1 tablespoon shredded asadero or Jack cheese
1 lime, preferably a Mexican limón (see page 30)

1. Scrub the clam shell thoroughly with cold water and a stiff brush, especially along the hinge area and lip of the shell; do not soak it in water. Shuck the clam (see page 82). Carefully remove the sandy "stomach" with a sharp knife and discard.

2. Chop the clam meat and replace in the shell along with the pico de gallo, wine, oyster sauce, and cheese. Close the shell and wrap tightly in two layers of foil.

3. Bury the clam in the coals of a barbecue or fire pit (it could also be cooked in a 400-degree oven or on a gas grill) for 3 to 5 minutes, depending on the heat of the fire.

4. Open the package and open the clam. Cut the lime in half and squeeze the juice over the clam.

Clams in Tequila Butter

This rich sauce is a bit swoony and over the top with all that tequila, but it showcases small, plump clams like no other. It's fantastic as an appetizer, with another shot of good *añejo* (aged) tequila to sip and crusty bread to sop up the sauce.

Whatever tequila you choose, make sure it is 100 percent agave. It will cost a little more, but you will be able to appreciate the true herby flavor of real tequila. Don't use *reposado* (the very best grade) here; its subtlety will be lost.

Makes 4 to 6 servings

3 pounds small manila clams or cockles
8 tablespoons (1 stick) butter
2 tablespoons chopped garlic
2 ripe Roma tomatoes, seeded and diced
1 large fresh serrano chile, minced (wear rubber gloves)
$\frac{1}{3}$ cup water

2 tablespoons freshly squeezed lime juice, preferably from a Mexican limón (see page 30)
$\frac{1}{4}$ cup 100 percent agave tequila
10 cilantro sprigs, stemmed and chopped
2 green onions, finely sliced

1. Scrub the clam shells thoroughly with cold water and a stiff brush, especially along the hinge area and lip of the shell; do not soak the clams in water.

2. Melt the butter in a large frying pan with a lid over medium heat. Add the garlic, tomatoes, and chile and stir for a minute or so; don't brown the garlic or butter.

3. Add the water and increase the heat to high. When it is boiling, add the clams and shake the pan gently to even them out. Reduce the heat to medium, cover, and allow to cook for 5 to 7 minutes, or until all the clams are opened. Discard any that do not open.

4. Pour the lime juice and tequila over the clams and scatter the cilantro and green onions over all. Shake the pan again to blend.

5. Cook for a minute more and serve immediately in heated bowls.

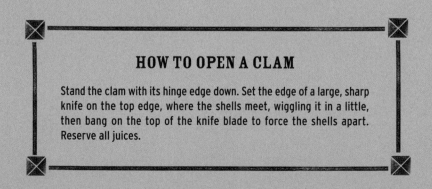

HOW TO OPEN A CLAM

Stand the clam with its hinge edge down. Set the edge of a large, sharp knife on the top edge, where the shells meet, wiggling it in a little, then bang on the top of the knife blade to force the shells apart. Reserve all juices.

Grilled Oysters with Baja Mignonette

Remote campsites and fish camps up and down both sides of Baja are often littered with oyster shells from past feasts. The big, meaty oysters are shucked and eaten raw or grilled in their shells over a wood fire.

Grilling serves two purposes: The oysters stew in their own delicious juices and then the shells pop themselves open—no messing around with oyster knives.

To reduce the possibility of illness, oysters should always be purchased from a reputable farm—your fishmonger will have the inspection tags.

Mignonette is traditionally a combination of shallots, black pepper, and champagne vinegar. This spicy version will wake up your taste buds. It is great on raw or broiled oysters. Grilled oysters can also be served with limes or hot sauce.

Makes 2 servings as an appetizer

¼ cup finely minced white onion
1 teaspoon minced fresh serrano chile, or to taste (wear rubber gloves)

2 tablespoons freshly squeezed lime juice, preferably from a Mexican limón (see page 30)
12 oysters

1. Make the mignonette: In a small bowl, combine the onion, chile, and lime juice.
2. Scrub the oysters thoroughly with a stiff brush. Grill rounded side down directly over a low fire, until they open slightly and are bubbling hot inside. Remove to a serving tray (*caution:* shells will be very hot) and carefully pry the shells open, reserving all juices. Discard any that do not open.
3. Serve with the mignonette on the side.

Note: Some people like to add a few drops of bottled hot sauce to their oysters. The mignonette is also delicious on freshly shucked raw clams.

Broiled Oysters with Chorizo and Cheese

Pacific oysters are large and meaty, with a briny taste that can stand up to substantial flavors like the spicy chorizo, onions, and hot chiles in this recipe.

Makes 2 servings

12 oysters
¾ cup shredded Oaxacan, asadero, or Jack cheese
½ cup Homemade Chorizo (see page 19), cooked

1 green onion, thinly sliced
1 fresh serrano chile, thinly sliced (wear rubber gloves)

1. Adjust the oven rack to 10 inches below the broiler. Preheat the broiler.
2. Shuck the oysters, rounded side down. Reserve the juices.
3. Cover each oyster with a layer of cheese and sprinkle the cheese with chorizo and green onion.
4. Broil the oysters until the cheese is lightly browned and the oysters are bubbly in their shells, about 5 to 7 minutes. (Or bake the oysters at 400 degrees on a bed of rock salt until the cheese is bubbly—8 to 10 minutes.)
5. Serve immediately with the chile on the side.

Deep-Fried Whole Fish

The ultimate Baja fish! Certainly a dramatic presentation and a delicious way to prepare fish if you're the adventurous type. In Baja you might choose *huachinango* (red snapper) or any small white fish, which are sold at the fish market trimmed and slashed, ready to fry. In the United States, buy farmed tai snapper, striped bass, or even small catfish. To eat, squeeze limes over the fish and fill your tortilla with chunks of fish, tomato, and onions. When you're done with one side, turn the fish over and do the same on the other side.

Important: Please refer to Safe Frying (see page 248) before you begin.

Makes 2 servings

1 small whole fish (about 1½ to 2 pounds)
Vegetable oil, for frying
1 cup all-purpose flour or cornstarch
4 teaspoons kosher salt (divided use)
1 teaspoon garlic salt
1 large ripe Roma tomato, seeded and cut
   into ½-inch pieces

¼ white onion, thinly sliced
1 green onion, thinly sliced
Leaves from 4 cilantro sprigs
Lime wedges, preferably from Mexican limones
   (see page 30)
8 fresh corn tortillas, warmed

1. Make sure the fish has been gutted and scaled but still has the head on.

2. Before you proceed, choose a large pan (such as a wok or wide brazier) to fry the fish. It must be deep enough so there's at least 2 inches of clear headroom between the surface of the oil (when the fish is in it) and the top of the pan. Lay the fish in the pan and add water until the fish is submerged by ½ inch. Remove the fish from the pan and measure the water. This will tell you how much oil you will need for frying. Discard the water and dry the pan.

3. Pat the fish dry with paper towels. With a sharp knife or scissors, trim the side and belly fins from the fish. Cut several slashes ½ inch deep down both sides of the fish.

4. Place the correct amount of oil in the pan and heat to between 350 and 365 degrees on a deep-fry thermometer.

5. Put the flour into a lasagna-type pan and stir in 2 teaspoons of the salt. Lay the fish in the pan and work the flour well into the slashes, rubbing it into the skin. The idea is to have a well-coated fish. Pick the fish up by the tail and shake off excess flour. Carefully slide the fish into the hot oil and move the pan gently for 30 seconds to keep the fish moving, so it does not stick to the bottom.

6. Do not attempt to turn the fish; just let it cook, occasionally giving the pan a gentle swirl to keep the fish from sticking. It will take 10 to 15 minutes for the fish to cook completely, depending on the size of the fish. You may find it helpful to baste the upper side of the fish with ladles of hot oil.

7. Turn off the heat when the fish is firm and nicely browned. Carefully slide a couple of large slotted spoons under the fish and lift it out of the oil and onto a platter. Sprinkle with the remaining 2 teaspoons salt, garlic salt, tomato, onion, green onion, and cilantro. Serve with lime wedges and tortillas.

SAVING THE SEA OF CORTÉS
(GULF OF CALIFORNIA)

▪ ▪ ▪

The Sea of Cortés is more properly called the Gulf of California these days, but I love the romantic old name—and the irony of its reference to the great conquistador, since only this body of water beat back the war-hardened Spanish time and time again. Furious *chubasco* storms boiling up out of the northwest sent many a Spanish ship to the bottom, and the armies and missionaries that did set foot on land were often defeated by the incredibly arid and harsh conditions.

After centuries of exploitation and decades of overfishing and rapine, the Sea of Cortés won another round in 2005, when it was declared a World Heritage site by the United Nations. The area protected includes over 200 islands and surrounding waters and is home to 695 plant species (more than any other on the World Heritage list) and 891 known fish species (90 of which are found nowhere else in the world). Of all the world's species of marine mammals, 39 percent are represented here, as are a third of the world's whale and dolphin species.

Designation by UNESCO will not prevent runaway development or illegal overfishing in this threatened area, but it does shine a huge spotlight on what is going on and puts pressure on Mexico and foreign nations to conserve, preserve, and protect this most wondrous and fragile place before it is too late.

Salmon with Honey, Pepitas, and Tomatillo Salsa

Chef Martín San Román of Rincón San Román restaurant in Tijuana did this combination at a wine dinner several years ago. He prepared it with grouper, but I have done it since with other fish such as halibut and sturgeon. Wild-caught salmon looks gorgeous prepared in this manner with leaf-green *pepitas* (green pumpkin seeds) crusting the pink flesh and paler green tomatillo sauce on the plate.

Be sure to use wild troll-caught salmon.

Makes 6 servings

6 king salmon fillets (6 ounces each)
2 tablespoons honey
1 teaspoon kosher salt
½ cup raw unsalted pepitas, chopped

1 tablespoon olive oil
½ cup white wine or water
1 cup tomatillo salsa (see note below)

1. Preheat the oven to 350 degrees.
2. Pat the fish dry. Brush the top side of the fish all over with the honey and sprinkle with salt. Cover with a layer of pepitas.
3. Heat the oil over medium heat in an ovenproof nonstick skillet large enough to hold the fish in a single layer.
4. Set the fish in the pan, pepita side up, and cook for 1 minute; do not turn. Pour the wine into the pan and pop the pan into the oven.
5. Bake for 7 to 10 minutes, or until the fish barely flakes when pressed with a finger.
6. For each serving, pool a little of the tomatillo salsa in the middle of a warm plate. Set the fish on top and spoon a little of the pan juices over the top of the fish. Serve immediately.

Note: You may use either the cooked or raw version of tomatillo salsa (see pages 38–39). I like the acidity and crunch of the raw salsa, but the cooked is equally good.

FARMED VERSUS WILD

Many consumers believe that farmed fish is by definition an ecologically sound choice, but this is not always the case. Many wild fisheries (such as the Baja spiny lobster fishery) are sustainable. Even some threatened species may be enjoyed in season, if caught by certain methods and if the catch is carefully monitored. Modern aquaculture (fish farming) is an expanding and soon-to-be essential industry with growing pains, successes, and challenges. Baja California aquafarms raise plump abalone, mussels, clams, oysters, catfish, and tilapia, but shrimp farms along the Sonoran coast of the Gulf of California often destroy the estuaries and swamps where wild shrimp breed.

When it comes to choosing wild versus farmed seafood, research and education are essential.

Mariscos en Papelote
(SEAFOOD BAKED IN PARCHMENT)

The technique of cooking in parchment paper enhances the delicate flavors of light-flavored, low-fat seafood. The seafood steams inside the packet with aromatics, making its own light sauce and allowing the true flavor of the seafood to shine.

Serve diners individual packets and allow them to open the paper at the table, where the puff of heady vapor is nearly as tasty as a first course, but utterly virtuous. If you choose to eliminate the small amount of butter, the recipe is very lean—completely free of added fat. It's also quick to make, impressive to serve—and delicious.

Suitable fish could include any delicate white fish: halibut, striped bass, farmed catfish, or sole (in season). Add clams, shrimp, mussels, scallops, or anything else that takes your fancy and you have a feast.

Makes 6 servings

6 fish fillets (4 ounces each)
Kosher salt
Any combination of seafood: scallops, shrimp, squid, clams, mussels, cracked stone crab claws, or shucked oysters; choose several pieces per packet
18 cherry tomatoes, halved

$\frac{1}{4}$ cup diced shallots or white onion
1 fresh serrano chile, sliced into rings (wear rubber gloves)
1 lime, preferably a Mexican limón (see page 30), sliced
6 tablespoons Cilantro Vinaigrette (see page 169)
1 tablespoon butter, cold and cut into 6 slices

1. Preheat the oven to 350 degrees.
2. Carefully remove all bones from the fish, using clean tweezers or needlenose pliers. Sprinkle each fillet with a pinch of salt. Rinse the other seafood and pat dry.
3. For each serving, lay out a piece of parchment 18 by 12 inches and set a piece of fish in the center. If there is a thin tail, tuck it underneath the thicker part of the fillet so it cooks evenly.
4. Sprinkle the fish with 6 tomato halves, a teaspoon of shallots, and a few chile rings. Lay a lime slice on top. Arrange the other seafood on top of the fish.
5. Spoon the vinaigrette over everything and top with the butter.
6. Bring the top and bottom edges of the paper together and roll them together, creasing to make a tight seal. Fold the sides into a pointed V shape and roll up tightly.
7. Set the packets on a cookie sheet or baking dish and bake for 20 minutes. Serve the packets still sealed and allow diners to open their own "presents."

Note: Bake the fish skin-on for added flavor and moisture.

Variations: Marinate the fish for 30 minutes in the marinade from Grilled Fish Tacos (see page 7). Top with the other seafood, a spoonful of diced tomatoes, and a whole basil leaf. Cook as directed above.

Substitute diced tomatillos for the tomatoes and sprinkle each fillet with a teaspoon of chopped cilantro. Top with the other seafood and cook as directed above.

Fish Baked in Banana Leaves with Achiote and Sour Orange

Since before the arrival of the Spanish, New World cooks have made little packets, called *mixiote*, of highly seasoned foods wrapped in *maguey* (agave), banana leaves, or avocado leaves, all of which impart subtle flavors to the food inside. This centuries-old culinary tradition lives on, as in this tropically tinged recipe inspired by the old colonial town of Cabo San José, with its languorous atmosphere. The achiote-orange combination is typically Yucatecan.

Makes 6 servings

¼ cup achiote paste (available in Latin markets)
1 tablespoon vegetable oil
Kosher salt
¼ cup very finely chopped red onion
1 garlic clove, chopped
⅛ teaspoon cayenne pepper
1 tablespoon white vinegar, preferably Heinz
Grated zest and juice from 1 orange

Juice from 1 lemon
6 fish steaks (7 ounces each)
1 package fresh or frozen banana leaves
  (available at Latin and Filipino markets)
½ bunch cilantro, chopped
Thin lemon or lime slices, preferably from
  Mexican limones (see page 30)

1. Combine the achiote, oil, 1½ teaspoons salt, onion, garlic, cayenne, vinegar, orange zest and juice, and lemon juice to make a runny paste; add more juice if necessary. Coat the fish with the paste on all sides and refrigerate for at least 1 hour.

2. Rinse the banana leaves under cold water. Pat dry with paper towels.
Preheat the oven to 350 degrees. Cut the banana leaves into 6 long strips or squares and smear with a little achiote paste. Set the fish in the center of each. Sprinkle with salt and the cilantro. Top with a lemon slice.

3. Wrap the fish into neat packages. Tie with a long "string" pulled from the banana leaf.

4. Set in a casserole without crowding. Add a little splash of hot water to the casserole and bake for 12 to 15 minutes, or until the fish reaches 150 degrees when tested with an instant-read thermometer.

5. Serve in the wrappers and let the guests open their "presents."

Roasted Fish with Wild Mushrooms, Garlic, and Poblano Chiles

I love the taste of seared mushrooms and fire-roasted poblano chiles together, a classic combination that really enhances meaty fish like halibut, yellowtail, or albacore, which can stand up to the flavors of the vegetables.

　　Searing the mushrooms in a hot skillet until they are lightly browned is the key to bringing up the flavors.

Makes 6 servings

3 large fresh poblano chiles — *ROASTED*
3 tablespoons olive oil
$\frac{1}{2}$ medium white onion, thinly sliced
2 large garlic cloves, thinly sliced
8 ounces oyster, shiitake, or king trumpet mushrooms, trimmed and cut into thin lengthwise strips

$\frac{1}{2}$ teaspoon kosher salt
6 fish fillets (6 ounces each and at least 1 inch thick)
$\frac{1}{4}$ cup white wine
$\frac{1}{4}$ cup very light fish or shellfish stock
2 tablespoons butter (see note below)

1. Prepare the chiles as for Rajas con Crema (see page 179). Cut into $\frac{1}{2}$-inch strips.

2. In a 10-inch skillet, heat 1 tablespoon of the oil over medium heat. Add the chile strips and sauté, stirring, until they are softened. Add the onion and garlic; continue to cook for 1 minute, stirring frequently. When the onion is translucent but still a bit crunchy, turn the vegetables onto a plate.

3. Wipe out the pan. Turn the heat to medium-high and add 1 tablespoon of the oil. Add the mushrooms; cook, stirring to brown them slightly. Sprinkle with $\frac{1}{4}$ teaspoon of the salt.

4. Return the vegetables to the pan. Cook a minute longer, then turn into a dish and keep warm.

5. Lightly dust one side of the fillets with the remaining $\frac{1}{4}$ teaspoon salt.

6. Wipe out the pan, return it to medium heat, and add the remaining 1 tablespoon oil. When the pan is hot, sear the fillets on one side until golden.

7. Turn the fish over and add the wine to the pan. Reduce the heat to low, cover, and cook for 5 minutes, or until the fish is barely cooked in the middle. With a slotted spatula, remove the fish to a warm plate and cover loosely.

8. Add the stock to the pan and increase the heat to medium. Reduce the liquid in the pan by half (about $\frac{1}{3}$ cup should remain). Whisk the butter into the simmering liquid. When it is incorporated, strain the sauce into a warm bowl.

9. To serve, divide the mushrooms and chiles evenly among 6 warm plates. Set a piece of fish on top; drizzle the sauce on top of the fish and around the plate.

Note: To reduce fat, eliminate the butter and thicken the sauce with $\frac{1}{4}$ teaspoon cornstarch mixed with $\frac{1}{2}$ tablespoon cold water.

Grilled Harpoon Swordfish with Olives and Two Warm Salsas

Simple and quick is the way to go when cooking swordfish. Here, grilled fish and a pair of simple, colorful salsas come together into a lovely entrée. As well as harpoon swordfish, sustainable choices include yellowtail tuna, catfish, Alaskan halibut and cod, ono, wild salmon, and bluenose bass.

Makes 6 servings

Grilled Chile and Tomato Salsa (see page 43)
Warm Avocado Sauce (recipe follows)
1 teaspoon olive oil

6 fish steaks (7 ounces each and at least 1 inch thick)
½ cup pitted kalamata olives, cut in half

1. Make the salsa and the avocado sauce. Keep both warm over gentle heat.
2. Heat an outdoor grill or grill pan over medium to high heat. Lightly oil the grill and the fish. Grill the fish for 3 to 5 minutes per side, or until firm but still juicy and a bit pink in the center. Don't overcook the fish.
3. On warm plates, place a few spoonfuls of each sauce next to each other. Set the fish on top, scatter a few olives over the fish, and serve immediately.

Warm Avocado Sauce

This creamy sauce is a perfect foil for spicier salsas. If you want to make the flavor more assertive, try adding a few spoonfuls of Roasted Poblano Chile Sauce (see page 92) or Cilantro Sauce (see page 94).

Makes 1½ cup

1 ripe Hass avocado
⅛ teaspoon kosher salt

1 teaspoon freshly squeezed lime juice, preferably from a Mexican limón (see page 30), or white vinegar, preferably Heinz

1. Pit and peel the avocado, then dice it into the bowl of a food processor. Pulse several times, then add the salt and lime juice. Puree until absolutely smooth, scraping the sides down several times.
2. Scrape the puree into a small saucepan and add water, a teaspoon at a time, until the puree is thinned to a sauce-like consistency. (To achieve the silkiest possible texture, press the sauce through a fine-mesh sieve.)
3. Warm the sauce over gentle heat; do not boil. Taste for seasoning, adding more salt or lime juice to taste.

SWORDFISH

Meaty, light-flavored, and firm, swordfish is one of the most desirable commercial and sport fish—and a victim of its own popularity. The Baja California population has been hunted with long-lines and gillnets to the point of collapse, yet the seasonal harpoon fishery in other areas and oceans shows signs of rebounding. Before buying swordfish, consumers need to ascertain where it comes from and how it was caught: It should be American caught and harpooned, never gillnetted or long-lined (using 20-mile lines, which kill other species indiscriminately). Most offshore-sourced swordfish is not sustainable.

Pan-Seared Fish with Roasted Poblano Sauce and Avocado

Pan-searing is a simple way to cook fish fillets on the stove, keeping the fillets deliciously moist while the pan juices make a little glaze for the fish. This recipe is well suited to thinner fillets of delicate fish, such as farmed bass, catfish, or ono, as well as Alaskan halibut and wild salmon. Shiny, dark green poblano chiles give an amazing depth of spicy flavor to the sauce.

Makes 6 servings

1 tablespoon all-purpose flour
1 teaspoon kosher salt
6 fish fillets (6 ounces each)
2 tablespoons olive oil

Juice of ½ lime, preferably a Mexican limón
  (see page 30)
⅓ cup Roasted Poblano Chile Sauce (see below)
½ ripe Hass avocado, diced

1. Combine the flour and salt and lightly dust the fish on all sides. Brush off the excess.
2. Heat the oil in a large frying pan over medium heat. Add the fish and cook for 3 minutes, until golden brown. Turn the fish and sprinkle the lime juice over the fish. Cover the pan and reduce the heat to low. Cook for 5 minutes, or until the fish is cooked through and flakes easily when gently pressed.
3. Pool the chile sauce on each of 6 plates and scatter the avocado over the sauce. Top with the fish.

Note: If the sauce is too spicy, stir ⅓ cup of Warm Avocado Sauce (page 91) into the finished sauce. You may then delete the diced avocado or use it for a garnish.

Roasted Poblano Chile Sauce

Makes about 1½ cups

3 large fresh poblano chiles
1 tablespoon vegetable oil
1 large garlic clove, chopped
½ cup White Wine Sauce (recipe follows)
Pinch of kosher salt (optional)

1. Prepare the chiles as for Rajas con Crema (see page 179). Cut into small dice.
2. Heat the oil in a small frying pan. Cook the chiles over medium heat, stirring occasionally, until they're very soft; do not allow to brown. Transfer to a food processor.
3. Add the garlic and puree to a smooth paste. Scrape into a bowl. (Can be prepared ahead to this point and refrigerated.)
4. Heat the wine sauce over low heat, stirring occasionally. Add ⅓ cup of the chile puree to the sauce and stir to reheat. (Thin with a little water, if necessary, and season with salt, if needed.) The sauce can be pureed or strained at this point; reheat before continuing.

White Wine Sauce

Basic white wine sauce is a blank canvas—a starting point for additions, sudden inspirations, and tinkering: stirring in roasted or dried chiles, roasted garlic, fresh citrus juices and zest, or fresh tomatoes and herbs. The sauce may be made ahead and reheated.

Makes 1¼ cups, enough for 6 to 8 servings

1 tablespoon butter
2 tablespoons minced shallot or white onion
½ cup white wine
¼ teaspoon white vinegar, preferably Heinz

2 teaspoons cornstarch
1 cup Seven Seas Broth (see page 103) or water
⅓ cup whipping cream
½ teaspoon kosher salt

1. In a 1-quart saucepan, melt the butter over low heat. Add the shallot and cook slowly until soft; do not brown. Add the wine and vinegar, increase the heat to medium, and reduce by half.
2. Mix the cornstarch with the stock and whisk into the wine reduction. Continue whisking until the sauce comes to a boil.
3. Add the cream, reduce the heat, and simmer for 10 minutes on low heat. Season with salt. Strain.

THE PANGA TRADITION

The Baja California coastline is dotted with tiny villages where the fishermen make their living out of *pangas*. A *panga* is a sturdy, open, wooden or metal boat with high sides, powered by an outboard engine.

The quaint sight of colorfully painted *pangas* pulled up on the beach while the fishermen mend their nets in between fishing sessions can obscure the importance of the *panga* fishing industry. No one has a bigger stake in sustainable fisheries than the local independent *panga* fishermen and their families.

The individual *panga* fisherman is the antithesis of the big commercial trawler. He makes his living the hard, old-fashioned way, with hand lines or thrown nets. Most fishermen sell their catches to large cooperatives for marketing.

A big commercial boat can move into a fishing ground and clean out an area for an entire season, leaving these men with no income for their families. The long term is even more dire. Unrestrained commercial overfishing will completely destroy a generations-old livelihood, while a village has a vested interest in maintaining its local fishing grounds.

Chipotle Fish Steaks with Cilantro Sauce

If you have a can of chipotles and a few other ingredients, you can have this delicious fish on the table in 30 minutes flat. Suitable fish include yellowtail tuna, catfish, Alaskan halibut and cod, ono, wild salmon, and bluenose bass. Camotes with Sea Salt (see page 185) are excellent with this.

Makes 6 servings

½ cup chipotles in adobo
6 fish steaks (7 ounces each and at least 1 inch thick)
1 teaspoon vegetable oil
Cilantro Sauce (see below)

1. Puree the chipotles in a food processor. Coat the fish on all sides with the chipotle paste. (May be cooked immediately or refrigerated for up to 12 hours.)
2. Heat an outdoor grill or grill pan over medium heat and oil lightly. Scrape most of the chipotle paste off the fish. Grill the fish for 3 to 5 minutes on each side, until firm but still moist in the center. Do not overcook.
3. Spoon a few tablespoons of the cilantro sauce on each plate and set the fish on top. Serve immediately.

Cilantro Sauce

Makes 1½ cups

2 cups lightly packed cilantro leaves
2 tablespoons butter
½ cup White Wine Sauce (see page 93)
½ teaspoon freshly squeezed lime juice, preferably from a Mexican limón (see page 30)

1. Chop the cilantro in a food processor as finely as possible. Add the butter and process until a smooth green paste is formed.
2. Heat the wine sauce over low heat and stir in 3 tablespoons of the cilantro paste, or more to taste, and the lime juice. Reserve any leftover cilantro paste for another use. Serve immediately.

Fish on Pan-Roasted Potatoes with Smoked Paprika, Garlic Shrimp, and Mussels

Paprika closes a culinary circle when used in Mexican cooking. Chiles indigenous to Mexico were transported to Spain in the 16th century. Owing to the change in soil and climate, they eventually evolved into the mild paprika chile. Dried and ground, paprika is now fundamental to the taste of Spanish cooking, in *sofrito*, *brava* sauce, or dry Spanish chorizo. The same paprika is used extensively in Mexico.

This recipe is a Baja-inspired riff on a common one found throughout Mexico and the Iberian peninsula: fish and seafood cooked with potatoes (another New World ingredient), Spanish paprika, onions, and garlic.

Sustainable fish choices include farmed striped bass, catfish, American-caught flounder or sole, Alaskan halibut, American-caught wild striped bass, farmed black mussels, and wild shrimp.

Makes 4 servings

20 black mussels or clams
2 teaspoons olive oil
3 tablespoons butter or vegetable oil
1/2 red bell pepper, diced
1/2 green bell pepper, diced
1/4 medium white onion, diced
2 medium Yukon gold potatoes, peeled and diced
2 teaspoons kosher salt

3 teaspoons smoked paprika
6 fish fillets (4 ounces each)
1/2 cup white wine
2 garlic cloves, finely minced
12 best-quality medium shrimp, preferably Mexican, peeled and deveined (tails left on)
1 tablespoon chopped Italian parsley
Lemon or lime wedges

1. Scrub the mussels well with cold water and a stiff brush. Discard any that do not close when tapped. Keep covered with a damp cloth in the refrigerator. Just before cooking, remove the fibrous beards by cutting them off close to the shell.

2. Preheat the oven to 400 degrees.

3. In a 12-inch ovenproof skillet, paella pan, or brazier over medium heat, heat the oil and add 1 tablespoon of the butter. Add the red and green peppers and onion; cook until they begin to soften. Add the potatoes and cook, stirring occasionally, until they are cooked through; this may take as long as 15 minutes. Season the potatoes well with most of the salt and paprika.

4. Remove the pan from the heat. Set the fish on top of the vegetables. (If the fillets are long and thin, like sole or rockfish, roll them up starting at the narrow end or fold them in half.) Dust the fish with the last of the salt and paprika.

5. Arrange the mussels around the fish and add 1/4 cup of the wine to the pan. Set a square of parchment or foil loosely over the fish and bake for 15 to 20 minutes, or until the fish is cooked (flakes when pushed with a finger) and the potatoes are soft.

6. Remove the pan from the oven. Keep the foil on and set in a warm place.

7. Heat a medium skillet over medium-high heat. Melt the remaining 2 tablespoons butter. When it is foaming but not browned, add the garlic and then the shrimp; cook and stir until the shrimp are barely pink, about 30 seconds.

8. Add the remaining 1/4 cup wine, bring to a boil, and cook for 1 minute. Pour over the fish and mussels and shake to blend the flavors.

9. Scatter the parsley over the fish and serve immediately with lemon wedges.

Coconut Calamari with
Dried Orange and Sesame

This simple recipe is sure to become a favorite, especially since you can bread a large batch and freeze some for unexpected guests or a surprise treat. The coconut crumbs are great on chicken, shrimp, fish, and crab cakes.

Makes 6 generous servings

1 cup shredded sweetened coconut
1 ½ cups panko bread crumbs
1 cup all-purpose flour
1 teaspoon cayenne pepper
1 teaspoon granulated garlic
1 teaspoon kosher salt
3 eggs
8 calamari steaks, cut into strips ½ by 2 inches
Vegetable oil, for frying

TO SERVE

1 tablespoon ground dried orange peel
1 tablespoon sesame seeds, toasted
Cilantro sprigs
Sirachi, sambal, and Thai sweet chile sauce (see note below)
Blood orange, tangerine, or lime wedges

1. Pulse the coconut in a food processor until finely ground. Add the panko and pulse three more times, quickly.
2. Set up three wide, shallow bowls; this will be your breading line. In the first bowl combine the flour, cayenne, garlic, and salt. Beat the eggs in the second bowl. In the third, place a small amount of the coconut crumbs.
3. Drain the calamari and pat dry. Working with 6 pieces at a time, toss the strips with the flour and shake off excess. Drop into the eggs, swish around (I use chopsticks), fish them out, and let the excess drip off. Drop into the coconut crumbs and coat on all sides. Shake off the excess and set on a cookie sheet. Continue until all the calamari is breaded. (Can be prepared ahead to this point and refrigerated or frozen. If frozen, do not thaw.)
4. Place oil in a 12-inch skillet or wok to a depth of ½ inch. Set over medium-high heat. (See Safe Frying on page 248.) When the oil reaches 350 degrees on a deep-fry thermometer, add the calamari strips in batches, without crowding, and cook until golden brown. Remove from the oil and drain on paper towels.
5. Dust with the orange peel and sesame seeds. Garnish with the cilantro. Serve warm with the hot sauce and citrus wedges on the side.

Note: Sirachi, sambal, and Thai sweet chile sauce are available at Asian markets. Panko bread crumbs and dried orange peel are available at most supermarkets.

CALAMAR (SQUID)

Like octopus, squid are cephalopods; unlike octopus, squid sport 10 tentacles, are bioluminescent, and hunt in large nocturnal schools. The common or market squid grows to about a foot in length, but "flying" squid 2 feet in length are regularly caught off Baja, and winter currents sometimes bring 40-pound Humboldt squid close to shore, where they are a popular sport catch and sometimes beach themselves chasing fish into the shallows. Much larger squid have been recorded in deep canyons just offshore, and the mythologically big ones (*Architeuthis*) that are thought to lurk in mid-ocean may reach lengths of 90 feet—or more.

FIESTA DE LAS VENDIMIAS
PAELLA CONTEST

■ ■ ■

Under the cloudless Baja sky, in an oak grove tucked between hectares of laden grape vines, clouds of fragrant grape wood smoke curl into the air where 40 paella teams are beginning to work their magic. It's 1:30 and the Ensenada-Tecate highway is backed up for miles in both directions.

The sun beats down. The air is like a furnace, fueled by 6-foot logs of grape-vine trunks that pulsate with heat beneath paella pans. *Paelleros* gulp down icy beers, mop their foreheads with bandannas, and nurse their paellas along obsessively.

This is the last event of the annual Guadalupe Valley *Vendimias*: the Paella Competition and Wine Tasting, undoubtedly the most widely anticipated and fiercely contested event of the 2-week wine festival. It is a rice and seafood olympics, where as in old, the winners gain only glory and bragging rights.

The honor of best paella is something that these teams take seriously. Many entrants practice all year. Teams sport matching aprons, and defiant banners flutter in the sun (*¡La mejor paella de la familia Olivera!* says one). Presentation tables are draped and decorated with vines and grapes, and on each are two massive grapevine trunks, where the finished paella will be set for judging.

Tables of extended family are tucked into the shade of towering oaks, children dart and play among the crowds, and short-legged dogs loll with their tongues hanging out. The packed crowd sways to live *mariachi, norteña,* and *rock en español*, sipping beer and tasting wines from all the valley's *bodegas* as they wait for a taste of paella. And oh, what paella!

Seafood paella, celebrating the bounty of the Pacific Ocean, is the theme, but every paella is as individual as its creators. The paellas are massive affairs, up to 4 feet across, cooked (per the rules) over the shriveled corpses of grapevines, gnarled and gray-black with shredded bark, pouring fragrant smoke and more ferocious heat into the still, hot midday air. There are more than a few welded, homemade contraptions, braziers both professional and impromptu—one of the best paellas cooks a foot off the ground on two concrete blocks, a single huge grapevine trunk wedged beneath, burning.

Sweating *paelleros* sauté the basic ingredients, tend the vast pans of glowing yellow saffron rice, and then set to work making intricate patterns of shrimp and mussels, octopus and clams, peppers, pork, lobster, and prawns. When the paellas are done, they are removed from the heat and tenderly wrapped in foil, napkins, or cheesecloth for the all-important cooling and steaming process that rehydrates the rice. The finished paellas are settled onto the grapevine displays on each table.

Lines begin forming early before the most spectacular paellas, but nothing will be served until the judges have seen and tasted each team's offerings. Only restaurant La Diferencia from Tijuana has brought other food, so we stand in line for *pastel de vegetales* (layered vegetables baked with cheese) with poblano cream sauce and *tostadas* with black beans, yellow pepper salsa, and a big bowl of fried grasshoppers (*chapulines*).

"Oh my," says an elderly American woman to my left, eyeing the crispy brown grasshoppers. "I think I'll try those." There are 20 valley wineries pouring tastes of their best wines, but no one is quite sure what to drink with the grasshoppers.

The judges taste from numbered white Styrofoam containers, without looking at the finished paellas. Some teams are not above sending something extra the judges' way, like little fried chorizos, especially plump shrimp, or a particularly nice clam. But at last the judges are done, and the teams call out to their waiting fans, "¡Provecho! ¡Prueba!" ("Come on! Let's try it!")

At last, we can eat, and the rush is on. With paella, it's all about the flavor of the rice, which carries the mingled tastes of the various recipes. Most paellas are tinted bright yellow with saffron, but a few brave souls eschew the obvious for more interesting interpretations: There are paellas with fresh artichokes, huge spiny lobster, tiny crayfish. Others feature homemade chorizo, chunks of pork and chicken, roasted peppers, octopus, and calamari. The variety is stunning.

The most spectacular presentation is at a professional table, where a team of rather large men in bright yellow aprons and panama hats pose proudly behind a magnificent paella 5 feet in diameter, intricate as fine cloisonné: In the center an enormous spiny lobster stands rampant like a lion on a coat of arms; radiating outward are clusters of "grapes" (made from finely chopped fish rolled into balls and colored purple with squid ink), along with *langostinos*, shrimp, and angry red crayfish. Amply decorated with grape leaves and cartoon colorful, this is the paella to beat, at least for looks.

But for flavor, the finest is the paella of restaurant La Diferencia, whose smiling, sweating chef has tended to his paella nonstop for over 3 hours. First he sautéed, in local olive oil, blue crabs and fresh prawns from Ensenada waters, along with little white clams, black local mussels, homemade chorizo, giant pismo clams, and his own style of *sofrito* (a mixture of garlic, onions, and tomatoes). His seafood stock is dark and rich with the lobster, chicken, shrimp, and calamari. At the end, he scatters saffron filaments over the rice as the paella bubbles away over the wood-burning grill. Behind him, his assistants clean huge prawns and shuck clams for the final garnish. The flavor is superb—light and fresh, redolent of the Pacific a few miles away, rich with local tastes and products.

Arroz con Mariscos (SEAFOOD PAELLA)

I like to think of Arroz con Mariscos as the less competitive form of paella: relatively thrifty, quick to make, and utterly delicious. I love *arroz* made with whatever is fresh and good at the market—shrimp, octopus, lobster, mussels, oysters, clams, fish, *calamar*, periwinkle, abalone . . . the list is endless. The more kinds of seafood you incorporate, the better it will taste. For special occasions, splurge on big shrimp and arrange them on top. For even splurgier events, toss a pinch of saffron into the stock.

I call for long-grain converted rice here because it gives consistent results. If you prefer to use regular long-grain rice, reduce the quantity of water by 1/3 cup.

Makes 6 to 8 servings

12 clams
12 black mussels
8 ounces best-quality medium shrimp, preferably Mexican, peeled and deveined
6 ounces sea scallops, side muscle removed, cut into quarters, about 12 pieces
8 ounces calamari, cleaned and cut into rings, legs trimmed, about 4 squid
1/3 cup olive oil
4 large garlic cloves, thinly sliced
1/3 cup finely chopped white onion
2 teaspoons kosher salt

2 cups long-grain converted white rice
1/2 green bell pepper, cut into strips 1/4 by 2 inches
1/2 red bell pepper, cut into strips 1/4 by 2 inches
1/4 cup thinly sliced green onions
4 ripe Roma tomatoes, cut into 1/2-inch chunks
1/2 cup white wine
2 cups Seven Seas Broth (see page 103)
1 1/2 cups water
4 ounces firm fish, cut into 1-inch chunks
2 tablespoons chopped Italian parsley
Lemon wedges

1. Scrub the clams and mussels well with a stiff brush under cold running water.
2. Discard any that do not close when tapped. Remove the fibrous beards from the mussels.
3. Rinse the shrimp, scallops, and calamari under cold running water and drain thoroughly.
4. In a 12-inch skillet or brazier with lid, heat half of the oil over medium-high heat. Add the garlic and cook, stirring, until the garlic just begins to turn golden around the edges. Add the onion and cook, stirring, until the onion is translucent—about 1 minute.
5. Add the shrimp, scallops, and calamari to the pan and cook quickly, stirring often, until the seafood is about half cooked. Season with 1 teaspoon of the salt. Remove the pan contents and juices to a bowl and return the pan to the heat. (Do not wipe out the pan.)
6. Add the remaining oil to the pan. Add the rice and cook, stirring, for 2 minutes, or until slightly golden.
7. Stir in the peppers, green onions, and tomatoes. Season with the remaining 1 teaspoon salt. Add the wine, stock, and water and shake the pan gently once or twice.
8. Stir the cooked seafood into the rice. Set the fish on top and shake the pan again, gently, to even out the rice and liquid. When the rice is almost boiling, arrange the clams and mussels on top of the rice and cover.
9. Turn the heat to the lowest setting. Cook the rice (without peeking!) for 25 minutes. At the end of this time, lift off the lid and give the pan a gentle shake to see if all the liquid has been absorbed. When you can no longer see any liquid in the pan, turn off heat, cover, and let the rice rest for 15 minutes before serving.
10. Scatter the parsley over the top and serve with lemon wedges.

Note: You can substitute bottled clam juice or fish bouillon for homemade stock, as long as you reduce the quantity to 1 cup and increase the water by the same amount.

Caldo de Siete Mares
(SEVEN SEAS SOUP)

Baja cooks excel at the creation of fish soups. Making a triumph out of necessity, they have learned to coax incredible flavor from a mix of leftover seafood odds and ends—using bones and heads from a variety of different types of fish as well as parts of shrimp, squid, mussels, clams, lobster, and whatever else comes along that day. Everything goes into the pot, and it all adds up to a complex mix of deep flavors—the essence of the sea.

Since home cooks generally don't have access to this kind of variety, many fish vendors at Ensenada's Mercado Negro sell premade "Seven Seas" bundles, ready to take home and cook. This usually consists of a meaty fish tail, a few shrimp, some crab claws, a chunk of squid, and celery, carrot, onion, and bay leaf.

Restaurant versions are typically more elaborate, like this recipe, which is finished with a flavorful lime aioli. This *caldo* is a meal in itself, extravagantly full of fresh seafood and richly flavored with a complex stock base that's well worth the time and expense. The extra stock can be frozen and used in seafood sauces.

Makes 6 to 8 generous servings

Seven Seas Broth (see the opposite page)
12 clams
12 black mussels
1 tablespoon vegetable oil
2 garlic cloves, chopped
¼ cup finely minced onion
2 ripe Roma tomatoes, diced
8 ounces calamari tubes, cleaned and sliced into ½-inch rings
8 ounces best-quality medium shrimp, preferably Mexican, peeled and deveined
8 ounces firm white fish fillet, such as striped bass, catfish, or bass

8–10 stone crab claws, cracked
8 large sea scallops, side muscle removed, quartered
1 tablespoon chopped Italian parsley

TO SERVE
3 tablespoons chopped cilantro
Lime Aioli (see the opposite page)
Salsa de Chiles de Arbol #1 (page 38)
Lime wedges, preferably from Mexican limones (see page 30)

1. Prepare the broth.
2. Scrub the clam shells thoroughly with a stiff brush, especially along the hinge area and lip of the shell; do not soak the clams in water.
3. Scrub the mussels well with cold water and a stiff brush. Discard any that do not close when tapped. Remove the fibrous beards by cutting them off close to the shell.
4. Heat the oil in a 2-gallon stockpot over medium-high heat. Add the garlic, onion, and tomatoes; sauté for 1 minute. Add the calamari and shrimp; sauté for 1 minute. Add the fish and crab claws, reduce the heat to medium, and cook for 1 minute more; do not stir.
5. Add the broth and bring to a fast simmer. Add the clams and mussels; simmer for 3 to 5 minutes, until they open. Discard any that do not open.
6. Stir in the scallops and parsley.
7. Use a skimmer to lift out equal portions of the seafood into warmed soup plates. Ladle the hot broth over the seafood.
8. To serve, sprinkle with the cilantro. Add a small spoonful of aioli and a few drops of salsa to each plate. Finish with a squeeze of lime.

Seven Seas Broth

May be made ahead and refrigerated or frozen.

Makes 3 quarts

3 pounds white fish frames (bones and tails)
6 ounces whole squid, cleaned and chopped
8 ounces broken shrimp pieces, with shells, or 1 quart shrimp shells and crushed lobster bodies
1½ tablespoons vegetable oil
2 garlic cloves, split
½ white onion, chopped
1 celery stalk, cut into chunks
1 medium carrot, cut into chunks
1 fresh serrano chile, split
2 large ripe Roma tomatoes, cut into 1-inch pieces
11 cups cold water
1 cup white wine
2 teaspoons kosher salt
½ teaspoon black peppercorns
1 bay leaf

1. Quickly rinse the fish bones, squid, and shrimp with cold water. Drain.
2. Heat the oil in a 3-gallon stockpot over medium-high heat. Add the garlic, onion, celery, and carrot and cook, stirring occasionally, until the vegetables are soft.
3. Reduce the heat and add the fish bones, squid, shrimp, chile, and tomatoes. Cover and cook slowly without stirring for about 10 minutes.
4. Add the water, wine, salt, peppercorns, and bay leaf. Bring to a boil, then turn the heat to low and simmer, without stirring, for 1 hour.
5. Strain through a colander. Do not press down on the solids, but allow the stock to drain for 15 minutes. Discard the solids. Let the stock settle and pour through a fine sieve.

Lime Aioli

Makes about ½ cup

2 garlic cloves, mashed to a smooth paste with ¼ teaspoon kosher salt
1 tablespoon best-quality extra-virgin olive oil
¼ cup mayonnaise
2–3 teaspoons freshly squeezed lime juice, preferably from Mexican limones (see page 30)

About 30 minutes before serving, mix all the ingredients and set aside.

Baja-Style Hot-Smoked Fish

Baja California is famous for its fish-smoking houses, a trade that developed out of the need to quickly preserve big fish like marlin and bluefin tuna in the days before refrigeration and canning. Smokehouses still dot the back streets of every coastal town from Rosarito to Cabo San Lucas, and stands at Ensenada's Mercado Negro sell dark bricks of oily fish infused with a delicious sweet/salty/smoky flavor.

Smoked fish is amazingly versatile, made into smoked fish salad or crumbled up, mixed with mayonnaise, and served as an *antojito* atop *tostaditas* with raw onions and lime. It can be stuffed into golden güero peppers with a flaming-hot Mango Salsa (see page 47) or eaten straight up, on crusty bread with a squeeze of lime.

The commercial hot-smoke method used in Baja is difficult to replicate in the home kitchen, but setting up a grill smoker is surprisingly easy and renders delicious results, as long as you are willing to sacrifice a cheap pan and experiment a little with times and temperatures. Depending on your ambitions (and the size of your refrigerator and grill), you can easily make 5 to 10 pounds of smoked fish in one session. Marinating and smoking require very little active time, but the preparation does spread over 2 days, so it's a great weekend project.

I came up with this smoking method when I was presented with four huge albacore, more than 120 pounds of first-quality fish, only hours out of the water. I suggest you start with a *much* smaller quantity.

And yes: The secret ingredient in many marinades is Coca-Cola.

Suitable fish include any firm, full-flavored fish such as pole-caught tuna, wild troll-caught king salmon, pole-caught albacore, ono, onaga, mackerel, yellowtail, grouper, harpooned swordfish, or Alaskan halibut. Fresh shrimp, scallops, mussels, clams, and oysters smoke beautifully.

Try to purchase the fish in one large piece and trim it yourself. The quality will be better. Don't cut the fish too thinly, as it will dry out.

Makes 5 pounds

MARINADE

3 cups raw cider or apple juice (or substitute Coca-Cola)
1 cup crushed piloncillo or packed dark brown sugar
1 cup best-quality Japanese soy sauce
¼ cup kosher salt
Juice of 2 limes, preferably from Mexican limones (see page 30)

2 tablespoons finely chopped fresh ginger
3 garlic cloves, finely chopped
1 teaspoon freshly ground black pepper
1 fresh serrano chile, split lengthwise (optional)

5 pounds thick fish fillets, cut into 4-inch pieces

1. Mix the marinade ingredients in a 1-gallon resealable freezer bag. Add the fish to the bag, squeeze out excess air, seal, and refrigerate for 24 hours.
2. Remove the fish from the marinade, drain, and pat dry on all sides. Set on a rack over a shallow pan and refrigerate, uncovered, for 2 hours, or until the outside is quite dry.
3. Soak 1½ cups of small hickory chips in water for 1 hour. (Try to find ¼- to ½-inch pieces.)
4. Set a rack in the smoking pan so it clears the bottom by an inch. Lightly oil the rack and set the fish on the rack with a little space in between the pieces so the smoke can circulate.
5. Drain the wood chips and put into a pie tin you're willing to sacrifice. Heat a grill and set the heat or arrange the fire so one side is hot and the other is medium heat. Set the tin with the chips on the grill over the hot side.

6. Close the lid. It will take about 5 minutes for smoke to appear. Quickly set the pan with the fish on the cooler side of the grill and close the lid again.

7. Monitor the temperature inside the lid to make sure it is around 325 to 350 degrees and set the timer for 20 minutes. Don't peek. After 20 minutes, open the lid, stir the chips, and test the internal temperature of the fish with an instant-read thermometer. Close the lid again and cook a further 20 to 25 minutes, to at least 145 degrees. Total cooking time will be between 40 and 50 minutes.

8. When the fish is cooked, remove it from the grill and wrap loosely in foil for 20 minutes. Then wrap the pieces individually in foil to prevent their drying out and refrigerate.

Notes: The thinner and smaller the pieces, the faster they will cook. Conversely, thick pieces will take longer.

Thin fillets of farmed catfish and striped bass take well to smoking, but be careful not to overcook the fish, which is very lean; 10 minutes in the smoke is enough.

Cut large pieces of fish into pieces the size of the palm of your hand and no more than 2 inches thick. This allows the marinade and smoke to penetrate without overcooking the fish.

If you want the smoke flavor to penetrate deeply, cook at a lower temperature for a longer time rather than adding more chips; too much smoke too fast will make anything taste like an old tire.

SMOKING EQUIPMENT

Good stove-top smokers are available, but I prefer the flexibility of making my own setup.

GRILL Gas grill with two or more burners, a tight-fitting cover, and an exterior thermometer

SMOKING PAN AND RACK Holds the food while it is smoking. Consists of a shallow pan with a rim and a raised rack that fits inside. The pan catches drips; the rack allows smoke to circulate all around the food. Can be a pie tin and a cake rack, a rimmed cookie sheet and a cooling rack, or anything else you like, as long as the grill cover can be fully closed.

You'll also need the following:

- Cheap pie tin for holding the smoldering chips
- Heavy-duty 1-gallon resealable freezer bags for marinating
- Small hickory chips, about $\frac{1}{4}$- to $\frac{1}{2}$-inch pieces—not powder
- Refrigerator space (for drying)
- Adjustable instant-read thermometer
- Aluminum foil wrap

3
SACRED ROOTS, NEW FIRE
NUEVA COCINA IN THE WINE COUNTRY

I drink when I have occasion,
And sometimes when I have no occasion.
—Cervantes

Few people associate Mexican food with great wine, but grapes have been grown and wine made in Mexico since the early years of the 16th century. Everywhere the Spanish went, grapes went too—including the farthest reaches of Baja California, where the first vines were planted by Dominican missionaries in 1791.

Four valleys in northern Baja California supply most of the table wines (and most of the best wines) sold in Mexico today. The region is made up of two distinct areas. The Guadalupe Valley (including San Antonio de las Minas) is only 90 minutes south of San Diego, a few miles northeast of the city of Ensenada. This area produces vast volumes of table wines, but it is also home to an ever-growing group of small, high-quality wineries that are revolutionizing Mexican wines. The second region, south of Ensenada and a few miles inland, is made up of Valle de Santo Tomás (the oldest wine-producing area in Baja) and Valle de San Vicente.

Thanks to a Mediterranean climate, this serenely beautiful part of Baja has everything it takes to produce spectacular wines—and great food to go with them. The valleys run from the inland desert toward the nearby coast, funneling in breezes from the Pacific Ocean, which bring cool foggy mornings, hot afternoons, and chilly nights. With lots of sun and heat, Baja wines, especially the new-style reds, tend to be big—deep colored, complex in flavor, with lots of fruit "up front." Wines like this can stand up to the robust flavors of the recipes in this chapter, inspired by the wine valleys of northern Baja California.

Here, in the ranchos and villages, the pace of life is relaxed; people often ride their horses through miles of vineyards to do the shopping and visit with neighbors. Chickens cluck in backyards and down dirt lanes; kids play soccer under oak and tamarisk trees filled with chirping birds.

Thriving olive groves yield Baja's wonderful olive oil. Local farms grow pomegranates and figs, baby vegetables, lettuces and aromatic herbs, artichokes, and avocados. In winter, citrus trees are laden with glowing fruit. White Charolais cattle graze the hillsides, lambs gambol through olive groves. Among the miles of grape vines, it seems that there's a good winery every hundred yards.

Local taco stands and restaurants might offer grilled quail along with fish and shellfish fresh from the Pacific Ocean via the markets of Ensenada (which is a mere 30-minute drive from San Antonio de las Minas at the southwest end of the valley). Cooks have access to grass-fed beef, local lamb and pork, free-range chickens, wild duck from the marshes and estuaries, and quail and rabbit, both wild and farmed. Freshly made farmhouse cheeses are sold in the little markets, along with the famous Real del Castillo cheese made near Santo Tomás.

In the new style of cooking called *nueva cocina*, some Mexican chefs mine their native and colonial heritage for indigenous ingredients, play with technique and presentation, and create something profoundly Mexican but completely new. Others might look globally for inspiration, incorporating Asian and other exotica with European technique and *criollo* attitude; many freely use super-premium ingredients, like foie gras and truffles, in their cooking.

In the wine valleys of northern Baja California, nueva cocina–style cooking transforms into a powerful statement of *terroir*—a French word meaning "the taste of the land." In food, as in wine, *terroir* means using what you have growing nearby, in its perfect season—the true expression of the very soul of this place on earth. In Baja, such expression means doing very old things but in a new way.

Cooking locally and seasonally also means eating better food, at its peak of flavor and freshness. It is environmentally responsible: Fewer chemicals are used on farm products, and less gas is needed to haul it to market. Water and other precious resources are used carefully. At its heart, local cooking supports neighbors and community and closes the circle from farm to plate—and from vineyard to palate.

Chef Jair Tellez of Laja restaurant in the Guadalupe Valley says firmly, "Other chefs tell me how lucky I am to be here. But it's not luck. It's a choice." Tellez built his own restaurant—from the ground up, with his own hands, using local stone. On the tables are arrangements of herbs intermingled with wild grasses. The wine list is a Baja oenophile's dream, with lost vintages, successful experiments, and bottles from Tellez's friends and the valley's tiny producers—wines found nowhere else in the world. Herbs and tomatoes grow outside the wooden doors to the restaurant. Lettuces, vegetables, and fruit are picked daily at El Mogor, an organic farm across the narrow highway. Beef fattened on El Mogor's carob occasionally finds its way onto the menu, which is deceptively simple—along with just-caught Pacific fish or some of the local cheese that Tellez ripens in his own cave. In Tellez's world, every bite must be truthful and of the land—of this place, of the *Valle*.

RECIPES

FROM SACRED ROOTS, NEW FIRE:
CHANGING STYLES IN WINE

■●■

January brings winter rains that profoundly transform the landscape of inland Baja California. Rocky gray, sun-blasted hills become green under the bluest of skies. Streams and rivers run with clear, ocher water. Fields of quick-growing wildflowers spring up and sway in cool winds off the sierra.

Throughout the many vineyards of northern Baja, grape vines sit bare and stark black amid the verdant extravagance of new growth. Wispy infant Merlot and Cabernet Franc, Viognier, and Chenin Blanc are interspersed with long rows of old, thick-trunked giants whose roots tap down 40, even 50 feet into the flinty grit, sand, and stone that lies beneath. The vines seem to know that this riotous, lush *jeunesse* will quickly pass. They save their energy for the months and years of drought and struggle ahead.

As the French saying goes, *Il faut souffrir pour être belle:* "One must suffer to be beautiful." When the vine suffers, the wine is beautiful—soulful and lingering, a long story on the palate. The tale told by Baja's wines spans two centuries of bitter drought, political and social strife, prosperity and privation, and heroic renaissance.

Wine has been made here more or less continuously since the padres planted their Mission grapes in the 1790s. Later, immigrants brought with them their favorite Old World vines and wine-making traditions. In the early 20th century, Russian settlers planted grapes and became the area's first commercial winemakers. And while Prohibition reigned for a decade north of the border, a few Italian winemakers raised grapes for sweet sacramental wines—the "sacred roots" of today's thriving industry.

After a slump in the 1960s, the wineries tore out many of the old sweet wines and began replanting with large swathes of more popular Chenin Blanc, Chardonnay, Cabernet, and Merlot.

Starting in the 1980s, a group of Mexican winemakers (the most influential of whom hold advanced degrees from the great wine schools of France) brought in southern French, Italian, and Spanish varietals more suited to the area's many microclimates. In this latest renaissance, an ever-expanding group of small, high-quality wineries have embraced both new and old: sacred roots revived by the fiery ambition of a new generation. The groundwork is finally laid for wines that fully express the earthy soul of Baja.

Varietals Grown in Baja California

Barbera
Cabernet Franc
Cabernet Sauvignon
Carignan
Chardonnay
Chasselas
Chenin Blanc

Colombard
Grenache
Mission—very old grapes,
    brought by the Padres and
    still grown in small patches
Malbec
Merlot

Nebbiolo
Petite Sirah
Sauvignon Blanc
Syrah
Tempranillo or Valdepeñas Viognier
White Málaga
Zinfandel

Two Tapenades with Warm Grilled Flatbread

The complex flavors of the two tapenades play beautifully against Baja California's powerful wines, especially when paired with warm fresh flatbread, right off the grill.

Both the flatbread dough and the tapenades can be made a day ahead. Bring the tapenades to room temperature before serving and roll and grill the flatbread at the last minute.

Serve the tapenades in small individual bowls or communally, on shallow plates. Raw vegetables, leaves of Belgian endive, breadsticks, or crackers make great accompaniments as well.

WINE Rich whites, such as barrel-fermented Chardonnay and Sauvignon Blanc; Spanish-style reds, such as Tempranillo-Cabernet blend; Grenache

Makes 8 generous servings

Green Olive Tapenade (see below)
Black Olive Tapenade (see opposite page)
Warm Grilled Whole-Grain Flatbread (see page 190)

Prepare the tapenades and serve with the warm flatbread.

Green Olive Tapenade

Makes 1 cup

1 cup green Mission olives, pitted
1 small garlic clove
3 tablespoons freshly squeezed orange juice

$1/3$–$1/2$ cup best-quality extra-virgin olive oil
$1/2$ teaspoon kosher salt

1. Rinse the olives to remove the brine and drain.
2. In a mini food processor or with a sharp knife, chop the garlic as finely as possible, almost to a paste. Add the olives and chop coarsely; a little texture is good. Place the olives in a small bowl.
3. Stir in the orange juice, oil, and salt. Cover and let stand for at least 1 hour before serving. Taste for seasoning—you may want to add a little more salt; the orange should be subtle. (Can be prepared 24 hours ahead and refrigerated.)
4. Bring to room temperature and stir well before serving.

Variations: Try adding lemon zest, black pepper, and a little chopped fresh rosemary. If you like anchovy, a tablespoon of chopped anchovy is delicious.

Black Olive Tapenade

Makes 1 cup

1 cup kalamata olives, pitted
2 large garlic cloves
2 tablespoons capers
Freshly ground black pepper
3 tablespoons best-quality extra-virgin olive oil

1 teaspoon finely grated lemon zest
1 ripe Roma tomato, very finely diced or chopped
2 tablespoons chopped basil
¼ teaspoon kosher salt

1. Rinse the olives to remove the brine and drain.

2. In the bowl of a food processor, pulse the olives, garlic, and capers together a few times until everything is finely chopped and sticking together, but not completely pureed.

3. Transfer to a small bowl. Stir in the pepper, oil, and lemon zest until thoroughly combined. (Can be prepared 24 hours ahead and refrigerated.) Add the tomato and basil just before serving. Taste for seasoning—you may want to add a little more salt.

OLIVES AND OLIVE OIL

So-called Mission olives came to Baja California with the Spanish missionaries. Later, in the early 20th century, large groves were planted in northern Baja to provide oil for the fish canning industry in Ensenada, but olives are grown on smaller scale throughout northern Baja.

In the Guadalupe Valley, the L.A. Cetto winery sells thousands of gallons of olive oil every year from its vast groves. Some smaller wineries in the region have planted interesting varieties of olives and have begun to produce their own extra-virgin olive oils through a local co-op. Estate-bottled olives and olive oils are a hot sales prospect for farmers, too.

Local oils are mostly golden green in color and light in flavor, with a hint of grassy bitterness, and may have a tinge of pepper or licorice. Mild-flavored, buttery-textured green olives are sold in local markets from 50-gallon plastic drums or in glass bottles, always unpitted. They are a popular *botana* (a nibble with drinks).

MISSION The original olive planted at the California mission, used mostly for olive oil; smaller than manzanillo and with a lighter-flavored oil.

MANZANILLO Originally a Spanish olive. Quick-ripening, prolific, and easy to cure; very rich fruit. Mostly used to make the mild-flavored pitted black olives. The oil is strong and a little bitter.

ARBEQUINE. Small, round, green Catalan olive. Now being planted in California and areas of Baja California. The oil is of the best quality.

PICHOLINE From the south of France, a small elongated olive with a light flavor.

Olives with Orange Peel, Chiles, and Garlic

An olive for olive lovers, seasoned with spices, garlic, and citrus. I make these to use in salads and sauces, but I'm not above eating them right out of the jar when no one is looking. At parties, set a bowl on a buffet table alongside sautéed salted almonds (see note below).

WINE Something subtle and citrusy, like Sauvignon Blanc

Makes 1 quart

1 quart green olives with pits
1 tablespoon cumin seeds
1 tablespoon fennel seeds
4–6 large dried chiles de árbol
10 black peppercorns
2 bay leaves
²/₃ cup best-quality extra-virgin olive oil, plus more to top up the jar

10 garlic cloves, thinly sliced
1 rosemary sprig (3 inches)
Thinly sliced peel from 2 oranges (preferably in a long piece each)
¼ cup red wine vinegar
Pinch of kosher salt

1. Rinse the olives to remove the brine and drain well. Dry on paper towels.
2. In a dry frying pan, lightly toast the cumin and fennel seeds, chiles, peppercorns, and bay leaves. Add the oil, garlic, rosemary, and orange peel.
3. Heat the oil and aromatics over medium heat until the oil is 145 degrees on an instant-read thermometer. Turn off the heat and let the oil cool for 30 minutes.
4. Pour the oil and spices into a very clean decorative jar. Add the olives, vinegar, and salt. Top up with more oil to cover the olives, if necessary.
5. Cover and refrigerate for at least 48 hours. The oil will solidify but will turn clear again at room temperature.
6. Keep refrigerated. Use within 2 weeks. Allow the olives to come to room temperature before serving.

Note: To make sautéed salted almonds, heat 2 teaspoons oil in a frying pan over medium heat. Add 1 cup blanched whole almonds (preferably raw). Cook and stir until the almonds are pale golden brown and crisp, about 2 minutes. Remove from the heat, toss with ¼ teaspoon kosher salt, and serve warm.

Homemade Sweet Potato Chips

Sweet potatoes, known as *camotes*, make wonderful chips: warm, crisp, and salty, with a hint of sweetness—completely addictive, in other words, the perfect snack. Packaged chips pale in comparison.

For best results, a mandoline-type slicer is essential. It's the only way to get thin, even slices. The other key to success is soaking and rinsing the slices in several changes of cold water, to remove all excess starch before cooking.

Make sure you use true sweet potatoes (which are pale yellow) and not the deep-orange yams. Or, if you like, substitute large Yukon gold potatoes for the sweet potatoes.

WINE Champagne, dry and bubbly, is the perfect match for rich, fatty, and salty foods. Try it—you'll like it.

Makes 6 servings as an antojito

4 large sweet potatoes, peeled (see note above)
3–4 cups peanut oil or other vegetable oil, for frying
Kosher salt

1. Cut the sweet potatoes in half crosswise. Using a mandoline, and working slowly and carefully, slice the potatoes into even rounds, as thinly as possible. (See note below.)
2. As you slice, immediately put the cut potatoes into a bowl with lots of cold water and swish them around. Let stand a few minutes, pour off the water, and repeat the process twice more, or until the water is absolutely clear.
3. In a heavy 4-quart saucepan, add the oil to a depth of at least 2 inches and heat to 350 degrees on a deep-fry thermometer (see Safe Frying on page 248). Drain the potatoes and dry thoroughly with paper towels. Cook a small handful of potatoes at a time, stirring to separate, and cook until golden brown. (Note: The oil should bubble at a slow, even pace. Lower the heat slightly if the oil foams.)
4. Skim out the potatoes with a slotted spoon or skimmer, let drain a few seconds, and then tip onto paper towels to drain.
5. Toss with salt before serving. Serve warm and fresh.

Notes: Peanut oil makes the best-tasting chips but costs about twice as much as regular vegetable oil. You can mix the oils 50–50 if you like. After the oil has cooled completely, it can be strained through a paper coffee filter into a clean container and refrigerated. It can be used several more times if filtered each time. **Never heat oil to the smoking point. It is very combustible.** Discard the oil if it smokes when heated or develops an "off" smell or color.

Mandolines are sold at cookware stores and in the housewares department in some Asian markets. You may want to try a few different thicknesses to see if you like sturdy (Hawaiian-style) chips or paper-thin, delicate chips. If your mandoline has a "waffle" blade, you can make waffle chips by turning the cut surface of the potato 90 degrees on each stroke.

Chipotle and Goat Cheese Tostadas with Piloncillo and Roasted Peanuts

Lots of big flavors in a little bite: creamy-funky goat cheese, spicy chipotle balanced by sweet *piloncillo* (raw brown sugar), crunchy peanuts, and tostadas topped off with the fresh zing of cilantro.

   Locally made fresh cheeses are sold at small markets throughout the wine valleys, and similar fresh goat cheese would be sensational if you can get some. Otherwise, use a quality creamy goat cheese with character.

WINE Chenin Blanc, Viognier—with balance of creaminess and acidity

Makes 24 antojitos

1 cup crushed piloncillo or packed dark brown sugar
1 cup water
1 can (7 ounces) chipotles in adobo
4 fresh corn tortillas
$\frac{1}{3}$ cup vegetable oil

Kosher salt
$\frac{1}{2}$ cup raw unsalted peanuts
6 ounces creamy, strong goat cheese
Cilantro leaves

1. Preheat the oven to 350 degrees.
2. Combine the piloncillo, water, and chipotles in a small saucepan. Bring to a simmer and mash with a potato masher until as smooth as possible. Cook over lowest heat until the syrup is thickened. Keep barely warm.
3. Meanwhile, brush the tortillas on both sides with the oil, stack, and cut into 6 wedges. Spread out on cookie sheets in a single layer and bake until crisp. Sprinkle with pinches of salt. Keep warm in the turned-off oven.
4. While the tortillas are baking, place the peanuts in a small pan and roast alongside the tortillas until golden brown. Cool and then chop roughly.
5. Mash the goat cheese until soft. Place a small spoonful on top of each chip, add a healthy drizzle of chipotle syrup, and top with a pinch of chopped peanuts and a single cilantro leaf.

Note: Save the extra chipotle syrup for use on grilled ribs or chicken.

Toritos

Mahi-Mahi is a wonderful seafood restaurant at the north end of Ensenada, near the port. At an outdoor *antojito* (appetizer) bar, you can sit and watch the cooks working in the open kitchen, sip a glass of local wine, and watch the world go by as you sample unusual treats like these *toritos*, which at Mahi-Mahi are made with smoked marlin. I usually use my own home-smoked albacore, but any hot-smoked fish will work.

Generically, toritos are small, hot peppers, such as güero (blond) or jalapeño chiles, stuffed with a savory filling and cooked on the *comal*. The name means "little bull" and probably refers to the shape of the little peppers, which do indeed look like horns—and can be spicy enough to lift you from the ground. ¡Ole!

They are deliciously rich and tasty, pleasantly hot—until you spoon on a little of the pretty pink "relish" that accompanies each order! Then the heat gets serious. This recipe calls for only half a habanero, seeds and ribs removed. You may add more, if you like!

WINE Riesling—or cold beer

Makes 16 toritos

RED ONION–HABANERO SALSA

$\frac{1}{2}$ cup finely diced red onion
$\frac{1}{2}$ teaspoon minced habanero chile with seeds and white ribs removed (wear rubber gloves)
$\frac{1}{8}$ teaspoon kosher salt
1 tablespoon freshly squeezed lime juice, preferably from a Mexican limón (see page 30)
1 tablespoon freshly squeezed orange juice
1 teaspoon olive oil

16 large fresh güero chiles
1 pound Baja-Style Hot-Smoked Fish (albacore, swordfish, marlin, salmon), shredded with a fork (see page 104)

1. Make the salsa several hours before you need it: Combine all the ingredients and allow to stand at room temperature until the onion turns pink and softens.
2. Line a heavy frying pan or comal with a sheet of foil and set over high heat. Roast the güeros until they begin to soften, about 5 minutes, turning several times. Remove from the heat, cool, and carefully cut a slit up one side of each. Remove all seeds but leave the stems on.
3. Fill each chile with as much smoked fish as you can stuff in. (An alternative method is to cut the tops off the chiles, forming a cone, and fill from the top.)
4. Return the stuffed peppers to the pan and continue to cook for 2 minutes per side, until the fish is heated through.
5. Serve right away with the salsa.

Grilled Beef Short Ribs with
Chipotle-Honey Glaze and Cucumber Salad

Another quick and delicious recipe off the grill, featuring a sticky, smoky-sweet-spicy glaze that contrasts with a refreshing cucumber salad.

The cut of beef called for here is a thin-sliced bone-in short rib known as a *kalbe* or Korean-style rib. It is available at Asian markets, or a butcher can cut the ribs for you.

Make sure the grill is very hot. The honey will char quickly, but don't be concerned—it tastes great!

WINE Zinfandel, Cabernet Franc, Cabernet Sauvignon

Makes 6 servings as an antojito

Cucumber Salad (see below)
1 can (7 ounces) chipotles in adobo
$\frac{1}{3}$ cup honey
3 pounds kalbe (Korean-style) short ribs,
    cut $\frac{3}{8}$ inch thick

1 teaspoon kosher salt
3 green onions, thinly sliced

1. Make the cucumber salad and refrigerate. It needs about 30 minutes to marinate.

2. In a blender, pulse the chipotles and honey to form a smooth paste.

3. Season the ribs with salt on both sides. Toss the ribs with about half of the chipotle paste and reserve the rest for a final glaze.

4. Preheat the grill until very hot. Grill the ribs for 2 minutes on each side, or until deliciously charred (it will be a smoky process) and medium-rare to medium.

5. Remove the ribs to a cutting board and cut between the bones. Serve each person some cucumber salad and a pile of ribs, with some of the reserved glaze spooned over top and a scattering of green onions.

Cucumber Salad

Makes 6 servings

1 seedless hothouse cucumber
$\frac{1}{2}$ small red bell pepper, cut into thin strips
$\frac{1}{2}$ teaspoon kosher salt
2 tablespoons sugar
2–3 tablespoons white vinegar, preferably Heinz
15 large mint leaves, sliced into thin shreds

1. Cut the cucumber in half lengthwise and then slice crosswise as thinly as possible into half-circles. Mix with the pepper in a bowl.

2. Toss with the salt and sugar and then add the vinegar and mint. The dressing should be strong but balanced in flavor.

Empanadas

Half-moon-shaped empanadas are an elegant nibble with drinks. Made in the Spanish style with dough that resembles a sturdy pie crust, these plump little pastries can be filled with rich tidbits of meat and sauce, various cheeses, or vegetables, but they're always meant to be eaten out of hand.

Empanadas may be baked or deep-fried. Fried empanadas have a crisp, delicate crust that is out of this world. Virtuously baked, the crust is just as delicious but sturdier.

Fillings can be as wild as your imagination or limited to leftovers. Whatever you choose must be fully cooked, but aside from that, the sky is the limit. See the opposite page for filling ideas.

Makes 24 (4-inch) empanadas

Empanada Dough (see the opposite page)
All-purpose flour

Filling (see the opposite page)
1 egg, beaten (if baking), or vegetable oil (if frying)

1. Prepare the dough and divide in half. Form each piece into a thick rope about 1½ inches in diameter and 12 inches long. Wrap in plastic and chill for at least 30 minutes.

2. Cut the cylinders crosswise into 1-inch slices. Turn each piece cut side up. Lightly dust the work surface with flour and roll the dough into 4-inch circles, about ⅛ inch thick. Stack with wax paper or plastic wrap in between and chill again before filling and baking.

3. Place a generous tablespoon of filling just off the center of each dough circle. Fold the dough in half and press the edges together. (Tip: Don't overstuff the empanadas.) Gently flatten the top. Proceed with baking or frying.

To bake: Preheat the oven to 400 degrees. Very lightly oil cookie sheets and set the finished empanadas on the sheets, leaving ample room between. Lightly brush the tops with a little egg. Bake for 15 minutes, or until light golden brown.

To fry: Pour ½ inch vegetable oil into a skillet and heat over medium-high heat to 350 degrees on a deep-fry thermometer (bubbles will immediately form around a scrap of dough and it will start to float; see Safe Frying on page 248). Fry the empanadas, turning once, until golden. (They will be very fragile.) Drain on paper towels.

To freeze and reheat: Let the cooked empanadas cool to room temperature. Chill, uncovered, in the refrigerator and then freeze on a plate or cookie sheet. When frozen, transfer to a doubled heavy-duty freezer bag, with as much air as possible squeezed out. To reheat, pop the frozen empanadas onto a cookie sheet and bake at 350 degrees until heated through.

Empanada Dough

Makes enough dough for 24 (4-inch) empanadas

3 cups unbleached all-purpose flour
1 cup masa harina (dry tortilla flour)
3½ teaspoons baking powder
1 teaspoon fine salt

1 teaspoon freshly ground black pepper
1 cup shortening
⅔–1 cup cold water

In the bowl of a food processor, combine the flour, masa harina, baking powder, salt, and pepper. Pulse to combine. Cut the shortening into small pieces and drop into the flour. Pulse until the mixture looks like large crumbs. With the machine running, add half of the water through the feed tube, then pulse as you add water a little at a time until the dough clumps together and forms a ball. (You may not use the full amount.) The dough is ready when it forms a ball, feels barely damp but not sticky, and holds together when pressed.

Crabmeat and Epazote Filling

Makes 2½ cups, enough for 24 small empanadas

8 ounces Dungeness or Alaskan king crabmeat, picked over
3 tablespoons butter
2 tablespoons finely diced white onion

1 teaspoon minced garlic
1 tablespoon minced epazote leaf or ½ teaspoon dried epazote
3 ounces Oaxacan cheese, cut into small dice

Melt the butter in a small frying pan. Cook the onion and garlic until softened; add the epazote. Stir into the crabmeat and add the cheese. Cool completely.

Black Bean Filling

Makes 2½ cups, enough for 24 small empanadas

2 tablespoons vegetable oil
¼ cup finely minced white onion
1 garlic clove, finely minced
2 cups cooked black beans
1 tablespoon minced serrano chile
½ teaspoon kosher salt

1 small ripe Roma tomato, seeded and diced
10 cilantro sprigs, stemmed and minced
1 teaspoon freshly squeezed lime juice, preferably from a Mexican limón (see page 30)
3 ounces cotixa, asadero, or Jack cheese, shredded (optional)

1. Heat the oil in a frying pan over medium heat. Add the onion and garlic and cook, stirring, for 1 minute, or until softened. Add the beans a scoop at a time and mash, adding bean cooking liquid or water as necessary to prevent sticking.
2. When the beans are mashed, fold in the chile, salt, tomato, cilantro, and lime juice. Cool completely. Add a pinch of the cheese to each empanada as you make it.

Garlic Cilantro Steak with Avocado and Tomatillo Salsa

I like to think of this as the white linen version of carne asada, still full of flavor but with wine in mind. You can serve the steak with tortillas and beans or a salad and crusty baguette—whatever you like.

WINE Nebbiolo, Cabernet, or Tempranillo-Cabernet blend

Makes 6 servings

2½ pounds flap meat, skirt steak, or thick rib eye steaks
4 garlic cloves, chopped
¼ red or white onion, cut into thin slices
2 teaspoons kosher salt
1½ teaspoons freshly ground black pepper
3 tablespoons olive oil

2½ tablespoons freshly squeezed lime juice, preferably from Mexican Limons (see page 30)
2 teaspoons ground cumin
Cilantro Paste (see below)
Raw Tomatillo Salsa (see page 44)
2 Hass avocados, pitted, peeled, thinly sliced, and sprinkled with salt

1. Cut the meat into 6 serving pieces. Place in a glass bowl and add the garlic, onion, salt, pepper, and oil. Squeeze the lime over the meat, sprinkle with the cumin, and toss to combine. Refrigerate for at least 4 hours.
2. While the meat is marinating, make the cilantro paste and set aside at room temperature. Make the salsa.
3. Preheat a clean grill until very hot. Wipe most of the oil from the surface of the meat. Press onto the hot grill and cook one side over very high heat until well marked and dark brown, then turn and cook the other side for 2 minutes for rare. (For medium, move the meat to a cooler part of the grill and cook a further 3 to 5 minutes with the lid closed.) Let the meat rest for 10 minutes before slicing. Slice the meat thinly across the grain.
4. Brush the warm sliced meat with the cilantro paste, so it "melts" into the meat. Top with a few slices of avocado and serve with a spoonful of the salsa on the side.

Cilantro Paste

Makes about ½ cup

1 garlic clove, roughly chopped
2 tablespoons roughly chopped white onion
½ teaspoon kosher salt

1 teaspoon freshly squeezed lime juice
2–3 tablespoons olive oil
1 bunch cilantro

1. Place the garlic, onion, and salt in a mini food processor. Pulse to chop, then process while adding the lime juice and oil. Process to a smooth paste.
2. Cut the thick lower stems off the cilantro. Roughly chop the upper half of the bunch, including the thin stems, and add to the processor. Puree until absolutely smooth, adding a little more oil if necessary. Taste for seasoning and add more lime and salt if you like. Scrape into a small bowl. Use immediately.

Chipotle Grilled Chicken with Avocado Salsa

Juicy roasters get a smoky, spicy kick from chipotles in adobo, which contrast beautifully with the creamy coolness of the avocado salsa. If you have no grill, roast the chickens in the oven.

WINE Zinfandel, Cabernet Franc, or Cabernet Sauvignon

Makes 6 servings

1 can (7 ounces) chipotles in adobo
4 large garlic cloves
2 tablespoons vegetable oil
1 teaspoon kosher salt
3 small whole chickens, cut into halves or quarters

TO SERVE
Fresh corn tortillas, warmed
Avocado Salsa (see below)

1. In a food processor, puree the chipotles, garlic, oil, and salt. Wipe the chickens with paper towels. Thoroughly coat the pieces on all sides with a layer of the chipotle paste.
2. Place in a nonreactive baking dish or in resealable bags and refrigerate for 2 hours, or as long as overnight.
3. Heat the grill to medium. With the lid open, grill the chicken on both sides until well marked but not burned—about 7 minutes per side. Turn the heat to low, close the lid, and cook the chicken, skin side up, until an instant-read thermometer inserted in the thickest part of the thigh reads 165 degrees. (Alternatively, bake at 350 degrees for approximately 30 to 40 minutes.)
4. Serve with the tortillas and salsa.

Avocado Salsa

This is not guacamole but chunks of buttery Hass avocado mixed with raw onion and cilantro—more like an avocado salad. The best avocados come from Southern California and Mexico, and the tastiest variety is the Hass. They are small, with pebbly black skins and smooth, rich flesh. For more about avocados, see page 35.

Makes 1½ cups

3 ripe Hass avocados, pitted, peeled, and cut into ½-inch pieces
Kosher salt
Juice of 1 lime, preferably a Mexican limón (see page 30)
⅓ cup finely diced white onion
3 cilantro sprigs, stemmed and chopped

Place the avocados in a bowl. Sprinkle with the salt and lime juice; mix gently with the onion and cilantro (don't mash; it should look diced).

Note: Avocado Salsa should be served within 3 hours. To hold longer, press a piece of plastic wrap directly onto the surface of the salsa and refrigerate until needed.

GRILLING ESSENTIALS

■ ■ ■

A GOOD GRILL A good grill is not necessarily expensive. The most important part of any grill is the grill bars. Coated cast iron is far and away the best grill material and will give the best results. The grill must also have a tight-fitting lid, and a thermometer is handy. Grills may burn wood, charcoal, or gas. Choose the type that suits your needs.

A CLEAN GRILL Keep your grill very clean throughout the inside as well as the grill bars themselves. Carbon deposits will accumulate and give an off taste to the food. To clean: Preheat the grill on high. Right before cooking, clean the grill with a wire brush and wipe the bars clean with a lightly oiled rag held with tongs.

VARIABLE HEAT Arrange the fire so you have a hot side (for searing) and a cooler side (for longer cooking).

SEASONING AND OIL Food to be grilled should be lightly salted and oiled. If the meat has been marinated, wipe the marinade off (otherwise it will burn).

SEARING Cook over the *highest possible heat* in the beginning, to create a dark crust and flavor on both sides. Do not allow flare-ups or allow the food to be engulfed in flames.

MARKING To make diamond grill marks on the presentation side: Lay the meat, best side down, on an angle to the grill bars. When the meat is well marked, turn on a 45-degree angle. Allow to cook a little more than halfway, then turn the meat over and finish cooking on the cooler side of the grill.

COVERING To cook larger items, such as whole chickens or legs of lamb, and give them a wonderful smoky flavor, close the cover and make an "oven" of your grill. First mark the meat all over on the hot side of the grill, then transfer it to the cooler side of the grill. Close the cover and cook until done to your taste (see below for temperature guidelines).

QUICK-SMOKING Soak a few hickory chips in water. Toward the end of the cooking, set a pan of soaked chips on the grill. When the chips begin to smoke, close the lid and smoke the food for a few minutes.

A GOOD THERMOMETER

Rare is 130 degrees, cool red center; meat juices are dark red

Medium-rare is 140 degrees, warm red center; meat juices are red

Medium is 150 degrees, pink center; meat juices are pink

Well is 165 degrees, gray throughout; meat juices are clear

Pollo al Asador

On the main street of Ensenada, the smell of grilling chicken starts wafting on the breeze just before the sun reaches its zenith, a siren scent that draws you halfway across town to where a busy *asadero* grills butterflied chickens on his huge wood-fired grill.

Nearby, the smell of wood smoke also permeates a restaurant, where plump golden brown chickens spin over blazing oak fires on makeshift rotisseries. A cook rolls out flour tortillas, flings them onto a huge *comal* to cook, and flips the cooked tortillas into a cloth-lined basket to be delivered to your table along with the roast chicken, a dish of *charro* beans, and lemon quarters. The chicken is juicy, smoky, and lightly charred. With a squirt of lemon, it might be the best chicken ever.

The process described below produces deliciously smoky, juicy chicken, without the fuss of a rotisserie. You can use any kind of chicken, but I like to use little Cornish hens—one per person.

WINE Red wines with a red cherry taste, such as Cabernet Franc and Zinfandel

Makes 4 servings

4 Rock Cornish hens or bone-in, skin-on chicken quarters
Olive oil
Kosher salt and freshly ground black pepper
1 cup hickory or mesquite chips ($\frac{1}{4}$-inch size)

TO SERVE
Flour Tortillas (see page 242)
Frijoles Borrachos (see page 246)
Lemon wedges

1. Rinse the hens and pat dry. With kitchen shears, cut out the backbone. Turn each hen breast up, grab both legs and bend the knees toward the center, popping the leg joints and flattening the hen. Take hold of the wings from behind, set your thumbs on the breastbone, and press down firmly. Tuck the wings joints behind. Coat with the oil and sprinkle generously with salt and pepper on all sides. Refrigerate until ready to use.
2. Soak the wood chips in water for 1 hour. Drain and spread out in a disposable pie tin. Prepare a medium fire in a barbecue or gas grill and set the pan of chips on the fire. Close the lid until the chips begin to smoke, about 5 minutes.
3. Turn down the heat on half of the grill to medium-low. Lay the hens breast side down on the cool side of the grill. Close the lid tightly to keep in heat and smoke and cook for 15 minutes. Turn and cook breast up for 15 minutes. Continue to cook, checking every 5 minutes, until an instant-read thermometer reads 170 degrees in the thickest part of the thigh.
4. Remove the hens to a warm platter and cover loosely with foil while you heat the tortillas.
5. Serve with the natural juices from the platter poured over each serving and with the tortillas, beans, and lemon wedges.

Note: You can also do a whole chicken this way. Cut out the back and flatten the chicken. It will take about 45 minutes to cook, turning every 15 minutes.

Warm Chicken and Spinach Salad Picadillo with Raisins, Olives, and Fig Balsamic Vinegar

With its unusual combination of meat with raisins, vinegar, and olives, traditional *picadillo* is clearly a medieval throwback. Here, those same ancient tastes are recombined into a thoroughly modern grilled chicken salad, spiked with flavors sour, savory, salty, and sweet. The fig balsamic vinegar is sure to become a staple in your pantry.

WINE Semidry rosé

Makes 4 servings as an entrée

CHICKEN

2 tablespoons Fig Balsamic Vinegar (see the opposite page) or balsamic vinegar
2 tablespoons olive oil
½ teaspoon kosher salt
4 boneless, skinless chicken breasts

SALAD

1 large bunch spinach, stemmed
1 cup large green olives, pitted and cut in half
½ cup large seedless raisins or dried currants
½ cup thinly sliced red onion
1 cup cherry or grape tomatoes, halved
¾ cup plus 2 tablespoons Fig Balsamic Vinegar or balsamic vinegar
2 tablespoons best-quality extra-virgin olive oil
Kosher salt and freshly ground black pepper

1. Make the chicken: In a resealable plastic bag, combine the vinegar, oil, salt, and chicken. Press out as much air as possible, close the bag, and knead gently to coat the chicken. Marinate, refrigerated, for several hours.
2. About 45 minutes before serving, cook the chicken on the grill, in a frying pan, or in the oven until cooked through. Set aside on a plate, but do not refrigerate.
3. Make the salad: In a large bowl, combine the spinach, olives, raisins, onion, and tomatoes.
4. Cut the warm chicken into thin strips or chunks and add to the salad, along with any cooking juices that have accumulated.
5. To make the dressing, combine the vinegar, oil, and salt and pepper to taste. (If you used regular balsamic, add 1 teaspoon honey to the dressing.) Taste and correct the seasoning; the dressing should be fairly strong.
6. Toss the salad with the dressing and serve immediately, making sure that each person gets some of everything—chicken, olives, raisins, onions, and tomatoes.

Variations: Char, peel, and seed 2 red bell peppers, toss with olive oil and salt, chop coarsely, and add to the salad. Or, rub thick slices of country-style artisan bread with a cut garlic clove and a little olive oil, grill alongside the chicken, and serve warm alongside the finished salad.

Fig Balsamic Vinegar

Vinegars of all types are pantry essentials, and I enjoy doctoring them up—adding garlic or herbs to make a special dressing or, in this case, adding honey, dried figs, vanilla, and citrus to the richness of balsamic vinegar to make a sumptuous, addictive syrup. It's dynamite in dressings and marinades, on the table for bread dipping, or even over ice cream and strawberries. It's a little extravagant, yes, but well worth it. The infused figs can be rescued at the end and added to salads or used for Peppered Lamb Loin with Figs in Port Wine and Orange (see page 136) or Mesquite-Grilled Quail with Figs and Pancetta (see page 143).

Makes 4 cups

1 pound good-quality dried black figs
4 cups water
1 vanilla bean, split
2½ cups balsamic vinegar
2 oranges, quartered (leave the peel on)
½ cup honey

1. In a heavy-bottomed 3-quart saucepan, combine the figs, water, and vanilla bean. Bring slowly to a simmer and cook very, *very* slowly over very, *very* low heat for about 1 hour, until the mixture becomes a thick syrup. Add the vinegar, oranges, and honey and heat until it just starts to boil; then turn off the heat and let stand until cool. Pour into a large glass bowl or crock, cover, and refrigerate for 2 to 3 days.
2. Strain the vinegar into a stainless steel or glass container. Discard the orange pieces and vanilla bean. Keep the figs for other uses (see note above).
3. Taste the finished vinegar. If it seems too sweet, add a couple more tablespoons balsamic vinegar. The figs can be refrigerated for up to 1 month; the vinegar will last, refrigerated, for up to 2 months, but you will use it before then.

Note: To make a glaze: After straining, reduce the vinegar to a thin syrup in a nonstick pan over low heat (watching carefully at all times to prevent scorching). Use on cooked chicken or pork, spicy caramelized walnuts, bruschetta, or fresh berries.

Variations: Use sweet Marsala wine or port wine in place of some or all of the water. Add 1 tablespoon black peppercorns with the vinegar, orange, and honey. Use lemons instead of oranges.

Paella of Chicken and Rabbit
with Local Olives
and Parsley-Garlic Oil

Ensenada takes paellas seriously. The genre is dominated by talented local cooks. The town has an informal school of paella, and the annual *Vendimia* wine festival ends with a hotly contested seafood paella competition (see page 98) featuring huge paellas cooked in the traditional fashion, over a fire of wood or grapevines.

Fortunately, paella also cooks very well in the oven! Paella is simple to make and does not have to include seafood—one of the oldest Spanish paella recipes is made with snails and rabbit. Paella is more about rice than anything else, and the cooking technique builds great flavor in layers, starting with an aromatic *sofrito* base of tomatoes, onions, and garlic. Variations on this recipe are limitless. Use all chicken, add a quail or two, or use cubes of pork shoulder instead of sausage.

Two paella essentials: the right pan and the right rice. The pan must be wide, with shallow, sloping sides and a wide bottom. This ensures even cooking, so the grains of rice stay separate and firm. If you don't have a paella pan (*paellera*), the paella can be cooked in any wide, shallow pan, such as a large frying pan. Imported Spanish short-grain rice (the traditional rice for paella) is best, if you can find it. Please note that Spanish short-grain is *not* interchangeable with *any* other form of short-grain rice (Asian, American, or Italian) as these will prove disastrous to your recipe! If you can't find Spanish rice, substitute long-grain white rice.

WINE Barbera or Tempranillo-Cabernet blend

Makes 8 servings

SOFRITO

¼ cup olive oil
1 small white onion, minced
4 garlic cloves, thinly sliced
1 teaspoon fennel seeds
1 green bell pepper, cut into ¼-inch strips
1 red bell pepper, cut into ¼-inch strips
1½ tablespoons Spanish paprika
3 ripe Roma tomatoes, chopped in a food processor

PARSLEY-GARLIC OIL

½ cup Italian parsley leaves
3 garlic cloves
1 teaspoon kosher salt
⅔ cup best-quality extra-virgin olive oil

PAELLA

1 teaspoon saffron threads
½ cup white wine
4 thin bacon or pancetta slices
1 fresh rabbit, cut into 8 pieces (see note on the next page)
8 small bone-in, skin-on chicken thighs
Kosher salt and freshly ground black pepper
¼ cup olive oil
4 ounces Spanish (dry) chorizo, andouille, or kielbasa sausage, sliced into thin half-circles
3 cups imported Spanish short-grain rice (or long-grain white rice)
4½ cups unsalted or low-sodium chicken stock
⅔ cup green olives, pitted
1 cup peas (optional)

1. Make the sofrito: In a sauté pan, heat the oil. Add the onion, garlic, fennel seeds, and bell peppers. Sauté the vegetables until they are soft, then add the paprika and cook a minute longer. Add the tomatoes to the pan and cook the mixture, stirring often, until the juice from the tomatoes is nearly all evaporated. Set aside.

2. Make the parsley-garlic oil: In a blender, combine the parsley, garlic, salt, and oil. Pulse until the parsley is finely chopped.

3. Set a rack in the middle of the oven and preheat the oven to 350 degrees.

4. Heat a small dry frying pan over medium heat. When it is hot, remove from the burner, add the saffron threads, stir them around a few times with a dry knife, and set aside. When cool, use the end of the knife handle to pound the saffron to a powder. Add the wine and set aside for 1 hour to bring out the saffron's full color and flavor.

5. Cut the bacon slices in half and wrap each piece of rabbit, securing the bacon with a toothpick. Season the chicken with salt and pepper.

6. Over medium-low heat, heat the oil in a 14-inch paella or frying pan (see the opposite page). Cook the rabbit and chicken pieces on all sides until golden brown, about 15 to 20 minutes (they will be undercooked inside), and set aside. Don't overcrowd the pan; you may have to cook in two batches.

7. Add the sausage to the pan and cook until the edges are crisp. Remove and set aside with the chicken and rabbit.

8. Add the rice to the pan. Stir the sofrito into the rice. Cook and stir until the rice has absorbed the color from the sofrito. Combine the saffron mixture and the stock (be sure to rinse out the saffron soaking pan with some of the stock to get every bit of color) and add to the pan. Gently shake the pan to settle the rice evenly over the bottom.

9. Arrange the sausage, rabbit, and chicken over the surface of the rice, pushing the pieces down into the liquid. Scatter the olives over the top.

10. Bake the paella, uncovered, for 35 to 45 minutes, or until the rice has absorbed all the liquid and the chicken is cooked through.

11. Remove from the oven and scatter the peas over the paella. Set the paella on top of the stove, out of any drafts. Drape two clean linen dish towels over the paella and cover loosely with foil. Let the paella rest, undisturbed, for 15 minutes; this allows the rice and meat to gently steam and become moist.

12. Drizzle some of the parsley-garlic oil over the paella and pass the rest separately.

Note: Fresh rabbit may be ordered from most good butchers. If rabbit is not available, substitute another 4 chicken thighs.

FIESTAS DE LA VENDIMIA

Each year, at the height of the wine harvest, Baja California winemakers celebrate the vintage and their thriving community with the *Fiestas de la Vendimia* (Wine Harvest Festivals). Best described as part street fair, part serious wine festival, and part consciousness raising, the *Vendimia* is an important cultural event created and run by the local community. It doesn't hurt that it's lots of fun, too.

The *Vendimia* has grown from a few casual bashes at small wineries to a network of more than 20 major events held over 2 weeks. The festivals kick off at Ensenada's Centro Cultural, in the historic old Casino, with a stroll-and-snack reception pairing local wines with food from the area's top restaurants.

The next morning, experts from the area and all over the world judge Baja vintages, a hotly contested competition for the next year's bragging rights. Chapters of the local *Cofradía* (Brotherhood of Wine) hold wine dinners in Tijuana, Mexicali, Ensenada, and Tecate to assay past and future vintages in congenial company.

For the two weekends following the judging, the *fiestas* move out to the Guadalupe Valley wineries. Past years have seen Russian dancing and food at Bibayoff, tango and lamb at Barón Balché, Japanese *bhuto* dancers at Casa de Piedra, the world-famous Romeros family guitar quartet at Monte Xanic, jazz at Mogor-Badán, bullfights at L.A. Cetto, and wine and Puerto Nuevo–style lobster under old oak trees at Santo Tomás's San Antonio vineyards.

The grand finale—and the most widely anticipated and fiercely contested event of the entire festival—is the legendary paella contest (see page 98). This veritable rice and seafood olympics, for which the only prize is glory, is a benefit for local charities and regularly sells out.

Chicken with Honey, Cumin, and Red Wine Lentils

Bees make honey from acacia, yucca, cactus, mesquite—indeed anything that flowers in the Baja desert. Desert honeys tend to be dark and strong flavored—perfect for cooking, where that sweetness blends well with savory elements. Using moist, dark-meat chicken thighs is another way to maximize flavor. The earthy lentils are as satisfying, in their own way, as the meat.

WINE Rustic reds, such as Grenache, Carignan, and Zinfandel

Makes 6 servings

Lentils with Red Wine and Caramelized Onion (see below)
2 tablespoons cumin seeds
12 bone-in, skin-on chicken thighs

$\frac{1}{3}$ cup dark honey
2 teaspoons kosher salt
$\frac{1}{2}$ cup chicken stock or water

1. Get the lentils going first, since they will take about an hour to cook.

2. Heat a small dry frying pan over medium heat. Add the cumin seeds and stir for about a minute, until the seeds are lightly toasted and fragrant. Pour onto a plate to cool, then grind in a spice grinder; set aside.

3. Preheat the oven to 350 degrees. Pat the chicken dry with paper towels. In a large bowl, toss the chicken with the honey and salt.

4. Arrange the chicken in a lightly oiled baking dish or on a rimmed cookie sheet just large enough to hold them without crowding. Dust with the ground cumin. Add the stock to the pan and cover loosely with foil.

5. Bake for 45 to 50 minutes, or until an instant-read thermometer inserted into the thickest part of a thigh registers 165 degrees. The chicken should brown under the foil. If it does not, remove the foil for the last 5 minutes of cooking.

6. Serve with the lentils.

Note: Toast and grind whole spices, such as cumin seeds, immediately before use.

Lentils with Red Wine and Caramelized Onion

Makes 6 to 8 servings

2 tablespoons olive oil
1 white onion, thinly sliced
1 teaspoon kosher salt
$\frac{1}{2}$ teaspoon freshly ground black pepper

$\frac{1}{2}$ cup red wine
4 cups water
1 cup dried green lentils

1. In a 2-quart saucepan, heat the oil over medium heat. Add the onion and cook, stirring occasionally, until very soft and golden brown, about 30 minutes.

2. Season with the salt and pepper. Add the wine and then cook and stir until all the wine has boiled off.

3. Add the water and bring to a boil over high heat. Add the lentils, reduce the heat to medium, and cook, stirring occasionally, until the lentils are softened but not mushy—about 30 minutes. If needed, add small amounts of water during cooking to keep the lentils barely submerged.

Pan-Roasted Duck
with Green Olives and Raisins

One of the more memorable meals I've had in Baja centered on a wild duck bagged by a (licensed) hunter in our party. We had been hunting quail, which, being smart birds, hid in impenetrable, rattlesnake-infested cactus thickets. An unfortunate duck had no such strategy, however. We simmered it for several hours with lots of ginger, onions, and soy sauce. It was dark, gamy, and delicious.

Farm-raised duck needs different handling. Long, slow roasting renders nearly all the fat out, leaving moist, tender meat and crisp skin. Red wine–soaked raisins added to a simple pan sauce give that hint of sweetness that goes so well with duck. Mild-flavored green olives, like the Mission olives planted by the *padres*, are a briny counterpoint.

WINE Merlot, Pinot Noir, or Tempranillo-Cabernet blend

Makes 2 servings; recipe may be doubled

1 duck, fresh or frozen, thawed
1 teaspoon kosher salt
¼ teaspoon freshly ground white pepper

RAISIN SAUCE
⅓ cup seedless raisins
1 cup red wine
1 tablespoon sugar
1 tablespoon red wine vinegar
1 teaspoon cracked black peppercorns
3 cups chicken stock
Green olives, rinsed

1. Cut the duck into 8 serving pieces. Pat dry with paper towels. Remove any obvious fat and discard. Season the duck inside and out with the salt and pepper.

2. Preheat the oven to 350 degrees.

3. Heat a 12-inch ovenproof frying pan over medium heat. Brown the duck pieces well on all sides, then put the pan in the oven and roast the duck pieces until the skin is crisp and the meat soft and tender, about 45 minutes. When done, the breast meat feels soft when pressed with a finger.

4. Make the raisin sauce while the duck is cooking: Combine the raisins and wine in a small saucepan over medium heat. Simmer on low heat for 30 minutes, until the raisins are soft; set aside.

5. Remove the duck from the pan and place on an ovenproof serving platter. Cover loosely with foil. Turn off the oven and keep the platter in the oven while you make the sauce.

6. Pour off the fat from the hot pan and reserve for another use (see note below). Do not wash the pan. Set the pan over medium heat and add the sugar; cook, stirring, until it melts and begins to caramelize. Add the vinegar, peppercorns, stock, and raisin mixture. Cook over medium-high heat, stirring often, until syrupy. Season with a little salt, if necessary.

7. Serve the sauce spooned over the duck, with a few green olives for garnish.

Note: The rendered duck fat may be used to sauté potatoes.

VALLE DE SANTO TOMÁS

● ● ●

The modern era began in 1791, with the founding of the Dominican mission of Santo Tomás de Aquino in a beautiful valley south of what is now Ensenada. The padres did the usual things — converting the local Indians, building churches and dwellings, and planting wheat, olives, and Mission grapes.

Compared with the other missions in Baja California, Santo Tomás was large and successful. True, it had a harrowing history of upheavals, disease, and disasters, but it did survive long enough to be secularized by the government. It was turned into a military base in the 1840s and was even, briefly, the capital of the territory.

In the 1930s, General Abelardo Rodríguez (later president of Mexico) acquired the vineyards of the Santo Tomás Valley and began an aggressive program of modernization under the direction of Esteban (Stefan) Ferro, an Italian winemaker. The company built a winery and bottling plant in the heart of Ensenada, which today has been converted to a restaurant/gallery/wine shop.

Despite (or perhaps because of) its remote location, Santo Tomás has been by turns the nursery, the capital-in-exile, and the refuge of the Baja California wine industry, weathering political upheaval, drought, and controversy in its quiet valley. More than once, the vineyards and winemakers of Santo Tomás kept winemaking alive in Baja California. Even when the offshoots withered, the root held firm.

Today, having changed hands several times, Bodegas de Santo Tomás is a fully modern winery producing 600,000 cases a year. Some of the wines are available in the United States.

Peppered Lamb Loin with Figs in Port Wine and Orange

The hardy fig tree has given pleasure and sustenance since Eden, so it was only natural that, along with grapes, wheat, and olives, the missionaries brought fig trees to Baja California. Heat-loving figs give shade in the summer, and the ripe fruit can be dried for use in less generous months. Green-skinned Mission figs have an interior the color of ripe watermelon; the dark brown, sticky-sweet Brown Turkey fig is another favorite variety. Figs are a natural companion to wines, cheeses, and gamy meats like lamb.

WINE Bordeaux blends

Makes 6 servings

6 boneless lamb loins or chops (about 6 ounces each)
2 tablespoons black peppercorns, crushed
Kosher salt

2 tablespoons good-quality olive oil
20 large mint leaves, chopped
Figs in Port Wine (see below)

1. Rub the lamb with the peppercorns, salt, oil, and mint. Refrigerate for several hours or overnight.
2. Make the figs.
3. Preheat the grill to high. Grill the lamb on the hottest part of the grill for about 3 minutes per side, or until lightly charred on the outside, medium-rare within—an internal temperature of 125 degrees. (Alternatively, heat a heavy frying pan over medium-high heat and sear the lamb on all sides in a small amount of oil. Reduce the heat and cook to medium-rare, turning several times.)
4. Let rest 5 minutes on a warm platter. Slice and serve with the natural juices and the figs.

Note: Lamb loin chops, rib chops, or shoulder chops may be substituted.

Figs in Port Wine

Makes 2½ cups

⅔ cup dried black figs, stems removed
Boiling water
1 large orange
1 cup red Port or Cabernet

1 clove
2 tablespoons dark honey
1 tablespoon balsamic vinegar

1. Cut the figs into quarters, place them in a 1-quart saucepan, and add just enough boiling water to barely cover. Simmer, covered, for 15 minutes.
2. With a sharp knife, peel the orange as thinly as possible in long strips, being careful to remove only the outside orange part of the peel and as little of the bitter white pith as possible. Add the peel to the figs, along with the Port, clove, and honey. Simmer over low heat. Add small amounts of hot water as needed to keep the figs just barely covered.
3. Cook until the figs are soft, about 30 minutes. Turn heat to high and stir until the juices have thickened and lightly coat the figs. Add the vinegar to the reserved liquid.
4. Serve at room temperature.

Pincho Moruno
(LAMB KEBABS)

Inspired by Baja's Spanish heritage, these bite-size pieces of tender lamb, grilled with a potent blend of garlic and spices, go perfectly with Baja's sun-drenched red wines. The combination of garlic, lemon, and cumin in this recipe reflects the Arab (Moorish) history of southern Spain; paprika and chiles originated in the New World.

WINE Bordeaux blends, Tempranillo, big Zinfandel

Makes 12 skewers

SPICE PASTE

1 tablespoon ground cumin
1 tablespoon Spanish paprika
1 teaspoon crushed red chile
1 teaspoon dried whole Mexican oregano, rubbed
   to a powder
1½ teaspoons kosher salt

1 teaspoon freshly ground black pepper
4 large garlic cloves, minced to a paste
¼ cup olive oil, or more as needed
2 tablespoons freshly squeezed lemon juice

2 pounds boneless leg of lamb
1 red onion

1. Make the spice paste: Combine the ingredients to make a thick but spreadable paste. Add a little more oil, if necessary.
2. Trim the lamb of all fat and silverskin and cut into 1-inch cubes. Massage the paste well into the lamb and marinate, refrigerated, for several hours.
3. Soak 12 (6-inch) bamboo skewers in cold water. Cut the onion lengthwise into sixths, then across to get chunks. Thread 3 or 4 lamb cubes onto each skewer, and poke a piece of onion on the end.
4. Grill over a very hot fire until nicely charred, about 2 minutes per side for medium-rare.

VALLE DE GUADALUPE

■ ■ ■

The mission of Nuestra Señora de Guadalupe del Norte was founded in the Guadalupe Valley in 1834 by Dominican Father Félix Caballero. The good father could not have known that this mission would be the last in Baja California. All his hard work was flattened by a storm of rebellious Indians, hard-scrabble drought, and political machinations in far-off Europe and Mexico City. The mission was abandoned.

Seventy years later, a group of pacifist Russians known as Molokans fled the last days of Czarist Russia. They settled the valley and caused it to bloom with grapes and olives and wheat. Descendants of the Molokan community proudly remember their Russian heritage. The Bibayoff family still makes wine on the land originally held by their family.

Wine making really began in earnest in the 1930s, mostly in sweet sacramental wines. Today the vineyards of Baja California supply most of the table wine sold in Mexico.

In the 1960s the Cetto family of Tijuana planted enormous vineyards at the northeast end of the valley. Though best known as a large-scale producer, LA Cetto has many small areas of high-quality varietals that produce premium wines under winemaker Camillo Magoni.

Monte Xanic winery, founded in 1988, changed everything. Instead of focusing on large-scale production of table wines, winemaker Hans Backhoff (an Ensenada native) was the first to plant high-quality European varietals, from which he made small quantities of premium wines that are highly idiosyncratic in style—true "boutique" wines.

Château Camou followed a few years later, with Dr. Victor Torres as winemaker. Influential winemaker Hugo d'Acosta left Bodegas de Santo Tomás in 1997 to found Casa de Piedra, and runs a school for local winemakers and olive oil producers.

With these wineries producing world-class wines and proving that quality could make money, many more new plantings and small wineries followed. Wineries like Adobe Guadalupe, Mogor-Badan, Viña de Liceaga, and many others are following the modern model of small, but beautiful.

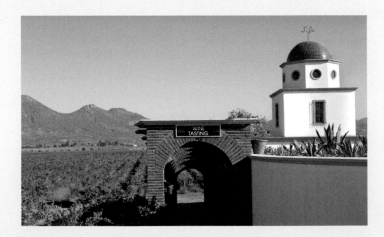

Grilled Leg of Lamb
with Huitlacoche Risotto

Boneless fresh leg of lamb may be oven roasted or marinated and grilled, depending on the season. The marinade is potent and caramelizes deliciously on the outside of the meat. Try to find fresh epazote or *yerbabuena*, which is similar to mint but with herby undertones.

Risotto is a perfect foil for lamb, and with the addition of *huitlacoche*, which some call "Mexican truffles," you have a remarkable flavor combination.

WINE Big reds, such as Cabernet Franc—Merlot blends, Cabernet Sauvignon

Makes 8 servings

1 small boneless leg of lamb (about 3 pounds)
1½ cups red wine
½ cup chopped garlic
1 cup best-quality Japanese soy sauce
1 small bunch epazote, yerbabuena, or mint, chopped

½ bunch oregano
1 tablespoon cracked black pepper
¼ cup olive oil
Huitlacoche Risotto (see page 181)

1. Trim the lamb of all fat and silverskin. Place in a large nonreactive dish. Combine the wine, garlic, soy sauce, epazote, oregano, pepper, and oil; pour over the lamb. Marinate, refrigerated, overnight.
2. Heat the grill to medium-low. Grill the lamb on all sides with the lid closed, turning every few minutes, until the thickest parts are 130 degrees when tested with an instant-read thermometer. This should take about 45 minutes. If the lamb gets too charred, turn off one side of the grill and move the lamb to the cooler area. Close the lid to finish cooking.
3. Let the lamb rest on a warm platter, loosely covered, for about 10 minutes. Slice thinly and serve with the carving juices and the risotto.

Mezcal-Brined Grilled Pork Loin
with Nopales Salsa

This is one of those recipes in which unusual ingredients produce harmonious results. Quality mezcal (and you shouldn't buy any other kind) is distilled from roasted agave hearts, often on small estates. It is meant to be sipped and appreciated like a fine cognac or single-malt scotch. In this recipe, the mezcal gives a smoky, rich flavor to the savory brine, which goes deliciously well with crunchy Nopales Salsa.

WINE Dry Sauvignon Blanc

Makes 6 servings

BRINE

3 cups water

¼ cup sugar

2 tablespoons kosher salt

1 bay leaf

5 black peppercorns, crushed

5 coriander seeds, crushed

1 tablespoon fennel seeds

Grated zest of 1 orange

1 cup good quality mezcal

1 boneless pork loin (2½ pounds)

Nopales Salsa (see page 174)

1. Combine the brine ingredients except the mezcal in a saucepan, bring to a boil, and simmer until the salt and sugar are dissolved, about 5 minutes. Cool the brine completely, add the mezcal and then immerse the pork loin in it (this can be done in a deep dish or a sealed freezer bag). Marinate for 12 to 24 hours.

2. Preheat the grill. Remove the pork from the brine and pat dry. Grill over high heat to brown on all sides, about 5 minutes per side. Move the meat to a cool area of the grill. Close the lid and cook until the thickest part is 145 degrees when tested with an instant-read thermometer. Remove from the grill, cover loosely with foil, and let rest.

3. Carve the pork into ½-inch slices and drizzle the meat juices over each serving. Serve with the salsa.

BRINING

When you plan to cook lean meats (pork or chicken) by roasting or grilling, I highly recommend a turn beforehand through a brine marinade. Brining saturates the meat with flavorful moisture that doesn't cook out. The result: juicy pork and chicken, every time.

For a basic brining solution, use 2 tablespoons kosher salt for every 2 cups of liquid. Customize with wine, spices, sugar or honey, citrus zest, or apple juice. (Pork always does well with a sweeter brine.) Bring all the ingredients to a boil, reduce the heat, and simmer for 10 minutes, or until the salt is dissolved. Cool completely before adding the meat. Completely immerse the meat in the brine and refrigerate small pieces for up to 4 hours, larger pieces up to 12 hours.

Sautéed Pork Tenderloin with Caramelized Fennel, Olives, and Dried Fruit

A lush combination of contrasting flavors sweet, salty, and herbaceous. This is a true sauté recipe, which means it is quick! Be sure to have all your ingredients prepared before you start to cook. A sauté must be served right away, so the caramelized fennel and the rest of the menu should be ready to serve before you start cooking the pork.

Pork tenderloins have almost no fat, so be careful not to overcook; a little pink inside (145 degrees) is perfectly safe to eat.

WINE Young Chardonnay or Chenin Blanc–Sauvignon blend

Makes 6 servings

2 medium fennel bulbs, trimmed and thinly sliced

6 tablespoons olive oil (divided use)

Kosher salt

2 large pork tenderloins (about 2 pounds before trimming)

2 tablespoons butter

⅓ cup all-purpose flour

Freshly ground black pepper

2 shallots, minced

1 garlic clove, minced

¼ cup white wine

¾ cup unsalted chicken or veal stock

1 thyme sprig, stemmed

¼ cup diced dried pear, pineapple, or mango

8 green or black olives, pitted and cut into strips

1. Make the caramelized fennel: In a small saucepan, combine the fennel with 2 tablespoons of the oil and cook over medium heat, covered, until the fennel is very soft and starting to caramelize—about 30 minutes. Stir occasionally, season with a little salt, and set aside.

2. Trim the tenderloins of the thin strip of meat and fat, known as the chain, that runs down one side. Carefully remove all silverskin and fat. Beginning at the larger end, cut each tenderloin crosswise into 2-inch-thick pieces (reserve the slender tails for another use).

3. Place each piece, cut side up, between sheets of plastic wrap. With the flat side of a meat mallet or a small frying pan, gently pound the meat into "scallops" 4 inches across and about ¼ inch thick.

4. Before starting to cook the meat, have the rest of the meal ready to go and all ingredients ready and at hand. Heat a 12-inch frying pan over medium-high heat. Add the remaining 4 tablespoons oil and then the butter.

5. Season the flour with salt and pepper. Working quickly, dredge the pork scallops, one at a time, in the seasoned flour, shake off the excess, and cook until golden brown, about 2 minutes per side. Cook in batches and do not crowd the pan. Keep warm. Be careful not to burn the little bits stuck in the pan bottom.

6. When all the pork is cooked, pour off the excess fat from the pan and return to medium heat. Sauté the shallots and garlic for 1 minute.

7. Pour in the wine, stock, and thyme; boil, scraping up all the bits stuck to the pan. Add the dried fruit.

8. Simmer the pan sauce until it is slightly thickened. Stir in the olives at the very end. Taste the sauce and season with salt if necessary.

9. Serve a couple of pork scallops to each person, topped with a spoonful of the fennel, some sauce and olives, and a few pieces of dried fruit.

Puesto-Style Quail in Achiote

In Baja California's back country, flocks of wild quail (*codorniz*) are everywhere. Some farms raise them for sale, so it's common to find grilled quail sold alongside tacos at local *puestos*. Half-boned quail are best eaten as finger food—just pick them up and have at it.

A favorite marinade for quail is achiote, a spice common in southern Mexico that has a taste similar to paprika but better. Jazzed up with some black pepper, garlic, and orange zest and tossed on the grill, this is sure to become a backyard favorite. If you can't find quail, skin-on chicken thighs are a perfectly delicious substitute.

WINE Soft, rustic reds, such as Grenache and Zinfandel

Makes 6 servings

ACHIOTE MARINADE
½ teaspoon kosher salt
½ teaspoon freshly ground black pepper
¼ cup olive oil
3 large garlic cloves, minced
2 tablespoons white vinegar, preferably Heinz
Grated zest and juice of 1 orange

2 tablespoons freshly squeezed lime juice, preferably from Mexican limones (see page 30)
1 teaspoon ground cumin
1 package (4 ounces) achiote paste, crumbled
6 cilantro sprigs, stemmed and finely chopped

12 deminboned quail or skin-on, bone-in chicken thighs (see note below)

1. Make the marinade: In a mini food processor or bowl, combine the marinade ingredients and puree or mash to a smooth paste. It should be the consistency of thick cream; add a little more orange juice to thin, if necessary.
2. Coat the quail thoroughly with the marinade and refrigerate for 1 to 3 hours.
3. Preheat a grill to medium. Grill the quail, turning often, until thoroughly cooked, 15 to 20 minutes total. If the birds darken too quickly, reduce the heat.
4. When the quail are cooked, remove to a warm platter and cover loosely with foil for a few minutes before serving.
5. To serve, cut the quail in half lengthwise. Quail are usually eaten with the fingers, so provide damp towels.

Note: Quail are available whole or deminboned, meaning that the breastbone and ribs have been removed. The quail lie flat, so they are easier to eat. If you use chicken thighs, they will take about 30 minutes to cook.

Mesquite-Grilled Quail
with Figs and Pancetta

This is a great campfire recipe—if camping for you includes skewered quail and delicious roasted figs wrapped in pancetta! Cooked over a fire of mesquite, the quail pick up a lovely tinge of smoke that enhances the flavor of a simple dry rub. Of course, you don't have to go camping to enjoy this recipe; any grill will do, or the quail can be oven roasted. The grilled figs are wonderful on spinach salad or with roast pork.

WINE Soft Grenache or Merlot

Makes 6 servings

SPICE RUB

10 black peppercorns
½ teaspoon fennel seeds
½ teaspoon coriander seeds
2 tablespoons Spanish paprika
2 tablespoons sugar
1 teaspoon kosher salt

12 whole or demiboned quail (see note below)

GRILLED FIGS

1 large orange
20 dried gold and/or black figs, stemmed
1 cup red wine
1½ cups water
⅓ cup sugar
1 clove
10 pieces thin-sliced pancetta
  or good-quality bacon

TO SERVE

6 cups strong salad greens, such as arugula or watercress
4 tablespoons best-quality extra-virgin olive oil
2 tablespoons freshly squeezed lemon juice

1. Make the spice rub: Toast the peppercorns, fennel, and coriander in a small frying pan until fragrant. Grind and mix with the paprika, sugar, and salt. Season the quail inside and out with the spice rub.
2. Make the figs: With a sharp knife, thinly peel the orange in long strips, being careful to remove only the colored part and not the bitter white pith. Put the figs in a small, deep saucepan along with the wine, water, sugar, clove, and orange peel. Bring to a gentle simmer and cook very slowly for about 45 minutes, adding water if necessary to keep the figs barely covered.
3. Discard the peel and let the figs cool to room temperature in the liquid. Cut the pancetta in half and wrap each fig with a piece, secured with a toothpick. Taste the poaching liquid; if it isn't thick and sticky, reduce slightly. Strain and reserve the cooking syrup. (Can be made a day ahead and refrigerated.)
4. Build a medium-hot fire of mesquite charcoal. Grill the quail and figs, turning often, until well cooked, about 15 minutes; push the coals to one side if the fire gets too hot.
5. To serve, toss the greens with the oil and then the lemon juice on a large platter. Set the quail and figs on top. Drizzle with the reduced cooking syrup and serve right away.

Notes: Quail are available whole or demiboned, meaning that the breastbone and ribs have been removed. The quail lie flat, so they are easier to eat. If you are using chicken thighs, cook for about 15 minutes per side, or until the meat is almost falling off the bone. If you are cooking on a gas grill, set a few mesquite chips in a pan on the burner to replicate the taste of a mesquite fire.

Baja California Grilled Turkey

Wild turkeys in Baja California? Anything's possible.

Guajolote (turkey) is a Mexican favorite—often the bird under the *mole* sauce on special occasions. Brining, marinating, and grilling ensures a succulent, savory bird. The brining process takes only 4 hours; try it and you'll be a believer! And the smoky edge from the marinade tastes fantastic with the juicy turkey.

The process of brining a whole turkey can be daunting, what with wrestling a heavy, slippery bird—not to mention turning the darn thing on the barbecue. Brining and grilling separate breast and legs works like a charm and is much, *much* easier to handle. And you'll need a 5-gallon plastic bucket or stainless stockpot (nothing galvanized) plus six frozen ice gel packs to keep the turkey cold while marinating.

WINE Riesling

Makes 12 servings

BRINE

4 cups kosher salt
2 gallons very cold water
2 cups packed brown sugar
1 cup granulated sugar
$\frac{1}{2}$ cup coriander seeds, crushed
$\frac{1}{4}$ cup black peppercorns, crushed
6 bay leaves, crumbled

1 bone-in turkey breast (about 7 to 9 pounds)
4 large whole turkey legs (about 7 pounds)

MARINADE

8 medium garlic cloves, split
1 tablespoon kosher salt
1 can (7 ounces) chipotles in adobo
$\frac{1}{2}$ cup olive oil or vegetable oil
$\frac{1}{4}$ cup best-quality Japanese soy sauce
$\frac{1}{3}$ cup freshly squeezed lime juice, or rice vinegar
$\frac{1}{2}$ cup ground California chile (see page 37)
$\frac{1}{2}$ cup ground cumin
1 heaping tablespoon dried whole Mexican oregano
1 tablespoon granulated garlic
$\frac{1}{2}$ cup freshly squeezed orange juice
$1\frac{1}{2}$ bunches cilantro, stemmed and roughly chopped

1. Combine the brine ingredients in a 5-gallon bucket (see the note above) and stir until the salt and sugar are completely dissolved. Put the gel packs in the brine. Completely submerge the turkey pieces in the brine and weight with a lid and a foil-wrapped brick to keep it under the surface. Marinate for 4 hours—no longer!

2. Make the marinade: Chop the garlic to a paste with the salt and chipotles. Stir in the oil, soy sauce, and lime juice. Add the ground chile, cumin, oregano, and granulated garlic. Stir in the orange juice and cilantro to make a paste the consistency of sour cream. Thin, if necessary, with a little more orange juice.

3. After 4 hours, remove the turkey from the brine and pat dry. Rub the marinade all over the turkey.

4. Heat the grill to medium hot. Grill the turkey pieces on all sides for about 30 minutes (total) until you have nice grill marks and the spices are cooked. Turn off one side of the grill and move the turkey pieces to a disposable aluminum pan on the cooler side. Brush with more of the marinade, close the lid, and cook with the burner on medium (325 to 350 degrees) for about 1 hour, or until an instant-read thermometer registers 170 degrees when inserted into the thickest part of the thigh and 160 degrees in the thickest part of the breast. (Alternatively, transfer the turkey to a 350-degree oven.)

5. Brush the turkey with the marinade twice more during cooking. If the turkey starts to turn black, cover with foil. Discard the marinade.

6. Let the turkey rest for 20 minutes before carving. Reserve the pan juices for sauce.

TRAVELING IN THE BAJA CALIFORNIA WINE COUNTRY

Highway 3 is the Ruta del Vino, which leaves the coast just north of Ensenada and runs through San Antonio de las Minas, Francisco Zarco, and Valle de las Palmas, ending at Tecate. There are some signs to wineries, but these are a bit random and you are better off with a good map and directions given to you by the wineries themselves. *Always* telephone ahead to make sure of hours of operation, since these may change without notice. Careful directions to the more remote wineries are *essential* and should be taken down when you make your reservation!

The interior of Baja is rough country with few services. If you are driving, make sure your car is in good condition and you carry emergency equipment and a spare tire. The dirt roads are very rough and should be avoided in wet weather and near dark. Last, always tell someone where you are going and when you plan to be back.

The two best sources for information on Baja wineries and the annual *Fiestas de la Vendimias* wine festival are:

Asociación de Vinicultores de Baja California
Lopez Mateos Avenue 582–208
Ensenada, B.C., Mexico
Phone: 011 52 (646) 178-3038
www.ensenada.com/wineries-events.html
E-mail: fiestasvendimia@hotmail.com

Government of Baja California State Tourism Secretariat
Site with links to maps, hotel and tourist information
www.discoverbajacalifornia.com

Here is a partial list of local Baja wineries:

Adobe Guadalupe
Barón Balché
Bibayoff—Bodegas Valle de Guadalupe
Bodegas de Santo Tomás
Casa de Piedra
Cava de Don Juan
Cavas Valmar
Château Camou
L.A. Cetto Boutique Ensenada
L.A. Cetto Valle de Guadalupe
Mogor-Badán

Monte Xanic
Shimul/Vinos Albarolo
Vides y Vinos Californianos
Viña de Liceaga
Viñas Pijoan
Vinisterra
Vinos Tanama
Vinícola Don Juan/Vinos Sueños
Vinícola La Farga
Vitivinícola Tres Valles

4
MI TIERRA
FOODS FROM FARMS AND GARDENS

Cuisine is when things taste like themselves.
—Curnansky

The United States is less than half a mile away, just across the river, but Tijuana's Mercado Hidalgo is fully immersed in traditional Mexico.

Visitors from the north are often shocked by the rawness and hurly-burly of the market, but most come to love it. The trip from field to market to table is short and direct, so the food is truly ripe and more flavorful. Everything for sale in the market is fresh, neatly arranged, and treated with respect by buyers and sellers alike. This is food that still has its soul.

Any time of year, the market is a vivid picture of the season: Zucchini flowers and all kinds of tender green *calabazas* (squash) are piled alongside bunches of wild and cultivated greens, like watercress, *verdolagas*, *guamuchil*, and others even more exotic: *quelite*, *papalotl*, *huazontle*, and *guajay*. Avocados, sugar cane, cabbage and carrots, garlic and onions, gourds and squash sit in crates. Perfuming the cool dim air are heaps of ripe fruit—guavas, mangoes, and enormous papayas—and gorgeous tomatoes.

Tucked into the space between two stalls, a trio of elderly men with machetes slice the spines off cactus paddles and laugh, cigarettes dangling from their lips, while a pigeon lands with a thump on top of a pile of paper-husked green tomatillos. A young boy wields a rusty cleaver, whacking the tops off green coconuts.

Everywhere there are neatly arranged mounds of fresh chiles like poblanos, serranos, Anaheims, jalapeños, blond güeros, and long, slender, twisted chilacas glowing in all shades of green from palest to near black, of satiny or shiny texture, a sight that likely has been seen day after day in Mexico for thousands of years.

Dried chiles in sacks and piles and *ristras* (strings) glow more subtly, from blood red to dark burgundy. Even chiles that look similar have different flavors—Mexican cooks use these subtle differences like notes on a piano. There are the common guajillos, Californias, and New Mexico chiles, which give the deep color and rich flavor to enchilada sauce. Dark wrinkled anchos and mulatos look for all the world like giant raisins.

Sneeze-inducing piles of hot chiles de árbol and chiles piquíns in near-lethal amounts invite cautious exploration. Leathery brown, smoke-scented chipotles and true mulatos or chiles negros share space with bell-shaped cascabels and dagger-like puya and japonés chiles.

Mercado El Paraiso, located within the larger market, specializes in all kinds of dried foods: bulk bins of pumpkin, squash, and sesame seeds, peanuts and *piñóns* (pine nuts), cooking and medicinal herbs, healing teas, cones of raw *piloncillo* sugar, different kinds of flours, and the all-important powdered chicken base. With all these ingredients, today's cooks could make *mole* from scratch, but few still do, judging from the huge tubs of premade *mole* paste—green, red, black. Blocks of red *ate* (guava paste) and *membrillo* (quince paste) gleam under glass at the front of the store. Out front, sacks in neat rows offer dried corn—white, yellow, blue, and red—for *posole* and *masa*. Dried beans abound in different sizes and colors, with melodious names like *flor de mayo* (May flower), *azufrado*, *mayocoba*, *bayo barrente*.

Just down the walkway crowded with shoppers, a green parrot sleeps in a large iron cage before a narrow, dim housewares shop. The place is crammed with cooking tools. Like something out of Alice in Wonderland, giant 3-foot-long wooden spoons for stirring carnitas keep company with tiny ones for serving salsas. Deep copper cauldrons will cook for a crowd. Braziers for charcoal and wood fires stand next to lava-black *molcajetes*, *metates* (flat lava rock tables for grinding *masa*), old-fashioned handled juicers, and rattle-like wooden *molinillos* for whisking chocolate to a heady froth. The shelves are piled high with round and oblong *comals* in black steel, brooms and scrubbers, stacks of earthenware cooking and serving pieces, glasses, and *pulque* pots. From the rafters hang *discas*, paella pans, kettles for steaming tamales. Tiny versions of everything, for children's toys, are charming.

Outside the *dulcerías* (sweet shops), dangling over shoppers' heads, hang huge brightly colored piñatas in the shapes of fish, stars, and various cartoon characters, all with colorful paper streamers fluttering. Inside, the store is packed floor to ceiling with brightly colored candy packages. There are bright pink and yellow coconut treats and slabs of fudge-like candy. Trays bearing swirls and chunks of a tan fudge-like confection share space with 6-inch disks of sticky caramel full of *pepitas* (green pumpkin seeds), peanuts, and sesame seeds. Outside, a rough wooden table is covered with pans of candied squash (*calabaza*), cactus (*chilicote*), and sweet potatoes (*camotes*)—an acquired taste, though not for the dozens of hornets and wasps dancing drunkenly in pools of liquid sugar.

A busy Oaxacan restaurant sells *agua fresca*, *moles*, and black beans and enormous sheets, several feet square, of *chicharrones*—pork skin deep-fried in lard until crisp, like giant cracklings. Upstairs is a small grocery selling Oaxacan ingredients, including *chapulines*—dried grasshoppers.

Much of the food for sale at Hidalgo is as unfamiliar as the *chapulines,* but the panorama of abundance captivates anyone who loves to cook. You experience with all your senses what is best to eat right now, on this day, in this season. The fresh smells and gorgeous colors of the market inspire wonderful meals. It makes you want to fill up a basket, go home, and *cook*.

RECIPES

Oven-Roasted Tomatoes and Garlic

Slow-roasting intensifies the sweet/acid joy of good tomatoes and improves the flavor of not-so-great ones. Use fleshy tomatoes, such as Romas, and make a batch when you have the oven on for something else. They take about an hour to cook and keep well for several days. Especially delicious warm from the oven, with garlic-rubbed toasted bread, olives, and a salty cheese. Gently rewarm any leftovers and use on salads or on grilled bread.

Makes 24 half tomatoes

12 ripe Roma or pear tomatoes
Kosher salt
1/2 teaspoon freshly ground or cracked black pepper

4–6 large garlic cloves
About 1/2 cup olive oil
Small rosemary sprig (optional)

1. Preheat the oven to 325 degrees.
2. Remove the tomato cores with the tip of a sharp knife and cut the tomatoes in half lengthwise. Scoop out the seeds and juice; turn upside down to drain for several minutes.
3. Season the tomatoes inside and out with the salt and pepper. Set hollow sides down on a rimmed cookie sheet with the garlic. Drizzle with several tablespoons of the oil and tuck in the rosemary sprig. Roast without stirring for about 1 hour, or until softened and shrunken.
4. Remove from the oven and cool; drizzle the pan juices over the tomatoes. Transfer to a small container and pour in the remaining oil and the pan juices. Cover, store in the refrigerator, and use within 3 days.

TOMATOES (JITOMATE)

Along with corn and squash, tomatoes are one of the foundations of traditional Mexican cooking, essential for salsas. The ordinary red tomato is still widely known by its Aztec name, *jitomate*.

Tomatoes were among the first New World products to be introduced to Europe — perhaps the original fusion food. Who can imagine Italian or Spanish cuisine without tomatoes? For that matter, ketchup and salsa are America's two top-selling sauces; pizza and pasta our favorite foods.

Mexican tomatoes are firm and fleshy, always picked ripe and sold at the peak of flavor, good for charring and peeling or chopping into pico de gallo. The best year-round variety for use in the United States is the oval Roma tomato. Choose dark red, fully-ripe tomatoes that you can actually *smell*. Store at room temperature and use quickly.

Heirloom Tomato Salad
with Croutons, Basil, and Red Onions

Heirloom tomatoes are older varieties of tomato that have enjoyed a renaissance in popularity over the past few years. They harken back to the ancestral *jitomate* with an exuberant variety of shapes and colors, from fat with green stripes, to bumpy and maroon, to flattened and orange. Different heirlooms are available from early to late summer, even into fall. Look for them at your local farmers' market.

This salad needs — no, *demands* — juicy, perfectly ripe tomatoes. This is summer at its best.

Makes 6 servings

4 thick (1-inch) slices firm home-style bread, crusts removed
½ cup olive oil
3 garlic cloves, minced to a paste
1 small tender rosemary sprig, stemmed and chopped
Kosher salt and freshly ground black pepper

2 pounds assorted ripe heirloom tomatoes, such as Cherokee, Brandywine, Green Zebra
2–3 tablespoons red wine vinegar
½ red onion, thinly sliced and rinsed with cold water
2 tablespoons shredded basil leaves (see note below)

1. Preheat the oven to 400 degrees. Cut the bread into 1-inch cubes.

2. In a large bowl, mix ¼ cup of the oil, garlic, rosemary, a pinch of salt, and a few grinds of pepper. Toss the bread with this and spread out in a single layer on a cookie sheet. Toast until golden, about 10 minutes; it's okay if the croutons are soft in the center.

3. While the croutons are baking, core the tomatoes and cut into chunks about 1½ inches square, reserving all juices. Place in a large bowl and sprinkle with the remaining ¼ cup oil, vinegar, and 1 teaspoon salt.

4. Remove the croutons from the oven and cool for a few minutes. Toss the tomatoes and croutons together and stir in the onion and basil. The salad is ready to serve when the croutons have softened slightly with the tomato juices.

Note: You could substitute fresh oregano, cilantro, dill, tarragon, or marjoram for the basil.

Grilled Corn

Just up the street from my favorite taco stand in Ensenada, a neatly dressed elderly gentleman will sometimes appear with a charcoal brazier and a basket of sweet corn. He sets up shop on the corner near the bus stop in late morning and carefully grills each ear of corn until it is perfectly cooked. By early afternoon, he has sold his basketful of corn and vanished. The slow-roasted corn he makes is something special—with a squirt of creamy, lime-spiked salsa and a dusting of fresh-ground guajillo chile perfect complements to the sweet, a bit chewy, and intensely smoky corn.

Brining seasons the corn and keeps it moist; it may be grilled as directed or wrapped in foil and roasted in the embers of a campfire.

Makes 6 servings, but may be doubled or tripled for a crowd

6 cups water
Kosher salt
6 ears sweet corn, shucked and trimmed
¼ cup mayonnaise

Juice of 1 lime, preferably a Mexican limón (see page 30), or to taste
1 tablespoon ground guajillo, California, or New Mexico chile (see page 37), in a shaker

1. In a nonreactive container or a 1-gallon resealable freezer bag, combine the water and ⅓ cup salt. Swish to dissolve the salt.

2. Add the corn to the brine and refrigerate for 4 to 12 hours.

3. Heat a grill on medium-high heat. Wrap each wet ear in foil and grill for 20 minutes, turning every few minutes to roast on all sides. The corn is done when the kernels are softened.

4. While the corn is grilling, mix the mayonnaise and lime juice to make a sauce. It should have the consistency of heavy cream; add water to thin, if necessary. Pour into a squeeze bottle.

5. Serve the corn still in the foil. Let diners season the corn to their taste with drizzles of sauce and sprinkles of ground chile and salt.

COCKTEL DEL ELOTE

At every saint's day fair and seasonal carnival in Mexico, someone will be selling sell cups of *cocktel del elote*—corn cocktail—from a truck or stand. Fresh corn kernels are seared on a hot griddle or *plancha* until the corn is golden brown. It is scooped into a paper cup and mixed with mayonnaise sauce, melted margarine, powdered salty cheese, and a pinch of ground mild guajillo chiles, then served with a lime wedge and a spoon.

Fresh Corn Strata with Crispy Onions and Oven-Roasted Tomatoes

I never tire of playing with the subtle and sweet flavor of fresh white corn, which here features a savory take on another home-style Mexican favorite: bread pudding *(capirotada)*. Leftover bread and silky corn custard are combined with layers (strata) of cheese and baked until firm and creamy. Crispy onions and slow-cooked tomatoes add color and crunch.

The bread needs to soak for several hours before cooking. The strata may be made the day before and baked before serving, which makes it ideal for brunch or buffet.

Makes 6 to 8 generous servings

3 ears sweet white corn
1 tablespoon vegetable oil
½ medium white onion, diced
2 cups water
¼ teaspoon baking soda
1½ teaspoons kosher salt
2 cups milk or 1 cup milk and 1 cup cream
½ teaspoon freshly ground black pepper
⅛ teaspoon freshly ground nutmeg
½ teaspoon cayenne pepper
4 eggs

1 tablespoon butter, softened
1 loaf (1 pound) firm white bread, crusts removed
2 cups grated Menonito, Chihuahua, or Jack cheese
Oven-Roasted Tomatoes and Garlic (see page 150)

ONIONS
½ cup vegetable oil
⅓ cup all-purpose flour
Kosher salt and freshly ground black pepper
½ white onion, cut into ¼-inch slices

1. Trim the ends of the corn and stand on end on a plate. With a sharp knife, scrape all of the kernels from the cobs; this should yield about 3 cups. Be sure to catch any corn "milk." Cut the cobs in half and set aside.
2. Heat the oil over medium heat in a 2-quart saucepan. Add the onion and corn; cook, stirring often, until the onion is softened. Add the water, corn cobs, baking soda, and salt. Simmer for 30 minutes. (Add a small amount of water during cooking to maintain the level, if necessary.)
3. When the corn is cooked, discard the cobs. Drain the corn, reserving the cooking liquid. Place the cooking liquid and half of the corn in a blender. Add the milk, pepper, nutmeg, and cayenne; blend on high speed for about 2 minutes, or until silky smooth. Taste for seasoning and add more salt and other spices if necessary; the custard should be highly seasoned. Add the eggs and blend on high speed for 30 seconds. You should have about 6 cups of custard.
4. Butter a shallow 3-quart baking dish (8 by 11 inches). Cut the bread into 1½-inch cubes. Cover the bottom of the baking dish with one-third of the bread cubes. Scatter on one-third of the cheese and half of the reserved corn kernels. Add another layer of bread, cheese, and corn. Top with the remaining bread and cheese. Pour the corn custard evenly over the bread; the mixture will be very wet. Cover and refrigerate for at least 4 hours.
5. Preheat the oven to 350 degrees. Bake the strata for 1 hour and 15 minutes, or until browned, puffed in the center, and firm to the touch. Be careful not to overcook or the custard will curdle and break. During the last 5 minutes of baking, place the tomatoes in the oven to heat.
6. Make the onions while the strata is baking: Heat the oil in a small saucepan over medium-high heat. Combine the flour and pinches of salt and pepper in a small paper bag. Add the onions and shake to coat. Shake off any excess flour and fry the onions in batches until crisp and brown. Drain on paper towels.
7. Serve the strata warm, with the roasted tomatoes and a scattering of onions.

Fresh Corn and Poblano Soup

An untraditional use of traditional ingredients makes this one of the best soups I've ever made. It's important to use only white sweet corn, not yellow. Out of season, use frozen white corn.

Makes 6 to 8 servings

3 fresh poblano chiles
4 ears sweet white corn
2 tablespoons olive oil
½ white onion, chopped
4 large garlic cloves, chopped
8 cups water

1½ teaspoons salt, or to taste
2 tablespoons uncooked white rice

TO SERVE
2 tablespoons Mexican crema or crème fraîche
Toasted, salted pepitas (green pumpkin seeds)

1. Char, peel, and seed the chiles as for Rajas con Crema (see page 179); cut into 1-inch pieces.
2. Trim the ends of the corn and stand on end on a plate. With a sharp knife, scrape all of the kernels from the cobs; this should yield about 4 cups. Be sure to catch any corn "milk."
3. Heat the oil in a 4-quart saucepan or small stockpot with a heavy bottom. Add the onion and garlic; cook until translucent, stirring often. Add the corn and corn juices, chiles, and 2 cups of the water. Reduce the heat to low, cover, and simmer for 10 minutes, stirring a couple of times.
4. Add the remaining 6 cups water, salt, and rice. Simmer for 45 minutes over low heat.
5. Let the soup cool for 15 minutes. Puree in several batches in a blender, until as smooth as velvet (this may take a couple of minutes). Add water, if needed, to make the soup the consistency of heavy cream; adjust the seasoning. Do not strain the soup after blending.
6. Serve the soup in heated bowls. Top each serving with a drizzle of crema and a few pepitas.

CORN (ELOTE)

Mexico has almost 300 indigenous languages, and every one has a multitude of words for *corn*. First grown in Central America untold thousands of years ago, it is still at the heart of everyday life. Its scent lingers in the air on every street and in every kitchen. Every garden and farm has a stand of tall corn stalks; the silk tassel is used as a medicine, the stalks are crushed to make a mildly alcoholic drink, and the cobs are burned for fuel or fed to animals.

Fresh corn, known as *elote*, is enjoyed grilled on the cob or seared and dressed with lime-spiked mayonnaise and ground chile. Cut-up cobs are boiled in home-style soups or stews. Corn-based *atole* is made from *pinole*, ground corn flavored with fruit and nuts. *Champurrado* is a chocolate drink thickened with dry masa, referencing Aztec flavors more than our idea of "hot chocolate." There is even corn *nieve* (ice cream), sometimes spiked with chile. Once dried, corn becomes *maíz*. The whole kernels are soaked with lime into swollen nubs called *nixtamal* (hominy), which is eaten in soups and *posole* or cleaned and ground to make the basic *masa* dough for tamales and tortillas. For more on making *masa*, see page 238.

Jícama with Lime, Salt, and Ground Guajillo Chile

Jícama is definitely odd looking—a large, flattened sphere covered with rough, hairy skin. But underneath the brown outer layer, the white flesh is starchy, sweet, juicy, and addictively crunchy all at once. The best way to eat jícama is with a squeeze of fresh lime and a sprinkle of salt and ground chile, but it also provides welcome substance to salads and can even be cooked, though it stays firm.

Jícama is a tuber that originated in Central America. When you buy it, it should feel as hard and heavy as a bowling ball, with no shriveling or moldy spots. To prepare jícama, strip off the skin and slice the white flesh into sticks or slices. It has no seeds and will not discolor on contact with the air.

Makes 6 servings

1 jícama (2 pounds)
Juice of 1 lime, preferably a Mexican limón (see page 30)
Ground guajillo or New Mexico chile (see page 37)
Pinch of kosher salt

Prepare the jícama as directed above. Squeeze the lime juice over the pieces, sprinkle with ground chile and salt, and munch away.

BOTÁNICAS

Every town and city has a number of *botánicas*, where dried herbs and other materials such as tree bark, seeds, or minerals are sold as medicines for body and soul. (In the United States, Europe, and Canada, specific medical claims cannot be made for such products, and no such endorsement is intended here.) In Mexico, these are considered "folk cures" and widely used. Mamá has her cupboard full of "teas" for every complaint, and many Mexicans visit the neighborhood *curandero* (herbalist) as often as they see a doctor.

Many of the herbs sold are gathered wild and are unfamiliar to Americans, such as *axocopaque*, used for rheumatism and arthritis, or the leaves of the *zapote* tree, used for high blood pressure. Others are common. *Anís* (fennel) is prescribed for digestive problems, gastritis, and mucous cough. Fenugreek, which is widely used in Middle Eastern cooking, is tagged for a list of complaints from hemorrhoids to arthritic pain. Rose petals are a laxative and make a soothing infusion for tired, sore eyes. *Gordolobo*, with its fat flowers similar to chamomile, is brewed during cold season for respiratory relief. Epazote is one of the commonest of such herbs; it not only alleviates flatulence but kills intestinal parasites. Rosemary leaves infused in hot water are used on sprains and aches. Lemongrass and *yerbabuena* (a variety of mint) comfort upset stomachs and aid digestion.

Foods, too, serve the body. Cactus and other desert plants are widely believed to be particularly health giving. And bee pollen is thought to sharpen the intellect and lift one's spirits; it is sold alongside raw honey in the comb.

Grilled Vegetables
with Tomato Emulsion

I don't know about you, but I return from every trip to the summertime market laden with armloads of fresh vegetables, far more than I can use. That's the time to make vegetables the main event on the grill.

All kinds of vegetables lend themselves to grilling. The process brings out their natural flavors and sweetness. It takes a little attention on your part, but the results are well worth it. Choose firm, medium vegetables; tomatoes are not really suited to this cooking method. My favorite vegetable to grill? Potatoes.

Your grill must be very hot on one side, a little cooler on the other. The vegetables will cook at different speeds; as each is cooked, remove it to a large serving platter. Only potatoes and eggplant need to be cooked until soft; other vegetables should be cooked until they are rubbery—not hard, but not too soft.

In order to keep down flare-ups, remove as much marinade from the vegetables as possible before grilling. Reserve extra marinade to pour over the vegetables after cooking to mingle with their cooking juices in a delicious, natural sauce, abetted by the fresh taste of the tomato emulsion.

Grilled vegetables should be served at room temperature within an hour or less of cooking. Never refrigerate and reheat.

Makes 8 to 10 servings

MARINADE

1 cup olive oil or best-quality extra-virgin olive oil
4 large garlic cloves, chopped to a puree
   or put through a garlic press
2 tender rosemary sprigs, finely chopped
4 thyme sprigs, chopped
$1\frac{1}{2}$ teaspoons freshly ground black pepper
1 tablespoon kosher salt

VEGETABLES

4 small Japanese eggplants, halved lengthwise
4 medium red potatoes, quartered
2 red or green bell peppers, halved top to bottom and seeded
1 large firm zucchini, cut into thick slices
1 large firm yellow crookneck squash, cut into thick slices
1 red onion
1 bunch green onions or leeks
2 Belgian endive or red endive (endigia), cut in half lengthwise
12 thick asparagus spears
6 baby carrots or other baby vegetables, split lengthwise
6 red jalapeño, green jalapeño, or güero chiles

TOMATO EMULSION

4 ripe Roma tomatoes, halved and seeded
$\frac{2}{3}$ cup olive oil
1 teaspoon kosher salt
$\frac{1}{4}$ cup red wine vinegar
4 large basil leaves

1. Combine the marinade ingredients.

2. Prep the vegetables and dry thoroughly. Toss with the marinade in a bowl about 30 minutes before cooking.

3. Make the tomato emulsion: Puree the ingredients and taste for seasoning. Set aside. Whisk again just before serving.

4. Grill the vegetables as directed below (in most cases, starting on the hot side of the grill and finishing on the cooler side). Remove each cooked vegetable to a serving platter and season lightly with salt. Serve the vegetables in their natural juices. Dress with reserved marinade and serve with a bowl of the tomato emulsion on the side.

JAPANESE EGGPLANTS Start by grilling cut side down until well browned; turn over and grill the skin sides until nearly charred. Move to the cooler side of the grill (indirect heat) and cook until soft.

RED POTATOES Grill cut side down until well browned; turn and finish cooking on indirect heat.

BELL PEPPERS Grill skin side down until nicely marked; do not turn upside down at any time. Move to indirect heat. Cook until still firm but not crisp.

ZUCCHINI AND YELLOW SQUASH Grill on both sides until well colored; remove from the heat while still a bit firm.

RED ONION Leave the root end intact. Cut from top to bottom into eight wedges. Grill until marks appear, then remove to indirect heat to cook until soft.

GREEN ONIONS AND LEEKS Grill until well colored, then cook until soft on indirect heat.

ENDIVE Grill until marks appear, then move to indirect heat and cook until nearly soft.

ASPARAGUS AND BABY VEGETABLES Grill until colored and remove immediately to the platter while still a bit crunchy; they will soften.

ALL CHILES Grill, turning several times, until lightly charred.

Note: You can make a great-looking platter of baby vegetable crudités with an assortment of quickly grill-marked young vegetables, such as tiny new asparagus, zucchini, pattypan squash, potatoes, and other little, very fresh vegetables. They're barely cooked—just marked and served almost raw: crunchy and sweet with a bit of smoky taste from the grill.

Chayote Sauté
with Tomatoes and Garlic

If you like summer squash and zucchini, you should become acquainted with chayote, a pear-shaped gourd native to Central America. In this country, chayote are smooth skinned and pale green, with a mild taste. Mexican chayote are dark olive green, covered in soft spines, with a more pronounced flavor. All chayote have a large, soft white seed, which can be cooked and eaten. Use the flesh as you would any summer squash, in sautés, vegetable stews, or ratatouille or grilled, deep-fried, or pickled. In other countries, chayote are used in sweet dishes (even as a substitute for apples in apple pie!). Leaves, young shoots, and roots are also cooked and eaten. Smooth-skinned varieties do not need to be peeled. Chayote is also called *chocho, mirliton,* or *christophine.*

Makes 6 servings

2 large smooth-skinned chayote
2 tablespoons olive oil
2–4 large garlic cloves, thinly sliced
$\frac{1}{4}$ red onion, sliced $\frac{1}{4}$ inch thick

2 ripe Roma tomatoes, cut into $\frac{1}{2}$-inch dice
Leaves from 2 thyme sprigs
$\frac{1}{2}$ teaspoon kosher salt, or to taste
Freshly ground black pepper

1. Cut each chayote into 1-inch chunks or wedges (leave the seed intact; it is considered a treat).
2. In a large frying pan, heat the oil over medium heat. Cook the garlic, stirring, until it is soft but not brown.
3. Add the chayote and onion; cook, stirring occasionally, until the vegetables are tender, about 20 minutes. The chayote will remain somewhat firm.
4. Add the tomatoes and cook for 5 minutes, stirring occasionally; the idea is to have the tomatoes soft but not turned to mush. If the mixture becomes wet, turn up the heat and stir until it dries out.
5. Just before serving, stir in the thyme, salt, and a few grinds of black pepper.

Quick Chayote Pickles

Chayote makes an excellent pickle, crunchy and tangy sweet. This easy version is not processed (canned) and so must be refrigerated and used within 2 weeks, which, if you are a pickle lover, is not a problem.

Makes 1 quart

4 large smooth-skinned chayote
2 cups white vinegar, preferably Heinz
1 cup sugar
1 tablespoon kosher salt
1 small white onion, sliced
¼ cup pickling spice

1 teaspoon coriander seeds
2 cloves
6 garlic cloves, peeled
6 dried chiles de árbol, stemmed and seeded (wear rubber gloves)

1. Slice each chayote into wedges ½ to ⅝ inch wide and remove the seed.
2. In a 4-quart saucepan, combine the vinegar, sugar, and salt. Stir over low heat until the sugar is dissolved.
3. Add the onion, spices, garlic, and chiles. Bring to a simmer and cook for 5 minutes.
4. Add the chayote and boil slowly for 6 minutes, stirring every minute or so, until the chayote are barely tender.
5. Remove the pan from the heat. Weight the spears down with a lid so all is submerged. Let the chayote cool in the pickling liquid. Pack into clean storage containers. Keep refrigerated and use within 1 week.

Cucumber and Melon Salad
with Yerbabuena

Cucumber and melons go very well together, especially with the addition of *yerbabuena* (variously known as *hierba buena* or *acoyo*), which translates to "the good herb." It is a wild herb of the prolific mint family, native to North and Central America, where it was much appreciated by the indigenous population.

The flavor is strongly minty, with an undertaste almost like fresh oregano. It combines happily with cilantro, oregano, basil, and many other fresh green herbs.

Dried or fresh, *yerbabuena* gives a zing to soups, stews, and broths; it is oddly good in salsas and on seafood and makes a wonderful *digestif* sorbet. Dried, it is a frequent addition in medicinal teas, where it is thought to aid digestion and alleviate gastric problems. Dried or fresh spearmint may be substituted.

Makes 6 servings

1 large English or hothouse cucumber
1½ teaspoons kosher salt
1 small ripe honeydew or cantaloupe
2 tablespoons sugar
2 tablespoons white vinegar, preferably Heinz

3 tablespoons shredded yerbabuena or mint leaves or
 1 tablespoon dried yerbabuena or mint
1 tablespoon roughly chopped tarragon leaves
¼ cup Mexican crema or crème fraîche

1. Cut the cucumber into lengthwise quarters, then cut the quarters crosswise into ¼-inch slices (you should have about 3 cups). Toss with the salt and set aside for 1 hour.
2. Peel the melon, cut in half lengthwise, and scoop out the seeds. Cut into lengthwise slices and then cut into pieces the same size as the cucumber. You should have about 3 cups.
3. Drain the cucumber slices and pat dry with a towel. Combine the melon and cucumber in a serving bowl. Toss with the sugar and then the vinegar. Stir in the herbs. Just before serving, stir in the crema. Serve very cold.

Variation: Add ¼ cup thinly sliced red onion, rinsed under cold water.

Seared Sesame Spinach
with Golden Garlic

You won't have any problem getting people to eat their spinach with this quick sauté, which is uncompromisingly garlicky—but that's part of its charm. The key is to cook the garlic over medium heat until it turns a light golden color, which flavors the oil; then toss in the spinach to stop the browning.

Sesame seed (*ajonjolí*), which is widely used in Mexican sauces and sweets, should be freshly toasted in a dry frying pan just before use, to bring out its delicate flavor.

Use a large frying pan for this recipe and move fast or the garlic will burn.

Makes 4 servings

2 bunches spinach, stemmed (see note below)
2 teaspoons sesame seeds
2½ tablespoons olive oil

8 garlic cloves, cut lengthwise into slivers (don't use chopped; it will burn)
¼ teaspoon kosher salt

1. Wash the spinach in several changes of water. Drain well and spin dry.
2. Heat a small frying pan over medium heat. Add the sesame seeds and gently shake the pan until the seeds start to lightly brown. Immediately pour the seeds out of the pan into a container.
3. Heat a large frying pan over medium heat and add the oil. When the oil is shimmering, add the garlic and salt and start stirring immediately.
4. Cook the garlic until it turns a light golden color. Immediately add all the spinach at once, stir, and increase the heat to medium-high. Cook and stir the spinach until it is completely wilted, about 1 minute or less.
5. Tip the pan to drain off excess oil. Serve the spinach with the sesame seeds sprinkled on top.

Note: To eradicate any grittiness, swish the stemmed spinach well in a large bowl full of water, then let the spinach float on top for a couple of minutes so any sand can settle to the bottom of the bowl. Lift the spinach out of the water into a colander and drain off the dirty water. Rinse the bowl, refill, and repeat the process once or twice more. Even so-called cleaned spinach should be washed before use.

Spinach and Watercress Salad with Strawberries and Balsamic Vinaigrette

Late spring brings an explosion of freshness and color to the markets, before summer's heat wilts all but the toughest crops. Here, tender spinach and the first strawberries of the year combine with acid-sweet balsamic vinegar and hints of peppery *berro* (watercress).

Watercress grows wild up the canyons of Baja California, in year-round streams. It was an important food for the region's indigenous peoples. Cultivated watercress is a very popular green throughout Mexico.

Makes 4 servings

1 pint strawberries
10 black peppercorns
½ teaspoon sugar
1 bag (9 ounces) baby spinach

2 large bunches watercress, stemmed
A few radicchio or treviso leaves (optional)
½ cup thinly sliced fennel
Basil Balsamic Vinaigrette (see below)

1. Hull the strawberries, core, and cut in half. Place in a small bowl.
2. Crush the peppercorns with a mallet or the bottom of a pan. Toss the strawberries with the peppercorns and sugar. (May be done 1 hour ahead.)
3. Wash the spinach and watercress; spin dry. Tear up the radicchio leaves, add to the greens, cover, and chill until needed.
4. Just before serving, toss the greens and fennel with the vinaigrette. Divide the salad among chilled salad plates. Arrange the strawberries around the edge of the salad.

Note: Crumbled Cabrales (blue) cheese is excellent on this salad.

Basil Balsamic Vinaigrette

Makes 1 cup

1 garlic clove
1 teaspoon kosher salt
½ cup canola oil
¼ cup olive oil

1 teaspoon Dijon mustard
¼ teaspoon freshly ground black pepper
¼ cup balsamic vinegar
6 medium basil leaves, stemmed and finely chopped

In a bowl, mash the garlic and salt together with a fork to make a paste. Whisk in the oils, mustard, and pepper until well combined. Beat in the vinegar to make a thick, creamy emulsion. Taste for balance—you may want to add more vinegar. Stir in the basil.

The Best Caesar Salad

A traditional Caesar salad involves a lot of tableside showmanship, with a tuxedoed headwaiter mashing garlic and anchovy, adding dashes and flourishes of this and that, flinging lettuce in the air with oil and coddled egg and cheese, and presenting the salad with a bow.

The results often vary wildly, depending on who's making it. And while the use of coddled (semiraw) eggs in the dressing adds a certain unctuous richness, the risk of contracting salmonella isn't worth it. The recipe that follows contains no raw egg, but you won't miss it.

Makes 6 servings

Caesar Dressing (see the opposite page)
3 heads romaine
¼ cup olive oil
4 large garlic cloves, finely minced
6 very thin slices from a baguette or artisan
    sourdough loaf

Chunk of Parmigiano-Reggiano cheese
Anchovy fillets (optional)
Freshly ground black pepper

1. Make the Caesar Dressing; it gets better with age, so you can make it up to 10 days ahead.
2. Strip away the outer leaves from the romaine and reserve for another use. Only the crisp, pale green hearts should be used. Trim the ends and separate the leaves. Wash well, dry, and chill thoroughly.
3. Make the croutons: Preheat the oven to 350 degrees. Combine the oil and garlic. Brush the bread with the mixture. Spread out on a cookie sheet and toast until crisp, about 20 minutes.
4. To serve: In a large bowl, toss the lettuce with just enough of the dressing to lightly coat each leaf. Divide the leaves among chilled salad plates, stacked neatly and all pointing in the same direction.
5. Take a sharp vegetable peeler and peel a few shards of cheese onto each salad. Top each salad with an anchovy and a crouton. Offer freshly ground pepper for each salad.

Note: If you prefer, cut the romaine hearts into 1-inch pieces and make the croutons square; this is easier to serve and eat. The jury is still out on which version is more "authentic," but it will taste the same.

Caesar Dressing

This version of Caesar dressing is potent and delicious and contains no raw eggs. Adjust the balance of anchovy, lemon, and vinegar to your taste. The dressing will keep, covered and refrigerated, for 10 days.

Makes 2½ cups

1 tablespoon anchovy paste or 1 anchovy fillet, finely chopped
1 teaspoon Dijon mustard
2 large garlic cloves
1 teaspoon Worcestershire sauce
¼ cup red wine vinegar
¼ teaspoon freshly ground black pepper

Juice of ½ lemon, or more to taste
¼ cup grated Parmigiano-Reggiano cheese
3 dashes Tabasco sauce
½ teaspoon kosher salt, or more to taste
¼ cup best-quality extra-virgin olive oil
1½ cups olive oil

1. In a blender or food processor, combine all ingredients except the oil and process well.
2. With the motor running the whole time, pour the oil in a steady stream through the hole in the top. Stop as soon as all the oil is in. If the dressing is very thick, add water a little at a time to thin it out to a creamy consistency.
3. Taste for salt and add more lemon juice if necessary. The dressing will be strongly flavored.

TIJUANA: HOME OF THE ENSALADA CAESAR

It's a quirk of culinary history that an utterly Italian salad should become an American classic by way of Tijuana, Baja California—and all because of Prohibition.

In the 1920s, Tijuana was one of the West Coast's more sophisticated urban centers, visited by a steady stream of Hollywood stars and wealthy socialites, who could dash across the Mexican border to Tijuana to drink, gamble, stay up late, and generally misbehave. Naturally, industries catering to these baser impulses sprang up and, along with them, fine hotels and restaurants.

One of the restaurateurs who set up shop in Tijuana was a talented chef with a flair for marketing. Caesar Cardini may (or may not) have been Italian. Whoever he was, wherever he came from, he had a genius for self-promotion that has taken a version of his name around the world. The recipe he is famous for is an utterly Italian concoction of romaine, eggs, anchovies, Parmesan, garlic, and olive oil; it has absolutely nothing to do with Mexico or Mexican ingredients. Today, you can still get a pretty fair version of his original salad at Hotel Caesar in old downtown Tijuana, near Avenida Revolución.

New World Salad

Like this salad, we really do have the best of both worlds. Much of what we eat today in the United States springs from the melding of Old and New World cultures. While this salad celebrates some of the indigenous flavors gifted by Mexico to the rest of the globe, notably tomatoes and avocados, it also contains cilantro, which originated in the Mediterranean region; romaine, the ancient salad green of Italy; and cotixa cheese, a European transplant gone native.

I like to serve this salad on a large platter, with the colorful ingredients in neat rows on top. This is a very substantial salad, suitable for potluck or buffet.

Makes 8 to 10 servings

1 head romaine	2 ripe Hass avocados
$^2/_3$ cup finely shredded red cabbage	$^1/_2$ cup raw unsalted pepitas (green pumpkin seeds)
1 bunch radishes	$^1/_3$ cup crumbled cotixa or feta cheese
$^1/_4$ red onion	Cilantro Vinaigrette (see the opposite page)
3 ripe Roma tomatoes	

1. Remove the dark green outer leaves from the romaine and reserve for another use. Cut off the top quarter of the lettuce and discard. For this recipe, you want only the pale green, crisp inner leaves. Cut the head lengthwise into 4 pieces, then across into 1-inch chunks. Add the cabbage to the romaine, then wash the salad in a bowl of cold water; drain well and spin dry. Chill until ready to use.

2. Wash and thinly slice the radishes. Thinly slice the onion. (The onion can be rinsed with cold water to remove some of its bite.)

3. Cut the tomatoes lengthwise into quarters and then cut each piece into thirds. Pit, peel, and dice the avocados.

4. Heat a small frying pan and add the pepitas. Stir over the heat until the seeds are dry and crunchy.

5. To assemble the salad, mound the greens on a platter. Arrange the vegetables and cheese in neat rows on top; finish by scattering the pepitas over the whole salad.

6. You may present the salad and toss at the table with the dressing or let guests help themselves and pass the dressing separately.

Variations: Make the salad more substantial with the addition of any or all of the following: cooked shrimp, Sautéed Nopales (cactus paddles; see page 173), cooked black beans, diced or julienned jícama, or diced smoked turkey or chicken.

Cilantro Vinaigrette

Makes 1 cup

½ cup canola oil
¼ cup olive oil
2 tablespoons white vinegar, preferably Heinz
1 teaspoon kosher salt
1½ tablespoons freshly squeezed lime juice, preferably from a Mexican limón (see page 30)
1 green onion, chopped
1 cup cilantro leaves

Combine all ingredients in a blender and pulse until the cilantro is finely chopped, but stop before it turns into a puree.

CILANTRO

Cilantro is one of *the* defining tastes of Mexico, but it was brought to Mexico after the Spanish conquest, supplanting a similar-tasting native plant known as *papalotl* or *quelite*, which is still found in Mexican markets.

Cilantro leaves have a bright, clean flavor and aroma that can stand up to big flavors like hot chiles and the acidity of limes and tomatoes. It is best friends with the power of chopped onions and the creaminess of avocados. Cilantro is most commonly used in fresh salsas, but fresh chopped leaves added at the last minute of cooking impart flavor and scent to hot foods as well (see Mexican Onion Soup Dorado, page 176).

There is no substitute for fresh cilantro, also known as fresh coriander or Chinese parsley. If you can't find cilantro at a supermarket, try any Asian or Latin market.

Cilantro leaves are fragile. Buy a lively looking bunch that has no blackened leaves. Stick the whole bunch into an unbreakable container filled with water and cover loosely with a plastic bag. Refrigerated, your cilantro "bouquet" will last up to a week.

Immediately before use, pluck as many sprigs as you need from the bunch. Rinse well under cold water and shake off excess water. Pull the leaves off the stems and roll in a paper towel until dry. Chop coarsely and use immediately. The chopped leaves from six sprigs of cilantro equal one generous tablespoon.

Gardeners: Note that cilantro grows well in almost all zones in season, though it dislikes extremes of heat or cold. It should be planted every couple of weeks to ensure a steady supply.

DESERT EDEN

●●●

Baja California is a country of surprises. Though it looks like a desert, in among the stony hills are tucked remote little farms and *ranchos* where life goes on much as it has for centuries.

Small-scale farms like these that are ecologically friendly, are water wise, and grow a variety of produce for local consumption are an old idea whose time may have come—again.

At Rancho El Mogor in the Valle de Guadalupe, 21st-century ideas are overlaid on tradition. The El Mogor rooster greets every visitor as his harem scratches for bugs and bits of corn. A few dogs lope lazily up to check out visitors. Their barks alert Dr. Antonio Badán, who ambles down the rutted dirt road, cell phone pressed to his ear, to greet visitors.

Badán and his sister Natalia are not your typical farmers. Rancho El Mogor is a vineyard, winery, organic garden, and cattle ranch, founded in 1948.

The garden began as a small project and grew "by itself" into a thriving enterprise; the ranch's products are so highly regarded that Natalia's car is often mobbed at farmers' markets before she can even unload it. She makes bitter orange marmalade from her oranges, jelly from her pomegranates, and *ate* and *membrillo* paste from guava and quince, and she coaxes honey from five hives of bees and eggs from a flock of hens. Soon she will have her own olive oil and cured olives from trees on the property. The forager from Laja restaurant across the road comes often to choose the best-looking produce to take back to chef Jair Tellez, who will write his menu partly from the garden. Beef from the ranch's carob-fed herd also makes an occasional appearance on his menu. The vineyard is planted with Cabernet Franc, Merlot, and Cabernet Sauvignon, which Badán blends into his wines.

But even this Eden has its problems. "The problem is water," Badán says. "The problem is always water. There isn't enough. Our wells are dry."

Baja California is an extension of the Sonoran Desert, one of the most arid regions on earth, with rainfall averaging less than 8 inches a year. In some places, there may be no rain for years at a time. Yet in oases and river valleys and deltas, or where the earth provides a natural reservoir called an aquifer, Baja blooms. The future of Baja California's farm economy and a traditional way of farm life depend upon how its scarce water resources will be managed.

In contrast to big agribusiness, small farms like El Mogor are finding that they can survive off local sales or band together as cooperatives to run efficiently and market in the United States. Smaller farms grow a wider variety of crops, and many are growing organically, such as the Del Cabo cooperative, based in Cabo San Lucas.

Many people, among them the Badán family, believe that carefully planned change and development will actually enhance Baja's agricultural future.

"Look around," Antonio Badán says. "Guadalupe wines are gaining worldwide attention. These wineries are the epicenter for a tourist industry that will support what we have now, not destroy it. And people need jobs. We understand that. But what kind of jobs? What kind of life?

"We must protect what is already here," Badán continues. "In Mexico, what we eat is more than just food. Food always has a bigger aspect of health and of nurturing body and spirit. We always say, '*¿Para que servile?*' What does the food do for you?

"It's not about money," Badán insists. "It's about life."

Quesadillas de Flor de Calabaza
(ZUCCHINI FLOWER QUESADILLAS)

Golden yellow zucchini flowers are one of the great treats of early summer for lucky gardeners or early visitors to the local farmers' market. Pick the male flowers (the ones without a little squash attached) while still dry and crisp. Just before cooking, wash with a quick swish through cold, lightly salted water and drain well. Examine them carefully inside and out and pinch out the pollen-bearing stamens.

   A recipe of great antiquity is *flor de calabaza* folded into fresh *masa* and roasted on the griddle to make a fine quesadilla. If you don't have any flowers, substitute very thin slices of tender little zucchini.

Makes 4 quesadillas; enough for 8 people as an appetizer

1 fresh poblano chile
Pico de Gallo, (see page 30)
2 tablespoons vegetable oil
3 garlic cloves, cut into long thin slices
¼ cup diced white onion

2 cups zucchini flowers, cleaned and cut up, or slivered tender zucchini
8 fresh corn tortillas
4 ounces Oaxacan or mozzarella cheese, shredded

1. Hold the poblano with tongs over a gas flame and char on all sides until the skin is blistered. (Or char under the broiler.) Wrap in a paper towel until cooled.
2. Rub off the blackened skin and remove the stem and seeds with the tip of a sharp knife. Cut the poblano into ½-inch dice.
3. Heat the oil in a skillet over medium heat. Cook the garlic until the slivers just start to turn golden in color. Add the onion and diced poblano and cook, stirring, until the onion is softened but not colored. Add the zucchini blossoms and sauté for 2 minutes, until the flowers are just wilted. Season with ½ teaspoon salt.
4. Heat a dry comal, a heavy griddle, or a cast-iron pan over medium-high heat. For each quesadilla: Set a tortilla in the pan and press down with a spatula. Turn the tortilla over and spread one-quarter of the cheese evenly over the surface. Add one-quarter of the zucchini flower mixture. Cover with another tortilla, press down, and flip over to cook the other side. Flip onto a plate and cut into quarters.
5. Serve hot with the salsa.

CALABAZA (SQUASH)

According to legend, squash, along with corn, was one of the sacred plants given by the gods to humanity in the time before time. There are thousands of varieties of squash and gourds, and they come in all shapes and sizes, with skins smooth or warty, creamy white to jet black. All sprouted from prehistoric South American roots and spread throughout the Western Hemisphere. Squash are hardy, easy to grow, exceptionally prolific, and adaptable to nearly all climates.

Sautéed Nopales

With little to eat but spiny cactus and agave plants, early indigenous peoples in inhospitable desert regions had to be tough and ingenious to survive. Somehow they learned to transform the difficult plants into delicious foods and drinks, many of which still feature prominently in traditional Mexican cooking.

Nopales, the young, flat paddles from various beavertail cacti *(opuntia)*, are widely used fresh for salsas, soups, and salads and are believed to have health-giving properties. Hot-pink cactus pears are enjoyed fresh or made into jams, jellies, candies, and cactus "wines."

A classic Mexican breakfast is eggs scrambled with nopales, served with *frijoles refritos* with crumbled cotixa cheese, hot salsa, and warm tortillas.

Makes 1½ cups, about 4 servings

1 tablespoon vegetable oil
1 cup cleaned and diced fresh nopales (cactus paddles; see below)
¼ red onion, cut into ½-inch dice
1 large garlic clove, thinly sliced
½ teaspoon kosher salt
½ teaspoon freshly ground black pepper
1 teaspoon white vinegar, preferably Heinz
¼ teaspoon whole dried Mexican oregano, rubbed to a powder

1. In a nonstick skillet, heat the oil over medium-high heat. Add the nopales and onion; cook, stirring, until the onion is softened but still a bit al dente.
2. Add the garlic, salt, and pepper and reduce the heat to medium. Add the vinegar and oregano. Serve hot or at room temperature.

COOKING WITH CACTUS

Latin markets often sell fresh *nopales* already cleaned and diced. If you absolutely must use canned or bottled nopales, rinse well before using. They are already cooked, so skip that step (below).

If you find a market that sells fresh paddles, you can easily prepare them yourself if you take care and follow a few simple steps. Always wear heavy gloves and be cautious when handling cactus, as tiny spines can work their way into your skin.

Wearing thick gloves, use a sharp knife to trim around the edges of the paddle. Then hold the paddle at the base with one hand and use a very sharp, 12-inch, straight-bladed knife almost flat against the paddle and scrape off all the spines. Cut the flesh into dice or batons (2-inch sticks).

Drop the cut-up nopales into boiling salted water and cook for 5 to 7 minutes. Drain and refresh with ice water. Drain again. They are now ready for use in any recipe.

Nopales Salsa

I particularly like *nopales* prepared as a substantial salsa—delicious with tostadas and a little cotixa cheese on top. It may also be used in any recipe calling for prepared nopales or with scrambled eggs, in salads, as a side dish, or as an addition to soups.

Makes 3 cups

2 tablespoons olive oil
$\frac{1}{2}$ medium white onion, diced
2 garlic cloves, chopped
2 fresh serrano chiles, sliced into rings
2 cups cleaned and diced fresh nopales (cactus paddles; see page 173)
2 ripe Roma tomatoes, seeded and diced

$\frac{1}{2}$ teaspoon whole dried Mexican oregano, rubbed to a powder
$\frac{1}{2}$ teaspoon kosher salt, or to taste
Freshly ground black pepper
$\frac{1}{2}$ bunch cilantro, stemmed and chopped
$\frac{1}{4}$ cup crumbled cotixa or añejo cheese (optional)

1. Heat the oil in a large frying pan over medium-high heat. Add the onion, garlic, and chiles. Cook, stirring, until the onion is just starting to soften. Add the nopales and sauté until crisp-tender, about 2 minutes.
2. Add the tomatoes and oregano; cook, stirring, until the tomatoes are just warmed through. Season with salt and pepper. Immediately before serving, stir in the cilantro and sprinkle the cheese lightly on top.

Ensalada with Verdolagas Greens, Nopales, Shrimp, and Queso Fresco

This unusual salad combines two vegetables you won't come across every day: *Verdolagas* or purslane *(Portulaca oleracea)* is a low, trailing plant with bright yellow flowers that grows like a weed worldwide. It has a lemony taste reminiscent of sorrel and soft, juicy leaves. *Nopales* are cactus paddles. They are delicious even if the idea of eating cactus does take a bit of getting used to.

Makes 8 servings

4 cups verdolagas (purslane), watercress, or baby spinach

1 teaspoon olive oil

1½ cups cleaned and chopped fresh nopales (cactus paddles; see page 173)

¼ cup diced white onion, rinsed under cold water

2 teaspoons minced garlic

Pinch of whole dried Mexican oregano, rubbed to a powder

1 teaspoon kosher salt

2 tablespoons freshly squeezed lime juice, preferably from Mexican limones (see page 30)

1 tablespoon white vinegar, preferably Heinz

2 ripe Roma tomatoes, seeded and cut into ⅜-inch dice

¾ cup cooked and peeled best-quality shrimp, preferably Mexican, cut into ½-inch pieces

¾ cup crumbled queso fresco, cotixa, or feta cheese

Cilantro Vinaigrette (see page 169)

1. Wash and stem the verdolagas, spin them dry in a salad spinner, and place in the refrigerator to chill.
2. Heat the oil over medium heat in a nonstick frying pan. Add the nopales and cook, stirring constantly, until they begin to dry out. Add the onion, garlic, and oregano; cook for 1 minute. Allow the mixture to cool and then stir in the salt, lime juice, and vinegar. Refrigerate until ready to use.
3. Immediately before serving, toss the greens, nopales, tomatoes, shrimp, and cheese with the dressing in a large bowl. Serve immediately.

Mexican Onion Soup Dorado

Sure, Paris's Les Halles market was the birthplace of the famous onion soup gratinée. But why should the French have all the fun? Big sacks of mild, sweet white onions fill the markets of Mexico, ready to be slow-cooked into a soup that is a fragrant tonic for the soul, flavored with oregano, tomato, and guajillo chile. Topped with crunchy tortillas, creamy cheese, and a spoonful of diced avocado, it is substantial enough to be the centerpiece of a light meal.

Makes 8 to 10 servings

8 medium white onions (about 4 pounds; see note below)
$\frac{1}{4}$ cup olive oil
1 tablespoon sugar
4 dried guajillo chiles
$\frac{1}{2}$ cup boiling water
4 large garlic cloves, sliced
1 teaspoon whole dried Mexican oregano
1 tablespoon kosher salt
1 teaspoon freshly ground black pepper
1 ripe Roma tomato pureed with $\frac{1}{4}$ cup water (or 2 tablespoons tomato paste)
6 cups Chicken Stock (see page 252)

GARNISH

4 stale tortillas, cut into strips
2 tablespoons vegetable oil
16 cilantro sprigs, stemmed and chopped
8 ounces Oaxacan or asadero cheese, cut into thin slices
1 cup diced avocado mixed with the juice of $\frac{1}{2}$ lime, preferably a Mexican limón (see page 30)

1. Cut the onions in half lengthwise and then cut into $\frac{1}{4}$-inch slices. Heat the oil in a heavy 12-inch frying pan.
2. Add the onions and cook over low heat, stirring occasionally, until soft. Sprinkle with the sugar. Increase the heat to medium-high and cook, stirring, until the onions are a rich golden brown color—let them get as dark as you can without scorching. (If they start to burn, add a little water just to the scorched area and continue to cook. This will add great color to your soup.)
3. While the onions are cooking, stem and seed the chiles. Toast quickly on both sides in a hot frying pan. Tear into small pieces and place in a bowl. Pour the boiling water over the chiles, stir a couple of times, and soak for 30 minutes. Puree the chiles and soaking liquid in a blender until fairly smooth.
4. When the onions are a dark golden brown, add the pureed chiles and cook, stirring, until the water has cooked off. Add the garlic, oregano, salt, pepper, and tomato. Stir over medium heat for 1 minute, then transfer to an 8-quart saucepan. Deglaze the frying pan with some chicken stock and scrape up all the bits stuck to the bottom; add to the saucepan, along with the rest of the stock.
5. Simmer the soup over low heat for 1 hour. Taste for salt. Keep the soup hot.
6. Cut the tortillas into $\frac{1}{2}$-inch strips. Heat the oil in a small frying pan and cook the strips in batches until they are just starting to harden. Remove to paper towels and drain.
7. Preheat the broiler.
8. Stir the cilantro into the soup. Ladle the hot soup into 6 onion soup crocks or other ovenproof bowls and set on a cookie sheet.
9. Divide the tortilla strips among the crocks and top them with an even layer of the cheese. Immediately run under the broiler to melt.
10. Top each crock with a spoonful of the avocado and serve right away.

Note: White onions are essential; they have a milder, sweeter taste than brown-skinned onions.

Cebollitas

(GRILLED SPRING ONIONS)

Every carne asada stand has great heaps of green onions stacked beside the grill, ready to cook in the flames alongside the meat. Charred, sweet, and still crunchy, grilled green onions are the ultimate breath mint!

 Cebollitas is the name given to the sturdy green onions we call scallions, slim and straight, as well as small baby onions on the stalk. Either may be grilled alongside carne asada or chicken until charred—sweet on the outside and a little crunchy within.

Makes 6 servings

1 bunch green onions or baby onions with green tops
2 teaspoons oil
Kosher salt

1. Wash and dry the onions. Trim the outer part and any fibrous roots, but leave the root end intact. Trim the green tops so the onions are 12 inches long.
2. Roll in a very small amount of oil and grill on a medium fire, turning several times. The onions should char a little on the outside but not overcook.
3. Sprinkle lightly with salt and eat immediately, alongside carne asada, chicken, or any grilled meat.

Rajas con Crema
(ROASTED POBLANO CHILES)

Chiles of all kinds are loaded with vitamins as well as flavor. Dark green, shiny poblanos have a deep, rich flavor that is accentuated by the process of charring and then cooking with onions and a touch of *crema*. (Charring chiles is an art in itself; see sidebar on page 43.)

Rajas means "rags" in Spanish—an offhand name for an absolutely addictive preparation! These are good with everything: fish, grilled beef, chicken, melted cheese (*queso fundido*), scrambled eggs, or roasted pork and by themselves on warm, fresh corn tortillas with a sprinkling of cotixa cheese.

Makes 4 servings

4 fresh poblano chiles
½ white onion
2 tablespoons butter
¼ cup milk

Kosher salt
1 tablespoon Mexican crema or crème fraîche
2 epazote leaves, chopped (optional)

1. Char the chiles over a gas flame or on a very hot grill until blackened. While still hot, wrap in paper towels to steam and cool. Remove the stem and seeds and rub off all the blackened skin and clinging seeds with the edge of a spoon or the paper towels. (Don't wash them; much of the flavor goes down the drain.) Don't worry if a little skin remains. If you want a milder taste, remove the ribs inside the chiles. Cut into lengthwise strips ¾ inch wide.

2. Slice the onion into thin strips, cutting the long way from stem to root instead of across (they hold their shape better this way).

3. Melt the butter over medium-low heat in a heavy frying pan and cook the onion and peppers together for 5 minutes, stirring often.

4. When the onion is softened, pour the milk over the vegetables and cook very slowly until it is evaporated. Season with salt to taste. (Can be made ahead to this point and refrigerated; reheat before serving.)

5. Just before serving, stir in the crema and epazote. Serve hot.

Note: The epazote isn't essential—many cooks don't use it with *rajas*—but I like the herby taste.

Pickled Jalapeño Peppers

Dishes of pickled jalapeños, usually with onions and sliced carrots, pop up on every table, every cart, and at every *puesto*.

The idea is to politely nibble on the chile as a palate cleanser, or if you're in a macho frame of mind, quickly wolf down the whole pepper and follow it with a long, hearty swig of something cold. (*Aficionados* know that the carrots are often much hotter than the jalapeños.)

This is a fresh pickle. It mush be refrigerated and used within a week. Remember to wear rubber gloves when handling any kind of chile!

Makes 2 cups

1 tablespoon vegetable or olive oil
6 fresh jalapeño chiles, cut in half lengthwise
10 thin onion slices
2 carrot slices
2 garlic cloves, cut in half
$\frac{1}{2}$ teaspoon kosher salt

1 bay leaf
4 black peppercorns
$\frac{1}{8}$ teaspoon whole dried Mexican oregano, rubbed to a powder
1 clove
$\frac{3}{4}$ cup white vinegar, preferably Heinz

1. Heat the oil over medium heat in a 2-quart saucepan. Cook the chiles, onion, carrot, and garlic for about 5 minutes, stirring occasionally, until half-cooked; do not let the vegetables brown.
2. Add the salt, bay leaf, peppercorns, oregano, clove, and vinegar. Bring to a simmer. Boil for 1 minute and set aside to cool. Pour into a clean storage container and refrigerate. Use within 1 week.

Pickled Red Onions

Bowls of these pale-pink pickled onions are found on taco carts and at *puestos*; they get better after a day or two. I like them alongside tacos, with pork of any kind, or on sandwiches.

Makes 1 cup

1 cup thinly sliced red onion
$\frac{1}{3}$ cup red wine vinegar
$\frac{1}{3}$ cup water
6 black peppercorns
1 bay leaf
1 clove
$\frac{1}{2}$ teaspoon kosher salt

Combine all the ingredients in a small saucepan and simmer until the onions are pink and still have a little crunch to them, about 5 minutes. Cool in the pickling liquid. Discard the bay leaf before using.

Huitlacoche Risotto

Huitlachoche isn't a pretty fungus: It invades corn kernels in the field like something out of a horror movie, turning them into swollen, purple-black caricatures of themselves. But the flavor is unparalleled, perfumed, and haunting; it is sometimes called the Mexican "truffle." Like the truffle, huitlacoche should be used in a preparation that enhances its marvelous taste and aroma, such as this risotto. If you are a mushroom lover, you owe it to yourself to indulge.

Huitlacoche is sometimes available fresh in season. Frozen huitlacoche is available from specialty grocers and wholesalers. Canned may be used, though while it offers an echo of the flavor, it is inky black and *ugly*. If you prefer, substitute highly perfumed oriental mushrooms such as shiitake, oyster, or maitake.

Makes 6 servings

1 fresh poblano chile, prepared as for Rajas con Crema (see page 179)
¼ cup olive oil
½ small white onion, finely diced
2 garlic cloves, chopped
½ pound huitlacoche
Kosher salt and freshly ground black pepper

1 cup carnaroli or Arborio rice (see note below)
½ cup white wine
2 cups chicken stock
1½–1¾ cups water
½ cup grated Parmigiano-Reggiano cheese or good añejo cheese

1. Cut the chile into ½-inch pieces.

2. Heat the oil over medium heat in a saucepan with a heavy bottom. Add the onion and garlic and cook until the onion is soft but not brown; adjust the heat as necessary. Add the huitlacoche and chile and cook until the fungus begins to soften. Season well with salt and pepper.

3. Add the rice and cook, stirring, for several minutes, until fragrant. The rice will absorb the oil. Do not brown.

4. Add the wine and continue to stir the rice until it is absorbed. Add ½ cup of the stock and keep stirring as the rice absorbs the liquid. Repeat until all the stock is used.

5. The risotto is done when the rice is cooked through and the risotto has a creamy consistency with a little "sauce." (You may need to add a little water to achieve the correct consistency.) Stir in the cheese and taste for seasoning.

Note: These short-grain rices are imported from Italy and are ideal for risotto. Carnaroli, when cooked, is a little firmer than Arborio.

Mushroom and Poblano Crepes with Manchego Cream Sauce

The Mexicans threw out the French after the Battle of Puebla on May 5, 1867, a date that lives on in those beery, commercial *Cinco de Mayo* celebrations. (Really, shouldn't we drink champagne instead?) Of course, Mexicans retained the aspects of French culture they liked—the food, in particular—while tossing Maximilian and Carlotta.

Mexican haute cuisine shows its French roots in the use of sauces especially, while foods such as crepes and *duxelle*-style mushrooms (chopped and cooked with aromatic vegetables) also outlasted French rule. The idea for this recipe originated with a client of mine from a wealthy Mexico City family. There it is made with extravagant amounts of fresh *huitlacoche*. Cultivated "exotic" mushrooms make a delicious substitute.

As with all crepe recipes, the various steps may be done at your leisure, ahead of time, and the crepes rolled and baked at the last minute.

Makes 16 plump or 24 thin crepes

Crepes (see the opposite page)
2 tablespoons butter, plus more for the baking dish
2 fresh poblano chiles, prepared as for Rajas con Crema (see page 179) and diced
3 large shallots, minced
2 large garlic cloves, minced
1½ pounds flavorful mixed mushrooms, such as button, crimini, oyster, or shiitake, chopped into ¼-inch pieces

½ teaspoon kosher salt
½ teaspoon freshly ground black pepper
1 tablespoon minced chives or parsley
1 teaspoon chopped thyme leaves

Manchego Cream Sauce (see the opposite page)
½ cup grated Manchego cheese

1. Make the crepes and stack until needed (extras may be frozen).
2. In a 10-inch frying pan, melt the butter over medium heat. Add the chiles and cook, stirring, for 1 minute. Add the shallots and garlic. Reduce the heat and cook, stirring occasionally, for 1 minute.
3. Add the mushrooms and increase the heat to medium-high. Season with the salt and pepper. Cook and stir the mushrooms until they begin to give off their moisture; the pan will be wet. Increase the heat and cook, stirring constantly, until the mushrooms cook down to a sticky paste, with no visible moisture in the pan.
4. Off heat, stir in the herbs and check the seasoning; you may want to add more salt and pepper. The mushrooms should be well seasoned.
5. Divide the mushrooms evenly among the crepes and either roll up in a cylinder shape or fold all four sides together to make a square "envelope." (The crepes may be made ahead to this point and refrigerated.)
6. Preheat the oven to 375 degrees. Butter a shallow baking dish or individual gratins and set the crepes in the dish.
7. Spoon the cream sauce over the crepes. Scatter the cheese over the sauce. Bake until the crepes are heated through and the sauce is bubbling. The sauce should brown lightly on top; if it does not, the dish may be set under a hot broiler for a few seconds to brown.

Crepes

Makes 25 (6-inch) crepes

1 cup water
1 cup milk
2 cups all-purpose flour
4 eggs

¼ teaspoon kosher salt
2 tablespoons butter, melted
Oil for the pan

1. In a blender, combine the water, milk, flour, and eggs. Blend on high speed for 1 minute. Add the salt and butter. Scrape down the sides with a spatula and blend again for 30 seconds. Chill for at least 1 hour. (The batter should be the consistency of light cream; add a small amount of water to thin if necessary.)
2. Heat an 8-inch nonstick pan over medium-high heat until a drop of water sprinkled in "dances" in the pan. Brush with a very small amount of oil.
3. Use a half-filled ¼-cup measure to pour the batter into the pan; you will need 2 to 3 tablespoons per crepe, depending on the thickness of the batter. Pour the batter into the hot pan and quickly swirl the pan to coat the bottom. Return to the heat. When the edges are lightly browned and the crepe is puffing, use a rubber spatula to lift the edge; quickly grab it and turn it over. Cook for a minute more, then slide onto a plate.
4. Continue until all the batter is used up, stacking the crepes. You will want to adjust the heat so the crepe cooks quickly; if the pan is smoking, it is too hot. Brush with a very small amount of oil every so often. (May be made ahead to this point, wrapped, and refrigerated.)

Manchego Cream Sauce

Spanish Manchego cheese is a firm-textured cheese with a nutty flavor. Ask for a Manchego with less age, as it melts better than the aged version. Imported Swiss Gruyère may be substituted.

Makes 2½ cups

2 cups milk
1 onion slice
1 bay leaf
10 black peppercorns
1 parsley or thyme sprig, or both
2 tablespoons butter

Scant 2 tablespoons all-purpose flour
¾ cup grated Manchego cheese
1 teaspoon kosher salt, or to taste
Pinch of freshly grated nutmeg

1. In a 1-quart saucepan, combine the milk, onion, bay leaf, peppercorns, and parsley. Heat over medium heat until bubbles form around the outside, but do not allow the milk to boil. Remove from the heat and set aside for 30 minutes.
2. Melt the butter in a 1-quart saucepan with a heavy bottom. Whisk in the flour and cook over low heat for 2 minutes, stirring often. Do not brown. (This is a roux.)
3. Strain the milk and discard the seasonings. Pour the milk onto the roux, whisking constantly. Return the pan to medium heat and whisk until the sauce comes to the boil, then reduce the heat and simmer for 5 minutes. Stir in the cheese. Season to taste with the salt and nutmeg.

Roasted Beets and Carrots
with Rosemary and Honey

Beets, with their dirt-sweet taste and dripping fuchsia interiors, are a year-round favorite in the markets for pickling and boiling as a side vegetable. In spring and summer, they are sold with the leafy green tops, which are cooked as a green or added to soups.

Roasting intensifies the earthy sweetness of all kinds of root vegetables besides beets. Firm red or white onions, parsnips, carrots, turnips, and rutabagas would be other candidates for this roasting technique.

Don't crowd the vegetables and don't turn them. Warning: You'll end up fighting anyone you serve this to for the crusty bits in the pan.

Makes 6 servings

3 large beets	2 tablespoons butter, melted
3 large carrots	1 tablespoon honey
1/4 cup olive oil	1 teaspoon chopped rosemary leaves
2 1/2 teaspoons salt (divided use)	Freshly ground black pepper

1. Preheat the oven to 400 degrees. Peel the beets (keep them dry—dry beets make far less mess) and cut into 1 1/2-inch wedges. Cut the carrots 1 1/2 inches thick on an oblique angle.

2. Toss the vegetables with the oil and 1 1/2 teaspoons of the salt. Spread out on cookie sheets. Roast for 1 hour, or until the vegetables are just soft all the way through. (Turn once only, after 30 minutes.)

3. Use a sharp-edged spatula to loosen the vegetables from the sheets. Remove carefully to a serving dish, drizzle with the butter and honey, and sprinkle with the rosemary. Season with the remaining 1 teaspoon salt and the pepper and serve as soon as possible.

Camotes with Sea Salt

Sweet potato (*camote*) usually refers to an ivory-fleshed elongated tuber with thin red skin. True sweet potatoes originated in South America and have been cultivated throughout Central America for millennia. (The so-called yam is really an orange-fleshed member of the sweet potato family and not a true African yam.) Chunks of camote are added to stews and soups. For a tooth-achingly sweet snack, they are cooked with dark sugar until crystallized or preserved in syrup—an acquired taste, to be sure.

I like them *au naturel* and came up with this recipe for fried slices—simple to make and so addictive! The outside gets crunchy, and the inside stays soft and creamy. I serve them as a side dish or as an appetizer topped with whatever takes your fancy—some ideas are listed below. Well-rinsed sweet potatoes also make dynamite potato chips (see page 115).

Makes 4 servings as a side dish or antojito

2 tablespoons vegetable oil
2 medium white or orange sweet potatoes, peeled

¼ cup fine rice flour (see note below)
About ¼ teaspoon sea salt

1. Heat the oil over medium heat in a 10-inch skillet. While it is heating, slice the sweet potatoes into slices ³⁄₈ inch thick.

2. Dust the sliced sweet potatoes with the flour and cook in the hot oil on both sides until well browned on the outside and soft in the middle. If the slices seem to be browning too quickly, reduce the heat a little.

3. Drain on paper towels and serve hot, sprinkled with the salt.

Note: Rice flour is available at Latin and Asian markets.

Variations: Heat 1 tablespoon honey and ½ teaspoon lime juice; drizzle over the slices just before serving.

Serve hot topped with a squeeze of lime and coarse salt.

Top with a small spoonful of Pico de Gallo (see page 30) or drizzle with Salsa de Chiles de Arbol #1 or #2 (see pages 38–39).

Red Potato Hash
with Roasted Corn and Onions

This hash makes a colorful and flavorful side dish with meat, pork, or chicken or a vegetarian entrée all on its own. It is delicious with cheese melted or crumbled on top.

I use a 14-inch round cast-iron griddle or *comal,* which heats evenly and cooks quickly without steaming the vegetables. If you do not have a griddle, a large frying pan will work.

Makes 4 servings

2 large red potatoes, about 1½ pounds
3 tablespoons olive oil
2 cups sweet white corn kernels
2 teaspoons kosher salt
½ white onion, finely diced

¼ cup diced red bell pepper
1 large fresh poblano or Anaheim chile, prepared as for Rajas con Crema (see page 179) and diced
2 green onions, finely sliced

1. Scrub the potatoes very well. Cut crosswise into ½-inch slices, then stack the slices and cut into neat ½-inch cubes. Immediately place in a bowl of cold water.
2. Heat 1 tablespoon of the oil on a griddle or in a heavy 12-inch frying pan set over medium-high heat. Add the corn and spread it out evenly. Do not stir the corn, but allow it to blacken on one side, which may take as long as 15 minutes. (It will be smoky, and the corn may "pop.") Spoon the corn onto a plate and wipe off the griddle.
3. Add another 2 tablespoons of the oil to the griddle. Drain the potatoes and pat dry. Add to the hot oil in a single layer, season with salt, and cook until browned. (If necessary, use two pans for this step.)
4. When the potatoes are browned, add the onion, bell pepper, chile, and corn. Cook, stirring with a metal spatula and scraping up the bottom, until the potatoes are cooked through. Add more salt if necessary. Stir in the green onions just before serving.

María's Drop-Dead Garlic Rice
with Spinach

This is only for garlic lovers, guaranteed to keep you healthy, smiling, and vampire free. The quality of the garlic is essential; it should be from whole heads, freshly peeled, firm, and not sprouted or shriveled. This recipe is adapted from one served by María Gomez in San Diego.

Makes 8 to 10 servings

1/3 cup vegetable oil (do not use olive oil)
1/2 cup finely minced white onion
2 cups uncooked converted long-grain white rice
1/2 cup dry white wine
3 1/2 cups chicken stock or water

1/2–1 whole large head of garlic, broken into cloves
   and peeled
1 tablespoon kosher salt
2 cups baby spinach, washed and stemmed

1. Heat the oil in a 2-quart saucepan with a tight-fitting lid. Add the onion and sauté until softened but not browned.

2. Add the rice and cook, stirring, until the rice has absorbed the oil and is lightly golden. Add the wine and cook until the rice has absorbed the wine. Add the stock, cover, and turn the heat to low. Cook without peeking until the rice is done, about 15 minutes. Keep warm.

3. While the rice is cooking, chop the garlic with the salt until it is almost a paste. The salt will bring the juices out of the garlic and help with the chopping as well as season the rice.

4. When the rice is done, fluff it with a chopstick or carving fork. Stir in as much of the garlic paste as you have the nerve for. Stir in the spinach and replace the lid for 5 minutes; the spinach will steam with the heat from the rice. Serve as soon as possible.

Variation: Try adding a handful of chopped basil or cilantro leaves in place of the spinach.

Herbed Requesón Cheese with Grappa and Garlic on Whole-Grain Flatbread

This appetizer is at once rustic and elegant, combining warm chewy flatbread with a spread of garlicky fresh cheese spiked with peppery grappa (a liquor distilled in the Guadalupe Valley from grape skins) and lots of fresh herbs. Serve with a bowl of marinated olives.

Requesón, similar in texture to ricotta, is the simplest cheese ever—sweet and creamy. If you don't feel like making cheese, whole-milk ricotta or purchased requesón cheese may be substituted. Making the flatbread is well worth the little time and effort required—make it once and it will become a favorite standby. If need be, you can substitute crisp whole-wheat crackers, whole-wheat pita, or lavash.

Make the dough and cheese the day before you want to serve them; both get better with time.

Makes 4 cups

1 gallon whole milk
½ cup white vinegar, preferably Heinz
3 garlic cloves, finely chopped
1 teaspoon kosher salt, or more to taste
¼ teaspoon freshly ground black pepper
3 tablespoons best-quality extra-virgin olive oil,
    or to taste

1 tablespoon chopped basil
1 tablespoon chopped chives
1 tablespoon chopped parsley
1 tablespoon chopped dill
1 tablespoon chopped chervil
2 tablespoons good grappa, or more to taste

TO SERVE

Whole-Grain Flatbread (see page 190)
Olives with Orange Peel, Chiles, and Garlic (see page 114)

1. Heat the milk over moderate heat, stirring occasionally, until it reaches 180 degrees on an instant-read thermometer (or until bubbles appear around the edges of the milk and it seems on the verge of boiling; but do not boil).

2. Remove from the heat and stir in ¼ cup of the vinegar. Stir once every 5 minutes, for 20 minutes.

3. Set a colander in a large bowl. Cut cheesecloth into squares large enough to hang over the edges of the colander; line the colander with at least four single layers of cheesecloth.

4. Carefully pour the milk from the pot into the lined colander and drain for 30 minutes.

5. Pour the whey (separated liquid) back into the pot. Repeat the process of heating and add the remaining ¼ cup vinegar. Drain and add to the first batch of curd (solids).

6. Fold the inner layers of cheesecloth over the curd, then tie the four corners of the outer layer together. Suspend the cheese from a dowel or spoon handle so it can drip freely into the bowl. Chill.

7. The soft cheese is ready for use when it stops dripping (about 5 hours), but the flavor improves the next day.

8. Stir the garlic, salt, pepper, oil, herbs, and grappa into the finished cheese. Cover and refrigerate for several hours to allow the flavors to blend. Taste again for salt just before serving.

9. Serve in a small bowl with warm flatbread and a bowl of olives.

Whole-Grain Flatbread

The flatbread is a simple yeast dough—easy to make ahead, easy to roll and cook. "Rested" dough is easy to handle and stretch, so make the dough 1 or 2 days before you need it.

Makes 8 flatbreads

2 cups warm water
1 teaspoon sugar
2 packages (1¼ ounces each) active dry yeast
3–3½ cups all-purpose flour

Kosher salt
½ cup olive oil
2 cups stone-ground whole-wheat flour

1. Warm a large mixing bowl. Pour in the water, which should be comfortably warm but not scalding (about 110 degrees). Stir in the sugar and then sprinkle the yeast evenly over the surface of the water. Set in a warm, draft-free place and let stand for 10 minutes, or until the surface is foamy.
2. Using a wooden spoon, stir in 2 cups of the all-purpose flour, 2 teaspoons salt, and 3 tablespoons of the oil. Mix thoroughly, then transfer to an electric mixer fitted with the dough hook (or continue to mix by hand). Mix in 2 cups of the whole-wheat flour. Mix in the white flour in ½-cup increments until the dough is no longer sticky. (Note: You might not use all the flour at this point. Use the remainder for kneading.)
3. Turn the dough out onto a clean surface, dust your hands lightly with flour, and knead the dough for several minutes. Add flour only as needed to prevent the dough from sticking (by flouring the dough and your hands). The dough should be bouncy and moist, rather like baby skin.
4. Find a mixing bowl that is several times larger than your dough ball. Lightly oil the inside and drop the dough into the bowl, turning once to coat with the oil. Cover the bowl with plastic wrap. Refrigerate immediately and let it rise in the refrigerator overnight. The first rising will take about 12 hours.
5. Punch down the dough and allow it to rise again in the refrigerator. It will rise faster each time; just remember to punch it down every time it doubles in size. The dough will keep in the refrigerator for up to 48 hours.
6. Poke the dough to deflate it, but handle it as little as possible otherwise. Divide the dough into 8 equal portions. Form into balls. Have a bowl of flour ready at hand.
7. Lightly flour your hands and roll each ball in the flour. Use your fingertips to poke the dough into a fairly even circle. Then roll the dough as thinly as possible into a 10-inch circle, dusting with flour as needed.
8. Heat two 12-inch cast-iron grill pans or nonstick skillets until medium hot (a drop of water sprinkled on the pan "dances"). Have a lid ready, also a bowl of salt, another of olive oil, and a pastry brush.
9. Lightly brush the hot pan with oil and lay in a round of dough. Brush the top with oil and sprinkle with salt. Put on the lid and let cook until the underside is golden brown and crisp and the dough is puffed—about 2 minutes.
10. Turn the dough and cook the other side for 2 minutes, then flip again.
11. Cut each flatbread into 6 wedges and serve warm.

Queso Fundido with Mushrooms, Green Onions, and Serrano Chiles

Queso fundido simply means melted creamy cheese . . . here made memorable with thin slices of mushrooms quickly sautéed with olive oil and garlic, plus the snap of onions and chiles. Regular mushrooms are yummy, but if you can get it, fresh *huitlacoche* (see page 181) is *sensational*. So is homemade chorizo.

It is worthwhile seeking out ball-shaped, woven Oaxacan cheese, which transforms into a creamy delicious mass at a fairly low temperature. Queso blanco, asadero, good-quality whole-milk mozzarella, or grated Jack can be substituted.

Fundido is better cooked and served in small individual dishes. Using heatproof gratins or *cazuelas*, or even a small frying pan, you can make fundido directly over low heat on the stovetop, in the oven, or perched on a corner of the grill while you cook something else.

Best with fresh corn tortillas, but crusty bread is a perfectly acceptable alternative.

Makes 6 servings as an antojito

1 pound Oaxacan, Monterey Jack, or asadero cheese
2 tablespoons olive oil
4 ounces mixed mushrooms, thinly sliced or julienned (see note below)
2 garlic cloves, finely chopped
Kosher salt and freshly ground black pepper

$\frac{1}{8}$ teaspoon dried epazote or 2 large epazote leaves, shredded
1 green onion, sliced
2 fresh serrano chiles, sliced in rings
Fresh corn tortillas, warmed, or sliced crusty bread

1. Grate the cheese or cut into very small cubes. Place about $\frac{1}{3}$ inch of the cheese in each of 6 individual shallow, heatproof gratin dishes.
2. Set over low heat (or in a 350-degree oven or over a medium flame on the grill) and watch carefully as the cheese begins to soften, then slump. Let it melt completely without stirring.
3. While the cheese is melting, heat the oil in a large frying pan. Add the mushrooms and cook, stirring, for 1 minute, or until the mushrooms begin to soften. Add the garlic, salt and pepper to taste, and epazote. The mushrooms will give off some moisture, and then the juices in the pan will begin to reduce and coat the mushrooms. Once the pan is fairly dry, spoon the mushrooms evenly among the gratin dishes.
4. Sprinkle with the green onion and chiles and serve immediately with the tortillas.

Note: Choose mushrooms like button, crimini, oyster, or shiitake. Or replace the mushrooms with $\frac{3}{4}$ cup fresh *huitlacoche* (see page 181).

Variations: Scatter any of these over the top: crumbled cooked Homemade Chorizo (see page 19); little daubs of pureed chipotles in adobo; Pico de Gallo (see page 30) or Salsa de Chiles de Arbol #1 or #2 (see pages 38–39).

MEXICAN CHEESES

Cheese making originated with the Spanish; the indigenous peoples of Mesoamerica used no dairy. Cheeses were originally made in small batches, heavily salted, and quickly consumed because of the lack of refrigeration. Nowadays, some large cheeses such as *Menonito* (made by Mennonites in the Chihuahua area) and *cotixa* are aged, but there is no tradition of blue cheeses or long-aged cheeses.

Baja has its own cheese-making tradition. Its most famous cheese is *Real del Castillo*, which is made on several ranches in the Ojos Negros region near Ensenada. The cheese bears the name of the ranch where it was made — Castro, Mancillas, Barajas, Gutiérrez. *Real del Castillo* comes in wheels of about 5 kilos, with a pale yellow rind. The cheese itself is creamy and dense, similar to a Muenster.

In the back country, most little markets sell salty homemade *queso fresco*. Volunteers at the Molokan Museum in Francisco Zarco sometimes make and sell a pressed, washed-rind cheese studded with chunks of roasted jalapeño. Many small *haciendas* also make aged cheeses from cow's milk, and some make fresh goat cheeses.

There are four basic types: fresh cheeses, which may be pressed and firm or soft and creamy; salty and crumbly cheeses; stringy melting cheeses; and firmer aged cheeses.

Cooked cheese dishes, such as *queso fundido*, are served with an appropriate salsa and warm tortillas. Young cheeses like *queso fresco* and *panela* are often eaten simply, with fresh fruit or with fruit pastes made from quince (*membrillo*) or guava (*ate*).

Below is a guide to the most common Mexican cheeses and suggestions for substitutions.

OAXACAN A creamy cheese with a delicate flavor that melts at low temperatures and has a tendency to run, string, and ooze. It is used in quesadillas or fundido, mixed into fillings and stuffings, or simply fried and eaten with tortillas. Substitute whole-milk mozzarella or Monterey Jack.

ASADERO Mild flavored with a distinctly rubbery texture. Asadero melts beautifully but keeps its shape and does not run. Useful in quesadillas, *gorditas*, sandwiches, and chiles rellenos or can be fried straight up in a hot pan. Sometimes called *queso quesadilla*. Substitute: Monterey Jack.

QUESO FRESCO Salty, rubbery, and wet, it crumbles easily, rather like a cow's milk feta cheese. Sprinkle on beans, tacos, salads, and enchiladas.

CHIHUAHUA OR MENONITO Mennonite immigrants from Germany brought this style of cheese to the border region in the 19th century. It is an aged cheese similar to a mild cheddar, made in large wheels.

PANELA Easy to identify by the distinct woven pattern pressed into the outside by the baskets used for molding. The flavor is mild and milk sweet. It's an excellent eating cheese, for dessert or as a *botana* (little nibble). It can be served hot. A good-quality fresh farmer's cheese or hoop cheese would be similar.

COTIXA (COTIJA) AND AÑEJO A crumbly, dry, and salty cheese, sometimes rolled in mild ground chiles to produce a reddish rind. Cotixa is widely used. It is the cheese crumbled over beans, atop enchiladas and tostadas, or in tacos. The flavor is always salty but runs the range from sweet to gamey, depending on age and origin. Substitute very dry, crumbly cow's milk feta. Añejo is aged cotixa.

REQUESÓN A soft fresh cheese with a creamy, sweet taste, similar to ricotta and used the same way.

192

DULCE POR
PIEZA
¡90° c/u

5

LA DULCE VIDA

SWEETS AND DRINKS

Into every day, a little sweetness should fall.
—Joe Saldana

While the Baja diet is generally a healthy one, serious meals nearly always include simple *postres* (pastries and desserts). Mexicans are brilliant confectioners, creating treats with an exuberant sense of color and fun, and there is a whole category of foods eaten purely for pleasure: *dulces*, or sweets. Mostly, *dulces* are for special occasions—and life here is full of reasons to celebrate, whether it is fancy cakes and *café de olla* with friends or a birthday *piñata* bursting with a bright shower of candy and toys.

Mexicans like their sweets very sweet indeed. Spain's tradition of heavy, sugar-soaked sweets (inherited from the Moors) took root here and flourished. From the mix of cultures and cuisines that so defines Mexican food come unusual sweets like candied cactus (pale green *viznaga*), sugar-crusted *chilacayote* studded with black seeds, and huge pans of sweet potato (*camote*) and squash (*calabaza*) cooked in heavy syrup until petrified with sugar.

The Spanish also imported the *churro*, my personal downfall. No one can resist these crunchy deep-fried fritters, cooked in front of you in a cauldron of bubbling hot oil and served hot, thoroughly coated with gritty cinnamon sugar. Served with a thick, chocolate *champurrado* drink, churros are proof that food doesn't have to be elaborate to be wonderful.

In the marketplaces, there are mountains of cone-shaped *piloncillo* (sugar), rich and spicy with natural molasses; combs dripping with wild-flavored desert honey; tubs of *aguamiel* (sticky agave sap, boiled down to a syrup); stacks of trimmed sugarcane; and huge cubes of purple *ate* (guava paste) and *membrillo* (quince paste).

Coconut treats—including fist-size coconut—sweet potato macaroons—are often dyed impossible shades of hot pink, lime green, and purple. Sugared coconut milk (*cocada*) is boiled down into thick white slabs and edged with a rim of magenta. *Leche quemada* (sweetened cow's milk cooked down to a caramel-colored fudge) is formed into fancy shapes, swirls, and cubes, all decked out with chopped nuts. Huge disks of shiny hard caramel are imbedded, like brittle, with peanuts, pine nuts, *pepitas* (green pumpkin seeds), and sesame seeds.

Chocolate is noticeably absent—in Mexico, chocolate is a drink (see page 228).

Unrepentant candy lovers revel in shops known as *dulcerías*, which are stacked from floor to ceiling with solid walls of sugary bliss. Nowhere else will you encounter such a bewildering array of sweets in such shamelessly unnatural colors and flavors. And the national penchant for truly shocking flavors is given full expression here. Tamarind candies, for example, rolled in chile powder, are salt/sweet/sour/hot all at once. They go off in the mouth like a bomb. Long strings of gooey caramel wafers and suckers (*chupes*) hang like streamers from the ceiling. Every corner is stuffed with sugar in its many forms, bedecked with insanely colorful wrappers—a mosaic of ultra-sweetness.

All this bounty is for stuffing into *piñatas*, hundreds of which hang in clusters from the rafters of stalls and marketplaces, papier-mâché feet swaying overhead, crepe paper streamers fluttering in the bright sun. For every child there is a piñata resplendent in juicy, riotous colors: trucks and princesses, cartoon heroes and giant fish, brave blue-green peacocks, brilliant suns, bristling silver stars, giant watermelon slices.

Frozen sweets, like *nieves* (ice creams and sorbets), tend toward the baroque—made of unusual ingredients, featuring surprising flavor combinations, and sporting floridly romantic names (see page 200). Vegetables are turned into refreshing sorbets—here again you might encounter sour, spicy, and sweet all in one mouthful. On street corners, the *helado* man sells fruit-flavored push-up pops from his cart alongside *raspados* (shaved ice doused in fruity syrup) and *paletas* (frozen fruit juices on a stick) that come in flavors from the obvious (watermelon) to the shocking (tongue-tingling sour *chamoya*).

Professional bakers in *pastelerías* create European-style cakes and petits fours as lovely as anything you could buy in Paris or Salzburg. In contrast, homemade desserts tend to be simple: usually fresh fruit, egg-rich flan in a light caramel bath, a simple cake with *dulce de leche* and sweet cream, or rice pudding dusted with cinnamon. Cookies are more like biscuits, for dunking into hot sweet coffee.

Sugar is (c'mon, admit it) *fun*. And *bajacalifornianos* are very good at having fun. In America, we sometimes forget that there should be a small place for things that exist purely for the joy of eating them. So enjoy a little of *la dulce vida*—the sweet life: gorgeous fruit, icy *paletas* and *nieves*, honey and gooey caramel, nutty treats, and simple, delicious desserts that bring home some of the best tastes of Baja.

RECIPES

Copas de Frutas
(FRESH FRUIT WITH LIME AND CHILES)

Where food carts gather, there is always at least one offering *copas*—clear plastic cups filled with pieces of perfectly ripe fruit, prepared to order, sprinkled with lime juice and ground chile, and served with a wooden pick and a smile.

Copas are the perfect antidote for a round of tacos and spicy salsas, no matter how full you might be. Choose four or five ripe seasonal fruits. Classic components include papaya, watermelon, mango, cantaloupe, pineapple, fresh coconut (see note below), banana, grapes, peach, and orange. Add jícama or cucumber for crunch and to heighten the sweetness of the fruit. Avocado may seem an odd addition, but it is a fruit, after all, and its velvety texture is fantastic. A squirt of sweetly acidic lime juice, a pinch of salt, and a light dusting of bitter, fragrant chile powder lift this into the stratosphere.

Makes 8 servings

4 or 5 kinds of ripe fruit (see note below)
Jícama (optional)
Cucumber (optional)
Avocado (optional)

TO SERVE

Fresh limes, preferably Mexican limones (see page 30), quartered

Ground guajillo or California chiles (see page 37) or Lucas Spice (see page 20)

Kosher salt (optional)

1. Bring the fruit, jícama, cucumber, and avocado to room temperature. Peel and seed as necessary and then cut into long spears or bite-size chunks 1½ inches in diameter. (The idea is to keep the juice inside the fruit. If you cut it up small, the juice will ooze out.) Combine in clear glasses or bowls, so you can appreciate the colors and textures.

2. Just before serving, squeeze some lime over each copa and sprinkle with ¼ teaspoon ground chiles and a tiny pinch of salt.

Note: Use enough fruit to allow one spear or chunk of each type per person. If using fresh coconut, you must crack it, drain, and pry the meat from the shell. Use a sharp vegetable peeler to remove all of the brown skin from the outside of the meat and then to pare the coconut into long strips. You can substitute dried unsweetened coconut shavings, or you can just sprinkle a little shredded unsweetened coconut on top.

NIEVE FROM HEAVEN

■ ■ ■

In keeping with the Mexican tradition of *big* flavors, *nieves* (ice creams and sorbets) tend toward riotous flavor combinations.

Standard *nieve* flavors include corn, rice, *horchata* (rice and almonds), peanut, *requesón* cheese, prune, fig, *leche quemada* (similar to *dulce de leche*), pine nut, and mamey (a tropical fruit with the texture of avocado and the color and taste of cooked squash). And yes, there's always vanilla.

In Tijuana, a chain of gourmet ice cream shops called Tepoznieves (named after the Aztec god of the wind) offers spearmint, cactus pear, tamarind, anise, and hibiscus, as well as chili-spiked sorbets of chamoya, jícama, cucumber, pineapple, or mango. Vegetable sorbets include avocado, beet, lettuce, carrot, or cactus (*nopal*). Other selections offer a boozy kick: coconut with gin, fig with mezcal, strawberries with wine, or straight tequila.

Many of the Tepoznieves' signature frozen desserts are as noteworthy for their fanciful names as for their unusual ingredients.

MOON'S LULLABY (*Arrullo de Luna*): Mango, peach, strawberry, and nuts

CINDERELLA'S KISS (*Beso de Cenicienta*): *Requesón* cheese, thick cream, strawberry jam, and honey

MERMAID'S SONG (*Canto de Sirena*): Sugar-crystallized pear, apple, pineapple, and peach

MAHONA (*Maona*): Rose petals, two kinds of chocolate, raisins, and almonds

THOUSAND FLOWERS (*Mil Flores*): Cream, almonds, and herbal tea

LOVE'S PRAYER (*Oración de Amor*): Marshmallow, cookies, almonds, mango, and peach

WIND'S PRAYER (*Oración del Viento*): Almond cake, chocolate, peanut, pistachio, and almond

ROSE PETAL (*Pétalo de Rosa*): Oven-roasted rose petals with honey and butter cream

QUEEN OF THE NIGHT (*Reina de la Noche*): Sesame seeds, three kinds of chocolate, and chopped fruit

LOVE'S LULLABY (*Serenata de Amor*): Coconut, pineapple, nuts, and cherry

SYMPHONY OF THE SEA (*Sinfonía de Mar*): Papaya, cherry, fig, cream, and almond

TEMPLE OF SILENCE (*Templo del Silencio*): Mango, peach, and pine nut

Basic Fruit Paletas

It seems like every corner in every town in Baja has a little shop selling colorful *paletas*, the Mexican version of the Popsicle. Old-fashioned freezer cases with sliding glass tops reveal neatly stacked rows of colorful paletas carefully wrapped in plastic, each on a sturdy wooden stick. Fuchsia cactus pear and watermelon, deep purple grape, tart tamarind, pale orange melon, pink papaya, white cherimoya, light gold guava . . . the list of flavors is often extensive, making it hard to choose just one. Paletas are made on-site, using only the very ripest seasonal fruit and a secret process known only to the *patrón*. The best paletas are laden with pieces of fresh fruit and are not overly sweet, often with a touch of lime instead. Any flavorful juice or drink may be used to make paletas.

Makes 12

8 cups finely mashed ripe fruit (see note below)   **1 cup sugar**
1 cup water   **Juice of ½ lime**

1. Mash the fruit very thoroughly, but don't puree; a little texture is nice. If the seeds bother you, remove them.
2. Combine the water and sugar; stir until dissolved. Add to the fruit and add the lime juice. Taste; the mixture should taste a little sweeter and limier than you would like, since freezing will dull the flavors slightly.
3. Pour the mixture into paleta or freezer pop molds and insert sticks. Freeze and enjoy.

Note: Choose ripe, fragrant fruit such as watermelon, melon, strawberry, Mexican papaya—whatever you like. Or use a powerful tamarind or lime drink.

Variation: For quick fruit juice paletas: Combine 1 cup water and 1 to 1½ cups sugar; boil until the sugar dissolves. Cool and add 2 cups pure fruit juice straight out of the box or can. (Prowl Asian and Latin markets for interesting juices. Some I have found: pomegranate, tamarind, cherimoya, and guava.) Add some chopped fruit (if you like) and the juice of 1 lime. Pour into paleta molds, insert sticks, and freeze.

Blackberry Cabernet Paletas

These *paletas* are strictly for grown-ups. You can enhance the flavor of fresh fruit with a judicious amount of alcohol; but if you add too much, the mixture won't freeze and you'll have a boozy slushie—which actually doesn't sound too bad.

This recipe offers a sophisticated flavor combination. See the variations below for a fun array of other alcohol-spiked options.

Makes 10

1 cup good Cabernet or other fruity red wine
1½ cups sugar
4—6 cups mixed fresh or frozen berries, mostly blackberries
Juice of 1 lime, preferably a Mexican limón (see page 30)

1. Combine the wine and sugar in a saucepan. Simmer gently for about 10 minutes to cook off some of the alcohol. Add the berries and cook for 10 minutes, or until softened and very mushy.
2. Strain through a coarse sieve into a bowl, pressing down well to force as much fruit puree through as possible (or use a food mill).
3. Measure the yielded juice; if necessary, add enough water to equal 3 cups of juice. Stir in the lime juice. Cool and taste for sugar; add more if you want it sweeter (I like this on the tart side, so I can taste the wine).
4. Pour into paleta or freezer pop molds and insert sticks. Freeze and enjoy.

Variations: For each of the following, start with 3 cups strong-flavored juice and ½ cup sugar; add other ingredients and adjust to taste.

Lime juice (preferably from Mexican limones, see page 30), grated lime zest, and ¼ cup vodka
Red Sangrita (see page 231) or Green Sangrita (see page 231) and ¼ cup tequila or mezcal
Tangerine juice and 2 tablespoons Cognac
Coconut milk, lime juice (preferably from Mexican limones, see page 30), and 2 tablespoons dark rum
Passion fruit juice and 2 tablespoons gin
Jamaica Agua Fresca (see page 227) made with sparkling wine instead of water
Pomegranate juice and 2 tablespoons cinnamon schnapps

Kumquats in Mezcal Syrup

With their glossy dark green leaves and bright orange fruit, tiny kumquats are one of winter's prettiest crops. Kumquats deliver a big flavor kick: The flesh is bitter and the skin is sweet. Here, they are poached quickly in heavy syrup that balances their natural bitterness. The whole spices add depth of flavor. The kumquats will keep, refrigerated and covered, for up to 2 weeks. They are delicious with creamy goat cheese, roast chicken or pork, and ice cream or sorbet. Or serve a spoonful with the Mexican Chocolate Bread Pudding with Apples on page 222.

Makes 5 cups

1 cup water
3 cups sugar
2 star anise pods
1 clove
1 cinnamon stick

1 piece (2 inches) fresh ginger, peeled
  and sliced
4 cups firm, very fresh kumquats, ends trimmed,
  thinly sliced
½ cup mezcal, brandy, or vodka

1. Combine the water, sugar, spices, and ginger in a large heavy-bottomed pan. Bring to a boil, reduce the heat, and simmer until the sugar has dissolved.

2. Add the kumquats and cook gently until the kumquats begin to look translucent, about 5 minutes. Stir several times during cooking.

3. Remove from the heat, add the mezcal, and cool the kumquats in the syrup. Store in the refrigerator for up to 2 weeks.

Fresh Citrus Curd

If life gives you lots of lemons (and other citrus fruits), be grateful—there are plenty of ways to enjoy their delicious scent and refreshing flavor. "Curd" is quick to make and useful to have around—think of it as instant dessert: a thick, rich, tangy-sweet sauce to slather between the layers of a freshly baked cake, dollop on ice cream, or use as filling for little tartlets.

   The same recipe may be used to make ravishing passion fruit curd (substitute passion fruit puree or juice for the citrus rind and juice). In fact, any naturally tart fruit can be substituted.

Makes about 2 cups

1 cup sugar

8 tablespoons (1 stick) best-quality unsalted butter

3 tablespoons grated rind and 1 cup juice from tart lemons,
   limes, grapefruit, tangerines, blood oranges, or other citrus

3 eggs, beaten

1. Combine the sugar, butter, rind, and juice in a 1-quart bowl. Set over a pan of simmering water; don't allow the water to touch the bowl. Stir over low heat until the butter is melted and the sugar dissolved.
2. Add the eggs and stir with a whisk until the mixture is thick and opaque. Do not boil at any time.
3. Pour the thickened curd through a strainer into a storage container. Press a piece of plastic wrap directly onto the surface and chill. Keep refrigerated and use within 1 week.

Arroz con Leche

(LEMON RICE PUDDING WITH COCONUT)

This is my absolute favorite rice pudding, both simple and rich, the perfect finale. It will make a rice pudding lover out of anyone. Cook it on the back burner as you make the rest of your dinner, so you can baby it along with lots of stirring, which develops the natural creaminess of the rice. You can also cook it in a double boiler. May be eaten warm or cold.

Makes 6 servings

1 cup medium-grain white rice (not converted)
2 cups water
1 cup heavy whipping cream
2¼ cups milk
1½ teaspoons pure vanilla extract
Grated zest and juice of 1 lemon
½ cup plus 2 tablespoons sugar

TOPPINGS

⅓ cup sweetened shredded coconut
⅓ cup heavy whipping cream
2 tablespoons confectioners' sugar
Fresh raspberries, blueberries, or other seasonal fruit (optional)

1. Place the rice and water in a 2-quart saucepan, bring to a boil, and simmer for 5 minutes.

2. Add the cream, milk, vanilla, lemon zest, and sugar. Bring to a simmer and cook over medium heat, stirring gently and continuously (a double boiler can be used for this step), until the rice is thoroughly cooked and very soft—about 20 minutes. The rice should be loose and very "saucy." It will thicken as it cools. Add the lemon juice.

3. Make the toppings: While the rice is cooking, preheat the oven to 350 degrees. Spread the coconut in a shallow pan and toast to golden brown. Keep a close eye on the coconut, stirring frequently; it will take 7 to 10 minutes.

4. Whip the cream and sugar until thickened.

5. To serve, spoon the rice pudding into champagne tulip glasses or martini glasses. Dollop a spoonful of whipped cream on top. Garnish with the coconut and berries.

Note: Thin as desired with milk.

Variations: Top individual servings with a simple meringue and brown it under the broiler.

For vegans, this dessert can be made with vanilla-flavored soy milk or coconut milk instead of heavy cream.

Omit the lemon and coconut. Soak golden raisins in hot water and a little rum. Drain and stir into the pudding. Sprinkle the top with ground cinnamon or freshly grated nutmeg.

Pineapple and Habanero Sweet Tamales

Sweet tamales are a Mexican tradition. In this recipe, sweet *and* hot makes for an enticing, surprising mouthful. Tamales take several hours to steam, so allow plenty of time before serving. Leftovers can be reheated in the microwave.

Makes about 20 small tamales

Dried corn husks for wrapping tamales (hojas)
1/3 cup best-quality unsalted butter, softened
1/3 cup shortening or lard
2 cups Maseca brand masa for tamales (dry masa)
1/4 cup finely crushed piloncillo or packed dark brown sugar
1 teaspoon baking powder

1/2 teaspoon fine salt
1 1/2 cups very ripe pineapple, well chopped
1 cup water
3 fresh habanero chiles, seeded and finely chopped (wear rubber gloves)
1/4 bunch cilantro, stemmed and chopped

1. Soak the dried corn husks in warm water for 15 minutes, or until pliable. Rinse under cold running water to remove any grit and stack neatly.
2. In the bowl of a standing mixer (or with a hand mixer), whip the butter and shortening together until well aerated, fluffy, and soft, about 5 minutes.
3. Sift together the masa, sugar, baking powder, and salt.
4. In a blender, puree 1 cup of the pineapple with the water. Stir the pineapple puree into the masa mixture and mix thoroughly.
5. Add half of the masa mixture to the shortening and beat well. Add the other half and beat in. If the dough seems dry (unlikely), add a bit more liquid. It should be very moist—thick enough to hold its shape but not crumbly.
6. Stir in the remaining 1/2 cup pineapple, chiles, and cilantro.
7. Set a corn husk with the pointed end facing away from you. Take a heaping tablespoon of masa and spread a layer about 1/4 inch thick over a 2 by 2-inch area in the center of the corn husk, leaving 1 inch on each side and 2 inches top and bottom. (If the husks are too narrow, overlap two side by side.)
8. Fold the two sides to the center, overlapping, and then fold the top down and the bottom up to overlap. (The packets should be about 3 1/2 inches long by 2 1/2 inches wide.) Tie with a strip of corn husk, if you like; it isn't essential. Repeat until all the masa is used up.
9. Take a deep stockpot with a lid. Position a round cake rack on ramekins, so there is at least 3 inches of clearance between the rack and pot bottom. Add water so there is an inch of air below the rack. Drop several pennies in the bottom of the pot. (The pennies will rattle as the water boils. When you can't hear them, you need to add more water.)
10. Set the finished tamales on the rack; place them on end, packed closely together, or shingled. Lay a damp towel over the tamales, cover the pot, bring to a boil, and steam on medium-high heat for 1 1/2 hours. When done, the tamales will still feel a bit soft. Wrap in foil to keep warm if not serving immediately.

Variation: Before folding, in the middle of the *masa* put a small piece of fresh pineapple, a couple of raisins or other small dried fruit, or half a fresh pitted cherry.

Sautéed Peaches with Brandy and Piloncillo

Stone fruit, such as peaches, nectarines, and apricots, grow well in certain areas of Baja. For a short season, usually in early summer, the tender fruit is available at the markets. Lucky people have their own trees, tucked against a sheltering wall. Peaches (or any other stone fruit, including cherries and plums) are wonderful quickly sautéed with cinnamon and *piloncillo*, then flamed with local brandy. The very simple technique is infinitely adaptable to apples, pears, and bananas as well.

   If you have a chafing dish and guests with nerves of steel, you can make this at the table after dinner.

Makes 4 servings

4 large firm peaches

3 tablespoons best-quality unsalted butter

4 cinnamon sticks

¾ cup crushed piloncillo or packed dark brown sugar

¼ cup brandy

4 small scoops vanilla ice cream

1. Peel the peaches: Dip them into boiling water for a count of 10, then drop into cool water. Peel and slice into a bowl, reserving the juices.

2. Set a heavy 12-inch frying pan over low heat and melt the butter. Add the cinnamon sticks, broken into 2-inch pieces, and cook for 30 seconds.

3. Add the peaches and piloncillo and increase the heat to medium. You want the sugar and peach juice to begin to melt together, but don't overcook the peaches.

4. Remove from the heat and pour the brandy over the peaches. Tip the pan slightly to one side and light the liquor with a long match. (Be careful that there is nothing flammable nearby—your sleeve, for example, or the curtains.) Return the pan to the heat and cook for 30 seconds. As soon as the flames have died down, spoon the peaches and sauce into bowls; top with a scoop of ice cream and a cinnamon stick.

PILONCILLO

Dark-brown cones of *piloncillo* sugar are sold in every Mexican market. It is made from boiled cane syrup mixed with a little dry lime (*cal*, the same mineral used for making *masa* for tortillas) and poured into molds to set. Coarse and moist, piloncillo tastes pleasantly of molasses; it is commonly used in *café de olla* (spiced, sweetened coffee) and *ponche* (a hot sometimes-alcoholic drink with spices served at Christmas). It is also used to sweeten crunchy cookies and to make the syrup in which yams and squash are preserved to make a popular, very sticky sweet. Dark brown sugar may be substituted, but piloncillo is less sweet and has a more complex flavor.

Date Babycakes with Nuts and Piloncillo

Dates, nuts, and molassesy *piloncillo* create charming little cakes with a buttery crust and a rich, moist, dense texture. For this recipe, use a mini bundt pan with six 6-ounce cups, which creates a hollow center ideal for filling with warm, oozing butterscotch sauce. Topped with a ball of melting vanilla ice cream, they will make you swoon with delight. (And yes, it is 3 tablespoons of vanilla!)

Makes 8 little cakes

BUTTERSCOTCH SAUCE

³/₄ cup crushed piloncillo or packed dark brown sugar
3 tablespoons milk
4 tablespoons (¹/₂ stick) best-quality unsalted butter

DATES

1 cup dates, pitted and cut into ¹/₂-inch pieces
1¹/₃ cups water
3 tablespoons pure vanilla extract
1 teaspoon baking soda

2 tablespoons best-quality unsalted butter, melted
2 tablespoons sugar

CAKE BATTER

4 tablespoons (¹/₂ stick) best-quality unsalted butter, softened
³/₄ cup granulated sugar
1 tablespoon grated orange or lemon zest
2 large eggs
2 cups all-purpose flour
1 teaspoon fine salt
1 tablespoon baking powder
³/₄ cup finely crushed piloncillo or packed brown sugar
¹/₂ cup chopped pecans or macadamia nuts

TO SERVE

Vanilla ice cream

1. Make the sauce: Combine the piloncillo, milk, and butter in a small saucepan. Bring to a boil and cook, stirring, for 2 minutes, or until slightly thickened. Remove from the heat. The sauce can be used warm or at room temperature (if you refrigerate it, gently reheat in a double boiler over simmering water).

2. Make the dates: Place the dates, water, and vanilla in a 2-quart saucepan. Bring to a boil and stir in the baking soda—it will foam up. Remove from the heat and let cool for 1 hour.

3. Brush the insides of 6 nonstick mini bundt cups with the melted butter. Sprinkle a little sugar in each cup and then rock and tap the pan around to lightly coat the insides.

4. Make the cake batter: Preheat the oven to 350 degrees. In a standing mixer, beat the butter, granulated sugar, and orange zest until well mixed. Beat in the eggs, one at a time.

5. Sift together the flour, salt, and baking powder. Stir into the butter mixture. Add the piloncillo and then the dates and all their soaking liquid. Fold in the pecans.

6. Spoon into the prepared bundt cups; fill them no more than two-thirds, since the batter will rise. (Reserve the remaining batter.) Bake in the center of the oven for 25 for 30 minutes, or until the tops spring back when poked. Remove from the oven, cool for 2 minutes, loosen the cakes carefully, and turn out onto a rack.

7. Butter and sugar the bundt cups again and bake the remaining batter.

8. To serve, wrap the cakes in foil and warm for 5 minutes in a 350-degree oven. Fill the center of each cake with warm butterscotch sauce until it spills down the sides. Top with a little scoop of ice cream.

Coconut Macaroons

Hardy coconut palms grow all over Mexico, and fresh coconut is a favorite snack. At a stand at the Mercado Hidalgo, a young man with a wicked-looking machete lops the top off a green coconut and offers you a straw and a squeeze of lime. When you are done drinking the refreshing juice, he takes back the green husk, chops it into several pieces, and digs out the jelly-like meat, which he hands to you in a plastic cup. You fix the coconut *al gusto* (to taste) with lime, chili powder, salt, or sour *chamoya*. It is light and soft-textured, hardly sweet at all.

Once dried, white coconut meat is cut into chewy unsweetened strips and added to fruit salads or dusted with chile powder and lime for a kind of tropical "chip." Shredded coconut is made into all kinds of little cakes, cookies, sweets, and candies. Creamy coconut milk is boiled down with eggs and sugar into a thick paste called *cocada,* which is sliced and eaten like fudge. (A little goes a long way.)

When I am at the market, I never fail to have a coconut macaroon. The best ones are large and deep orange; other coconut sweets may be dyed startling colors, such as lime green or hot pink.

Makes about 20 macaroons

3 cups sweetened shredded coconut

2 tablespoons all-purpose flour

1/4 teaspoon fine salt

1/2 cup sweetened condensed milk

1 teaspoon pure vanilla extract

3 large egg whites

1/2 cup sugar

1. Preheat the oven to 350 degrees. Lightly grease a nonstick cookie sheet.

2. In a large bowl, combine the coconut, flour, and salt. In a small bowl, mix together the milk and vanilla; add to the coconut. Mix very thoroughly.

3. Place the egg whites in a medium bowl and beat with a hand-held mixer until soft peaks form. Slowly add the sugar and beat until stiff. Fold one-third of the egg whites into the coconut and combine thoroughly. Gently fold in the remaining egg whites.

4. Drop by the tablespoon onto the prepared cookie sheet, forming little "haystacks" about 1 inch apart. Bake until golden brown and set, about 18 minutes.

Mexican Wedding Cookies

Easy and quick to make, these cookies always disappear fast. This recipe uses pretty bright green pistachios but also tastes fabulous with pine nuts, hazelnuts, walnuts, or pecans. Properly made, wedding cookies melt in your mouth.

Makes 36 (1½-inch) cookies

16 tablespoons (2 sticks) best-quality unsalted butter, softened
Grated zest of 1 lemon or orange
1 cup confectioners' sugar, sifted (divided use)

1 teaspoon pure vanilla extract
2¼ cups all-purpose flour
¼ teaspoon fine salt
¾ cup finely chopped pistachios or other nuts

1. Place the butter and lemon zest in a bowl. Beat with a hand-held mixer (or by hand) until light and fluffy. Stir in ¾ cup of the confectioners' sugar and the vanilla. Stir in the flour and salt. Add the nuts. Chill the dough for 30 minutes.

2. Preheat the oven to 375 degrees. Roll the dough into 1-inch balls and set on a cookie sheet about 1 inch apart. Flatten slightly.

3. Bake until just set, 7 to 10 minutes. The cookies should not brown. While still warm, dust generously with the remaining ¼ cup confectioners' sugar. Cool on a rack.

Variation: Place the dough between two sheets of plastic wrap. Roll into a rectangle 3 by 10 inches. Chill and cut crosswise into sticks ⅜ inch thick. Chill again and bake.

VANILLA

Real vanilla is expensive but worth every penny. The vanilla bean (actually a seed pod) is used in recipes with a lot of liquid, while pure vanilla extract is used in cakes and cookies. (Imitation vanilla should be avoided.) To infuse a vanilla bean: Split the pod lengthwise, scrape the black paste (which is the tiny seeds) into the liquid in the recipe, add the pod, and warm on gentle heat for about 10 minutes; do not boil. Remove the pod, which may be rinsed, dried, and used again or buried in white sugar to make vanilla sugar. Vanilla extract is simply added directly to the dough or batter.

Vanilla, an orchid, is thought to be native to tropical Mexico. It was certainly widely used by the indigenous peoples, much as it is used today, as a sweet flavoring, particularly in chocolate drinks. In the early days of Spanish domination, all vanilla came from Mexico—it is one of Mexico's gifts to cooking the world over. Today it is grown in tropical areas all over the globe, and those varieties are stronger and more perfumed; Mexican vanilla tends to be mild.

Obleas
(BUTTER COOKIES WITH DULCE DE LECHE)

Obleas are communion wafers, thin and translucent. But the term is also applied to nonecclesiastical rice paper wafers sandwiching a sticky layer of *cajeta* (a kind of *dulce de leche* made with goat's milk). They're the perfect delivery system for cajeta, since the wafers just melt in your mouth.

In this adaptation, the cookies sandwich a filling of gooey *dulce de leche*. Make the cookies any size from dainty (1 inch across) to overkill (3 inches). The dough is rich with butter and can be tricky to handle if it gets warm, so pop it in and out of the refrigerator as you work.

Makes 48 (2-inch) cookies

16 tablespoons (2 sticks) best-quality unsalted butter, softened

1 teaspoon pure vanilla extract

2⅓ cups all-purpose flour

1 cup sifted confectioners' sugar

¼ teaspoon fine salt

½ cup Dulce de Leche (see page 214)

1. In the bowl of a standing mixer, beat the butter until light and very fluffy. Add the vanilla.

2. Sift together the flour, sugar, and salt. Slowly beat into the butter. The dough should be silky soft, but not sticky; if it sticks, work in a little more flour. Divide the dough into 4 parts and shape into flattened disks. Chill for 1 hour.

3. Preheat the oven to 350 degrees. Place a piece of dough between two sheets of waxed paper or parchment paper and roll out to less than ⅛ inch thick—as thin as you can make it and still be able to handle the dough. (If the dough becomes sticky at any time, refrigerate it and work on another piece.) Chill the dough again.

4. Peel off the top layer of paper and turn the dough upside down onto a lightly greased cookie sheet. With a sharp metal cutter, cut out 2-inch circles, leaving ½ inch between the cookies. Peel away the excess dough, form it into a disk, and chill. Chill the cookies on the sheet for 10 minutes, then bake until lightly browned around the edges, 12 to 14 minutes (depending on size). Cool on a rack.

5. Roll and bake the remaining dough, including all scraps.

6. When cool, sandwich two cookies together with a layer of dulce de leche.

Variations: Filled cookies may be dipped in melted bittersweet chocolate. Or drizzled with melted chocolate. Dust the cookies with a little confectioners' sugar or cocoa powder.

Add a pinch of cinnamon or ground anise (not fennel) seed to the dough.

To make these cookies the traditional way, with cajeta, substitute half canned goat's milk in the Dulce de Leche recipe. Canned goat's milk is available in many supermarkets and Latin markets.

Dulce de Leche

Make no mistake. If you make *dulce de leche* once, you will make it forever.

Basically, both dulce de leche and cajeta are sweetened milk boiled until it caramelizes into a thick, light brown paste. Cajeta is made wholly or partially with goat's milk, which gives a gamey tang to the almost overwhelming sweetness.

The easiest way to make dulce de leche is to simmer canned sweetened condensed milk for hours, still in the can. The longer you cook it, the darker and firmer and more delicious it becomes. Once cooled, it has many uses: as a filling for prebaked tartlets or to sandwich small shortbread cookies together, as a sauce or base for ice cream, or as a filling for crepes. Dulce de leche may be thinned with more milk for use as a sauce, warmed, and poured over ice cream. Then there's always the possibility of finding yourself standing in front the refrigerator with a spoon.

Makes 1½ cups

1 can (12 ounces) sweetened condensed milk

Set the unopened can in a deep, narrow 2-quart saucepan with a heavy bottom. Add enough water to cover the can and simmer the can for 4 hours, turning it occasionally and replenishing the water as needed. Never leave the pan unattended. Allow to cool completely at room temperature before opening. Use a flexible rubber spatula to scrape the dulce de leche into an airtight storage container. Store in the refrigerator.

Churros

Churros are one of my guilty pleasures anytime I'm in Baja. Strolling down a busy street, munching them right out of a paper sack, still warm from the hot oil, gritty with sugar, and scented with cinnamon—I can't imagine anything better, except maybe a cup of thick, rich hot chocolate for dipping (see page 228). This recipe gives you authentic flavors with great ease of preparation.

Be sure to read Safe Frying (see page 248). A deep-fry thermometer is essential for best results.

Makes 20 (5-inch) churros

2 cups water
1 tablespoon sugar
1 teaspoon fine salt
2 tablespoons vegetable oil
2 cups all-purpose flour, sifted
4 large eggs
Grated zest of 1 lime, preferably a Mexican limón (see page 30)
2 teaspoons pure vanilla extract
3–4 cups vegetable oil, for frying

TO SERVE
½ cup sugar
1 tablespoon ground cinnamon

1. Combine the water, sugar, salt, and oil in a 2-quart saucepan. Bring to a boil quickly and immediately remove from the heat. Add all the flour at once and beat with a wooden spoon until well combined.
2. Transfer to the bowl of a standing mixer fitted with the paddle attachment. Beat the dough until smooth and no longer steaming hot, but still warm. Add the eggs, one at a time, beating well after each addition and scraping the sides of the bowl several times. (After each egg, the dough will break into lumps, but as you mix, it will come back together again.) Add the lime zest and vanilla.
3. Fit a small star tip (#5 or #7) in a pastry bag or cookie press. Transfer the dough to the pastry bag, filling the bag no more than halfway.
4. Pour the oil into a 12-inch frying pan to a depth of 1 inch and heat over medium-high heat to 360 degrees (measured on a deep-fry thermometer; see Safe Frying on page 248).
5. Pipe the dough in straight lines about 5 inches long, directly into the hot oil. Use a sharp knife or kitchen scissors to "cut" the dough off at the tip.
6. Fry on both sides until the churros are a deep golden brown and very crisp, 3 to 5 minutes. Drain well on paper towels.
7. To serve, combine the sugar and cinnamon. Dust the warm churros with sugar and eat immediately.

Variations: Split fat churros lengthwise and stuff them with Dulce de Leche (see page 214) or homemade raspberry jam; dust with confectioners' sugar. Or drizzle with melted chocolate.

Cream Cheese Flan
with Orange Sage Honey

Traditional flan is a heavy combination of sweetened condensed milk, eggs, and runny caramel. I much prefer this version, which despite the name is more like a light delicious cheesecake. The finished, chilled flans will pop right out of nonstick muffin pans or a soft silicone mold, or you can bake and serve in 6-ounce porcelain ramekins. Sara Polczynski developed the basic recipe, which I have adapted.

Makes 10 individual flans

ORANGE HONEY SYRUP

½ cup mesquite honey or other dark honey
(see note below)
1 fresh sage leaf
1 large orange

FLAN

1 pound cream cheese
7 large eggs
2 cups sweetened condensed milk
1 cup milk
1 teaspoon pure vanilla extract
Fresh berries or peaches (optional)

1. Make the syrup: In a small saucepan, combine the honey and sage. Remove long strips of zest from the orange with a vegetable peeler and add to the honey (reserve the rest of the orange for another use). Place over medium-low heat until warm. Let steep, off the heat, for several hours or overnight. Remove and discard the zest and sage.

2. Make the flan: Preheat the oven to 300 degrees. Set 10 (6-ounce) straight-sided soufflé dishes in a roasting pan just large enough to hold them.

3. In a blender, combine the cream cheese, eggs, condensed milk, milk, and vanilla; process until very smooth. Divide the mixture evenly among the dishes.

4. Pour hot water into the roasting pan until it comes halfway up the sides of the dishes.

5. Bake the flans for 40 to 50 minutes, or until they are no longer liquid, feel barely firm in the center, and jiggle only slightly when moved. Remove from the water bath, cool, and chill.

6. If you wish to turn out the flans, hold a dessert plate firmly over each mold and quickly turn upside down. Drizzle the tops with the honey and garnish with the fruit.

Note: The flan may be baked in one large dish, instead of individually. Increase the baking time to 1½ hours. Agave syrup (available at health food stores) may be substituted for the honey. The syrup is agave sap boiled down to a honey-like consistency, with a unique, gently herby flavor.

Chocolate Crepes with Dulce de Leche and Tropical Fruit

Crepes are a favorite fancy dessert in Mexico. This festive recipe, based on one developed by pastry chef Denise Roa, combines chocolate, caramel, cream, and fruit—in other words, perfection.

While the recipe may seem elaborate, most of the preparation may be done a day or more ahead of time. The crepes themselves can be filled and chilled several hours before dinner. This recipe makes a lot of crepes, but there are never any leftovers.

Makes 36 filled crepes

Chocolate Crepes (see below)

Dulce de Leche (see page 214)

Fresh tropical fruit and berries (see note on the opposite page)

¾ cup heavy whipping cream

¼ cup confectioners' sugar

1 teaspoon pure vanilla extract, brandy, or dark rum

½ cup purchased chocolate sauce or thick chocolate syrup (optional)

Cocoa powder or confectioners' sugar (optional)

1. Up to 1 day before serving, prepare the crepes, dulce de leche, and fruit. Keep both refrigerated.

2. Prepare the fruit and chill. Do not add sugar to the fruit.

3. Whip the cream in a chilled bowl. When it is thickened, sift in the sugar and whip until it is stiff. Stir in the vanilla. Fold a small spoonful of the whipped cream into the dulce de leche to lighten the consistency a little. Keep it fairly thick. Chill the filling and the remaining whipped cream until serving time.

4. To serve, set a single crepe in the center of a serving plate. Spoon a generous amount of fruit in the middle of the crepe. Dollop a couple of tablespoons of dulce de leche on top of the fruit. Fold the crepe in half toward you or roll into a fat cigar shape.

5. Add a tablespoon of the reserved whipped cream on top, drizzle the whole crepe with a tablespoon of chocolate sauce, and decorate the plate with more fresh fruit.

6. Put a tablespoon of cocoa powder or confectioners' sugar in a small sieve. Hold the sieve over the finished plate and tap gently to send a cascade of "snow" over the crepe and plate. Don't overdo it.

Chocolate Crepes

1 cup water

1 cup milk

1½ cups all-purpose flour

½ cup cocoa powder

4 eggs

¼ teaspoon fine salt

4 tablespoons (½ stick) best-quality unsalted butter, melted (divided use)

1. In a blender, combine the water, milk, flour, cocoa, and eggs. Blend on high speed for 1 minute. Add the salt and 2 tablespoons of the butter. Scrape down the sides with a spatula and blend again for 30 seconds. Chill for at least 1 hour. (The batter should be the consistency of light cream; add a small amount of water to thin if necessary.)

2. Heat an 8-inch nonstick pan over medium-high heat until a drop of water sprinkled into it "dances" in the pan. Brush with a very small amount of butter.

3. Use a half-filled ¼-cup measure to pour the batter into the pan; you will need 2 to 3 tablespoons per crepe, depending on the thickness of the batter. Pour the batter into the hot pan and quickly swirl the pan to coat the bottom. Return to the heat. When the edges are lightly browned and the crepe is puffing, use a rubber spatula to lift the edge; quickly grab it and turn it over. Cook for a minute more, then slide onto a plate.

4. Continue until all the batter is used up, stacking the crepes. You will want to adjust the heat so the crepe cooks quickly; if the pan is smoking, it is too hot. Brush with a very small amount of oil every so often. (May be made ahead to this point, wrapped, and refrigerated.)

Note: Plan on ½ cup of fruit per crepe. Use a combination of diced mango, papaya, pineapple, and guava, or substitute fresh berries.

FRUTAS

MANGO

Mango is a tropical fruit grown in mainland Mexico and imported to Baja. The variety most often seen is the bean-shaped, yellow manila variety, with its exquisite texture and flavor. Tiny versions known as *mangos niños* are popular. Find a perfect mango with your nose; they smell gorgeous and lush when ripe. The flesh should feel soft, but avoid bruised fruit.

PAPAYA

Spring brings heaps of huge orange papayas to the roadsides of Baja, where they are sold from makeshift stands or out of the back of pickup trucks. Some lunkers can weigh 6 to 8 pounds. The deep-coral-colored perfumed flesh and black seeds are a wonderful treat on their own or simply drizzled with a squeeze of fresh lime and some local honey, but most papayas wind up in delicious, refreshing *copas*. When perfectly ripe, a papaya's skin will be mottled orange and yellow, with some pitting. The skin will feel slightly sticky, and the fruit itself will be firm but yielding when gently pressed with a finger.

GUAVA

The perfume of ripe guava haunts the air of the outdoor markets, emanating from piles of golf-ball-size yellowish fruit with spiky little leaves on their undersides. When perfectly ripe, the skin is soft (it may mark or bruise easily, but this does not affect the flavor), and the inside is creamy, sweet, and delicious. Guavas are native to southern Mexico and have spread throughout Central and South America. Wild or cultivated, they grow easily and prolifically. There are many varieties. The larger, green-skinned feijoa is sometimes mistakenly called a guava. Guava is sometimes spelled *guyaba or guyava*.

PINEAPPLE

Pineapple (*piña*) is native to South America and was certainly known to pre-Hispanic Mexicans before Europeans took it around the world, planting as they went. Today, juicy-ripe *piña* is still among the most popular fruits in Mexico, in a *copa de frutas* or pureed into a refreshing *agua fresca*. Firmer pineapple may be grilled, caramelized, dried, or enjoyed as is. A mildly alcoholic beverage is made from the skins, fermented in water with sugar at room temperature for several days.

Quick "Dos Leches" Cake
with Damiana

Traditional *pastel tres leches* is made of homemade cake flavored with sweetened condensed milk, *dulce de leche*, and whipped cream, topped with meringue and fresh fruit; it is delicious but time-consuming. This rendition is not only quick but also light and sophisticated.

Damiana liqueur or syrup is derived from a wild herb gathered in Baja California. The herb has a long tradition of medicinal use by the indigenous peoples of Baja. Today, a liqueur made with damiana is reputed to be an aphrodisiac and comes in a risqué bottle. Regardless of your motive for putting this on the table, your guests will love it.

Makes 8 servings

DAMIANA SYRUP

2 cups sugar
1 cup water
1 vanilla bean
¼ cup damiana liqueur or 1 tablespoon
   dried damiana herb (see note below)

CAKE

8 ounces heavy whipping cream
¼ cup confectioners' sugar, sifted
6 slices (1 inch each) plain white cake or pound cake
1 cup Dulce de Leche (see page 214)
2 ounces bittersweet chocolate, grated on the coarse
   side of a box grater
Fresh berries (optional)

1. Make the syrup: Combine the sugar and water in a 1-quart saucepan. Split the vanilla bean and scrape out the seeds. Add the seeds and pod to the pan. Simmer until the sugar is dissolved. Remove the vanilla pod and save for another use. When cool, add the liqueur. You should have about 2 cups of syrup.
2. Make the cake: In a chilled bowl, whip the cream until soft peaks form. Add the sugar and whip until thickened. Chill.
3. Place each slice of cake on a dessert plate. With a skewer, poke holes in the cake about every ½ inch. Spoon the syrup over the cake and allow it to be absorbed before adding more. The cake should be moist but not saturated to the point of falling apart.
4. Gently warm the dulce de leche and spoon over the cake (thin with a little milk, if necessary, to make it oozy). Top with a cloud of whipped cream. Scatter some grated chocolate over the cream and decorate with fresh berries.

Note: Dried damiana herb is available at health food stores. To use it in this recipe, cook the sugar and water until the sugar is dissolved. Off heat, add the dried herb and set aside to steep for 30 minutes. Strain out the leaves and discard. Add the vanilla seeds and pod to the syrup and heat gently for 5 minutes. Remove the pod before serving.

If you don't have time to make dulce de leche, you may substitute Butterscotch Sauce (see page 208). But then you will have only *"Una Leche"* Cake.

Coffee Chocolate Mousse

Mexico, the birthplace of chocolate, is also the source of a terrific coffee-flavored liqueur. Coincidence? I think not. The two in combination are heavenly.

This is a super-simple mousse and looks wonderful served in demitasse coffee cups (about 4 ounces) topped with a froth of whipped cream, rather like . . . *chocolatl* (see page 228). Serve with warm, fresh Churros (see page 215) on the side.

Makes 10 demitasse servings

10 ounces best-quality semisweet chocolate, grated
   or chopped
2½ cups heavy whipping cream
⅓ cup coffee liqueur, like Kahlúa
4 large eggs, separated, plus 1 large egg white
¼ cup sugar
Ground cinnamon

TO SERVE
Cinnamon sticks

1. Dry a metal mixing bowl and set over a pot of hot, barely simmering water. Add the chocolate and allow to melt, stirring often. Be very careful not to get any liquid in the chocolate or it will harden and turn gray.
2. In a large bowl, beat the cream until medium stiff (just past soft peaks) and fold in half of the coffee liqueur. Set aside ⅔ cup of the whipped cream for decorating the mousses; cover and chill. Do not refrigerate the rest.
3. In a clean mixer bowl, beat the egg yolks with 4 teaspoons of the sugar until thick and the mixture forms a slowly dissolving ribbon when the beaters are lifted. Set aside; do not chill.
4. Thoroughly clean wire beaters and a metal bowl (preferably copper) with hot water and soap. Rinse well with hot water, then scrub with white vinegar and a teaspoon of coarse salt. Rinse again with hot water. (Bowl and beaters must be absolutely free of grease or your whites won't whip!)
5. Whip the egg whites until soft peaks form. Add the remaining sugar and beat until stiff and glossy.
6. Gently fold the egg yolks into the whipped cream. Fold the whipped cream gently into the melted chocolate.
7. Add a large spoonful of the beaten egg whites to the chocolate and stir in, then fold in the remaining egg whites, working quickly. Do not overmix; you should still be able to see little bits of the egg white.
8. Spoon into coffee cups, leaving ½ inch at the top. Wrap and chill overnight.
9. Before serving, drizzle the remaining coffee liqueur over the top of the mousses. Top with the reserved whipped cream, so it looks like chocolate froth. Dust the cream with a pinch of ground cinnamon and stick in a cinnamon stick at a jaunty angle.

Note: As this recipe contains uncooked egg, it should not be eaten by children or anyone ill or elderly.

Capirotada con Chocolate y Manzanas
(MEXICAN CHOCOLATE BREAD PUDDING WITH APPLES)

If you've never had chocolate and apples together, you're in for a treat. When this is warm, it tastes like Mexican hot chocolate with a hint of cinnamon and fruit.

The bread pudding may be baked in an 8 by 11-inch baking dish or in 6-ounce individual soufflé dishes; the cooking time may vary slightly. Either way, be sure to pull it out of the oven when puffed but still moist and creamy in the middle. The leftovers (if there are any!) make a terrific breakfast.

Makes 8 servings

3 cups milk

1¼ cups sugar, plus more for the baking dish

1½ cups chopped good-quality semisweet or bittersweet chocolate or chocolate chips

1 tablespoon ground cinnamon

1 teaspoon pure vanilla extract

¼ teaspoon fine salt

4 eggs, well beaten

8 cups firm bread cut into 1-inch cubes (see note below)

2 tablespoons best-quality unsalted butter, plus more for the baking dish

3 tart green apples, peeled, cored, and cut into ½-inch dice (about 3 cups)

TO SERVE

Crème fraîche, whipped cream, or vanilla ice cream

1. Preheat the oven to 400 degrees.

2. In a 2-quart heavy-bottomed saucepan, gently heat the milk and 1 cup of the sugar over low heat until barely warm, stirring with a whisk, until the sugar dissolves. Add the chocolate, remove from the heat, and stir until the chocolate melts.

3. Stir in the cinnamon, vanilla, and salt. Let cool. Stir in the eggs thoroughly.

4. Place the bread in a mixing bowl and pour the custard over the bread, stirring to combine. Let stand for 10 minutes while the bread absorbs the custard.

5. Melt the butter in a 10-inch frying pan. Add the apples and the remaining ¼ cup sugar. Cook, stirring constantly, until the apples are soft and the sugar has caramelized. (If the sugar begins to burn, quickly add a little water to the pan and continue.)

6. Butter an 8 by 11-inch baking dish or 8 (6-ounce) ramekins and dust the inside with a spoonful of sugar. (Overkill, but good.) Spoon the apples into the dish; top with the bread pudding mixture and any unabsorbed custard. Set on a cookie sheet and bake until puffed up but not dried out (15 minutes for individual dishes and 30 to 40 minutes for a large one).

7. Serve warm or cold, with a dollop of crème fraîche.

Note: Use a firm, homemade-style bread, a day or two old. You will also get wonderful results with day-old challah, egg bread, brioche, or even croissants.

Variations: Scatter fresh raspberries over each serving. Or add grated orange zest and a touch of Grand Marnier to the custard. Or use 1¼ cups good-quality white chocolate instead of semisweet chocolate.

Chocolate-Jalapeño Truffles

Strangely addictive! The combination of sweetness and heat, *dulce* and *picante*, is classic—it's just the ingredients that are a little unorthodox. The mixture can also be used, at room temperature, as a filling for a rich, sweet chocolate cake.

Makes about 36 (1-inch) truffles

1 tablespoon instant coffee powder

¼ cup boiling water

10 ounces best-quality semisweet chocolate, in small pieces or chips

10 tablespoons (1¼ sticks) best-quality unsalted butter, cold and cut into small pieces

2 or 3 jalapeño peppers, roasted, peeled, seeded, and finely chopped (wear rubber gloves)

½ cup unsweetened cocoa powder, sifted onto a plate

1. In a metal 1-quart mixing bowl, dissolve the coffee in the water. Add the chocolate and set on top of a pan of gently simmering water. When the chocolate has softened completely but is not hot, remove from the heat and stir until smooth.

2. Beat in the cold butter a small piece at a time, adding a new piece as soon as the previous one is almost absorbed. Beat with a hand-held mixer until creamy, about 10 minutes. Continue beating for a few minutes to cool. (This can also be done in a stand mixer, fitted with the whip attachment.)

3. Add half of the jalapeños and taste. Add more jalapeño to your taste; remember that the heat will intensify with time. Try for a balance of sweet and heat.

4. Scrape into a small, deep container, press a piece of plastic wrap on the surface, and chill overnight, until completely firm.

5. Scoop out small balls and roll in the cocoa powder. Keep refrigerated until ready to serve.

Variation: Roll the balls in finely chopped pistachios, almonds, or macadamia nuts.

BEBIDAS
(DRINKS)

Since ancient times, Mexicans have had a remarkable way with drinks. Along with their ingenious knack for combining flavors, they are lucky enough to live in a hot climate with ready access to delicious ingredients like fresh fruits, spices, sweet agave sap, and chocolate.

While Mexico is best known today for quality beers and tequila (see page 230), traditional nonalcoholic Mexican drinks are more like liquid meals—nutritious and sustaining. *Agua fresca* is a refreshing cold drink made from mashing very ripe fruit with water, sugar, and a touch of lime juice. Every *fonda* and *frutería* has a row of colorful aguas frescas on display in large, barrel-shaped glass jars, which show off the beautiful colors of the fruit. The most popular flavors are tamarind, watermelon, pineapple, guava, cucumber, papaya, melon, and hibiscus (*jamaica*).

Licuados are like light smoothies, made in a blender with fresh fruit, milk, ice cubes, honey, and vanilla. They usually incorporate banana in combination with other fruit.

Fresh extracted juices (*jugos*) are sold in *fruterías*, *paleterías,* and health food stores. They are sometimes aggressively healthful: Popular selections include fresh fruit juices as well as carrot, parsley, *chía*, alfalfa, potato, or celery combined with fruit juices. (If you add beet juice, the result is called *chupacabra*, after a fictitious vampire demon from central Mexico.)

Atole and *champurrado* are thick drinks that date back to ancient times. Both are based on ground dried corn (*masa*). Atole is dry masa mixed with salt, ground chiles, finely ground nuts, spices, and water. Champurrado is basically atole mixed with sugar and Mexican chocolate and served hot, with a *churro*.

Horchata is a milky-looking cold drink made from pureed rice and almonds, water, sugar, and lime juice. It is light and very refreshing.

Café de olla is strong coffee infused with spices—like clove and cinnamon—and sweetened with unrefined sugar (*piloncillo*). *Ponche* is a kind of spiced hot punch, more or less alcoholic, sweetened with piloncillo and tiny native apple-like fruits. It is a traditional drink during the Christmas season.

Frothy c*hocolatl* (chocolate) is sweetened with brown sugar, sugar, or honey and infused with spices, especially cinnamon. The drink is whipped to a froth with a special tool called a *molinillo* (see page 228).

Rompope is a very sweet, rich mixture, similar to eggnog, with medieval Spanish roots. It's made of spice-infused cream, honey or sugar, and egg yolks.

Opposite page:
Red and green sangritas (see page 231)

Watermelon Agua Fresca

This *agua fresca* recipe is a basic template for any soft fruit: watermelon, cantaloupe, mango, papaya, pineapple, strawberry, guava . . . the list is endless. Start by mashing the fruit and add water to make 1 gallon—but resist the urge to throw it into the blender, since good agua fresca usually has little pieces of fruit floating in it.

Make all aguas frescas a little stronger than you think you would like, as chilling dulls the flavor and ice will dilute it. Homemade aguas frescas are as healthy as they are delicious, since you can control the amount of sweetener or leave it out altogether.

Extra agua fresca can be used as a base for *paletas*.

Makes about 1 gallon

3 cups water
½–1 cup sugar
1 ripe medium watermelon
Juice of 1 lime, preferably a Mexican limón (see page 30)
Ice

1. Combine the water and sugar to taste in a saucepan and boil until the sugar dissolves. Cool.
2. Peel the watermelon, remove as many seeds as possible, and mash with a potato masher (or pulse in a food processor) until the fruit is fairly smooth. Add the water and lime juice. Taste and adjust with more sugar, lime, or water as desired. Serve over ice.

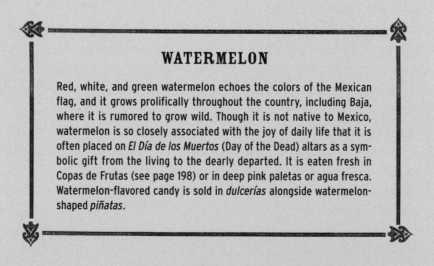

WATERMELON

Red, white, and green watermelon echoes the colors of the Mexican flag, and it grows prolifically throughout the country, including Baja, where it is rumored to grow wild. Though it is not native to Mexico, watermelon is so closely associated with the joy of daily life that it is often placed on *El Día de los Muertos* (Day of the Dead) altars as a symbolic gift from the living to the dearly departed. It is eaten fresh in Copas de Frutas (see page 198) or in deep pink paletas or agua fresca. Watermelon-flavored candy is sold in *dulcerías* alongside watermelon-shaped *piñatas*.

Tamarind Agua Fresca

Tart and sweet *tamarindo* is one of the most popular *agua fresca* flavors—so refreshing! Kids love it. See page 21 for more about tamarind and its multitude of uses.

Makes 10 cups

1 package (14 ounces) tamarind paste
2 cups boiling water
8 cups cold water
3/4 cup sugar
Ice

1. Break the tamarind paste into smaller pieces. Place in a large nonreactive bowl or 2-quart glass jar. Pour the boiling water over the paste and allow to cool. Mush it with your hands or a potato masher to make a paste.
2. Add the cold water and mix thoroughly. Add the sugar (it is supposed to be a little tart). Steep for 4 hours.
3. Strain through a fine strainer, pressing down hard to remove the tamarind seeds and fibrous strands. Chill and pour over ice.

Note: Tamarind paste is available at Latin and Asian markets.

Jamaica Agua Fresca

Jamaica are the dried ruby red blooms of the hibiscus. (Look for them in Mexican and Asian markets.) The flowers are steeped in water to a gorgeous red drink with an exotic and sensational flavor: tart, flowery, and delicious. See the "*sangría*" variation below.

Makes 3 quarts

4 ounces dried hibiscus flowers (jamaica)
12 cups water
1 cup sugar
Ice

1. Place the flowers in a large glass jar or other nonreactive container. Add the water and stir in the sugar. Refrigerate for 24 hours; it needs to be very strong. Strain and pour over ice.

Variation: To make Jamaica "Sangría": Scrub an orange, lime, lemon, and green apple. Slice the fruit and place in a large glass pitcher. Fill the pitcher with steeped hibiscus water and let stand for half an hour or so in the refrigerator. Pour over glasses full of ice, adding some of the fruit. I wouldn't blame you a bit if you wanted to add a splash of red wine, tequila, vodka, or gold rum to this.

Mexican Hot Chocolate

Light-flavored chocolate is spiced with cinnamon and nuts and whipped to a light, fluffy froth with a special wooden whisk, known as a *molinillo*. Try the drink less sweet and you will taste the chocolate more.

Makes 4 servings

1 disk Mexican hot chocolate (see note below)
1 quart milk
Sugar or honey (optional)

1. Using a cleaver or mallet, break the chocolate disk into small pieces. Heat the milk until bubbles form around the edges, stirring frequently, but do not allow the milk to boil.
2. Whisk in the chocolate and stir until melted. Remove the pan from the heat. Add sugar to taste. Froth the hot chocolate in the pan with a hand-held blender or pour into a blender jar and blend until light and frothy.

Note: Ibarra is the best-known imported brand of Mexican chocolate disks and is worth seeking out.

XOCOLATL

■ ■ ■

The Aztecs were as obsessive about chocolate as any modern society. However, instead of eating chocolate bonbons, kings and priests drank their frothy chocolate (*chocolatl* or *xocolatl*) unsweetened, spiked with vanilla, chiles, and spices and thickened with corn *masa*. Sometimes, just for fun, it would be tinted the color of blood with annatto seeds as an offering to their gods. Cocoa beans were even used as money.

The cocoa tree originated in the tropical regions of Central America and Mexico. Somehow, over millennia, the early inhabitants of the region figured out the long process of fermentation, drying, roasting, and grinding that develops the familiar bitter chocolate flavor. Even when the Aztecs dominated Mexico, they had to trade for their precious chocolate with the Olmeca and Mayan peoples who held the secret to the beans.

The sweets-loving Spanish enjoyed the energizing effects of the Aztecs' chocolate drink but not the bitterness; they added honey and sugar, more vanilla and cinnamon, to create a thick, luscious chocolate drink that sparked the first wave of chocolate mania (predating coffee) among Europe's elite class. Chocolate remained something one drank until the middle of the 19th century, when mechanical processes were developed to smooth, stabilize, and solidify chocolate liquor into the solid blocks we know today as chocolate. Chocoholics haven't looked back since.

Mexicans still like to drink their light-flavored chocolate Aztec style, rather than eat it—partly because of the difficulty of keeping such a temperamental substance in a hot climate, but mostly because they prefer it that way: heavily sweetened, spiced with cinnamon, and whipped to a froth with hot water or milk using a special wooden spindle with rings, called a *molinillo,* that looks like an elaborately carved child's rattle. Most large older cities still have special chocolate shops, where your chocolate is blended for you with your own preference of sugar and spices and your personal recipe kept on file.

Atole champurrado is a frothy drink of chocolate thickened with corn *masa* and usually eaten with Churros (see page 215).

BEYOND TEQUILA

■●■

If it's colored, don't drink it; at least that's good advice for most tequilas. But nothing can prepare you for a shot of rattlesnake mezcal, which I tasted at Mariscos Fili in Tijuana.

The colorless, slightly cloudy liquid was served after our meal in tiny shot glasses, meant to be downed in a flash. I sipped mine cautiously.

"How do they make this?" I asked. I have no problem with either rattlesnakes or mezcal in principle, though the two in combination were another matter.

"They put a rattlesnake in a big water jug," Liliaana Navarette explained, making it sound easy. "Then they fill it up with mezcal and wait until the rattlesnake dissolves." She tipped hers back with the ease of long practice. Regular mezcal has hallucinogenic properties and tastes a bit like gasoline; this was no different. I did not sense the strength or the spirit of the rattlesnake filling me, though I did have some interesting dreams that night and a slight headache the next day.

Mezcal and its better-known cousin, tequila, are certainly the most famous agave products. Tequila is made from only blue agave, grown and produced within a well-defined region within central Mexico (a controlled appellation, much like those designated for Champagne or Parmigiano cheese).

Mezcal may be made from different types of agave, anywhere in Mexico, and the fermentation process is a little different. Smoky and rich, the best mezcals are made and bottled in small quantities on a single estate and can become the focus of obsessive collecting. (Casa de Piedra winemaker Hugo d'Acosta plans to manufacture mezcal made from agave gathered in northern Baja.)

Both tequila and mezcal are made from the huge, starch-rich heart of the agave. This *piña* is pit-roasted and ground into mash with water, which is later distilled. The best tequilas and mezcals are as distinct and delicious as the finest European liquors.

Make sure that the tequila you buy is made from 100 percent agave. It is designated *blanco*, *añejo*, or—the finest grade—*reposado* (aged in wood). Which you prefer is a matter of individual taste.

Mexicans are experts at making alcohol out of just about anything vegetal and could probably make a nice drink out of the stones of the desert, were they so inclined. The sap of certain agave, known as *aguamiel*, is fermented into a drink called *pulque*. *Sotol*, a relative newcomer to the U.S. market, is made from a wild plant that grows in the Chihuahua/Texas region. The distilled liquor is comparable to tequila.

Other alcoholic drinks include *aguardiente*, meaning "fiery water." It refers to any clear, distilled liquor. The native "beers" of Mexico are made from whatever is on hand—usually fruit, cactus, or corn. *Tepache* is made from pineapple skins and water, fermented for a couple of days with spices and *piloncillo*. It is mildly alcoholic. *Pozol* is a drink made from fermented corn and water.

Colonche, or cactus "wine," is made of fermented cactus pears, or *tuna*.

Red Sangrita

Good tequila and mezcal should be treated with the same respect accorded an expensive Cognac or single-malt Scotch. Forget that silly business with salt and lime or blended margaritas; those are methods used to disguise the taste of bad tequila.

Fine tequila is *sipped* (not gulped) straight up from shot glasses, with a taste of *sangrita* to clear the palate.

Sangrita is basically a mixture of tomato, citrus juice, spice, and salt; it should be full flavored and spicy hot. This mixture has been enjoyed in Mexico for hundreds of years; it is obviously the inspiration for the Bloody Mary.

The *sangrita* should be served chilled in shot glasses alongside the tequila. A plate of cut limes is usually offered as well.

Makes 4 servings

½ cup tomato juice
½ cup freshly squeezed orange juice
¼ teaspoon fine salt

1 teaspoon bottled Mexican hot sauce
1 tablespoon freshly squeezed lime juice, preferably from a Mexican limón (see page 30)

Stir together and chill until needed.

Green Sangrita

A fun variation, spicy and tart.

Makes 4 servings

2 tomatillos, husked and washed
1 piece (1 inch) fresh serrano chile (wear rubber gloves)
5 tablespoons freshly squeezed orange juice

2 tablespoons freshly squeezed lime juice, preferably from Mexican limones (see page 30)
½ teaspoon fine salt

Cut the tomatillos into small pieces and chop the chile. Puree in a blender with the juices and salt. Chill until needed. It will separate, but stir just before serving.

Sangría

My favorite wine for making sangría is a fruity Barbera or Tempranillo blend from Baja's wine country. Nothing is more delicious on a hot day.

Makes 2 quarts

1 lemon
2 oranges
1 bottle (750 milliliters) dark fruity red wine
1 tablespoon sugar
1 green apple
Ice
Sparkling bottled water

1. Scrub the citrus fruit. Thinly slice the lemon and 1 orange. Place the fruit in a 2-quart container and mash gently with a wooden spoon. Add the wine and sugar. Let stand for a couple of hours.
2. Core and thinly slice the apple; slice the remaining orange. Put the fruit into a 3-quart pitcher. Strain the wine into the pitcher. Serve over ice and top up each glass with a little sparkling water.

CERVEZA

Mexican beers, both *güera* (blond) and *morena* (dark), are always served ice cold, preferably several at a time in small buckets packed with ice.

It's common to drink beer with a squeezed lime in the bottle, but I like mine *michelada*, which means the waiter brings a bucket of iced beers and a short tumbler made of thick, bubbly Mexican glass that has been frozen until frosty, rim dipped in chile powder and salt. You squeeze a couple of limes in and pour in the ice-cold beer. It's super frozen, colder than cold, smooth, bubbly, and salty—darn near perfection when the sun has beaten you down.

A variation on perfection, *preparada* is a michelada with a few plump, freshly cooked and peeled shrimp in the bottom of your glass. You drink down the beer and toss back the shrimp as your reward. The chabela is a supersized preparada—a bigger beer with more shrimp. It's the ideal mid-afternoon pick-me-up if you're too lazy to get up and eat a real meal.

Precios *

	Pesos	DLL
TACOS ASADA/BEEF	10.00	1.00
TACOS AL PASTOR	10.00	1.00
TACOS PESCADO/FISH	10.00	1.00
TACOS DE POLLO/CHICKEN	10.00	1.00
CONOS DE FRIJOL/CONE BEANS	10.00	1.00
BURRITOS	33.00	3.00
QUESADILLAS	10.00	1.00
QUESATACOS	15.00	1.40
QUESABURROS	38.00	3.60
CHIPS AND SALSA	10.00	1.00
CERVEZA/BEER	20.00	2.00
AGUAS FRESCAS	10.00	1.00
AGUA NATURAL 500 ML	10.00	1.00
SODAS	10.00	1.00

TACOS BEER...!

6
BAJA BASICS

If pale beans bubble for you in a red earthenware pot,
You can often decline the dinners of sumptuous hosts.
—Martial's *Epigrams*

I am still humbled and amazed by how many riffs can be played with a list of ingredients that look pretty similar until you introduce the subtle changes wrought by cooking technique, small recipe variations, and timing. I have infinite respect for the sheer ingenuity of a people who developed such a sophisticated, delicious cuisine thousands of years ago without metal implements or any of the other "necessities" of the kitchen. Today's Mexican cooks move easily among ancient and modern—European, New World, American, even Asian. Mexican cuisine is really a 500-year-old "fusion" experiment, the nuances of which are being redefined and debated still today.

Despite this culinary sophistication, knowing how to make the basics is still essential. Preparing these recipes from scratch will give your food authentic flavor along with a real understanding of the cuisine. Freshly made tortillas and home-cooked beans, for example, are amazingly good in a soul-satisfying way that cannot be captured by any commercial product. This chapter was designed to give you a thorough grounding in how to prepare the staples of the Mexican table.

In simple recipes like those that follow, cooking technique and quality of ingredients are paramount. Don't be afraid to make mistakes as you learn to handle unfamiliar products. The recipes may look long, but that is because the directions are thorough—read them through carefully to get a mental picture of the process. You will be an expert after a couple of sessions.

You do not need any special equipment, though such items as a *molino* for making fresh *masa* lend a certain air of authenticity to the proceedings. Just forge ahead with the recipes and enjoy yourself.

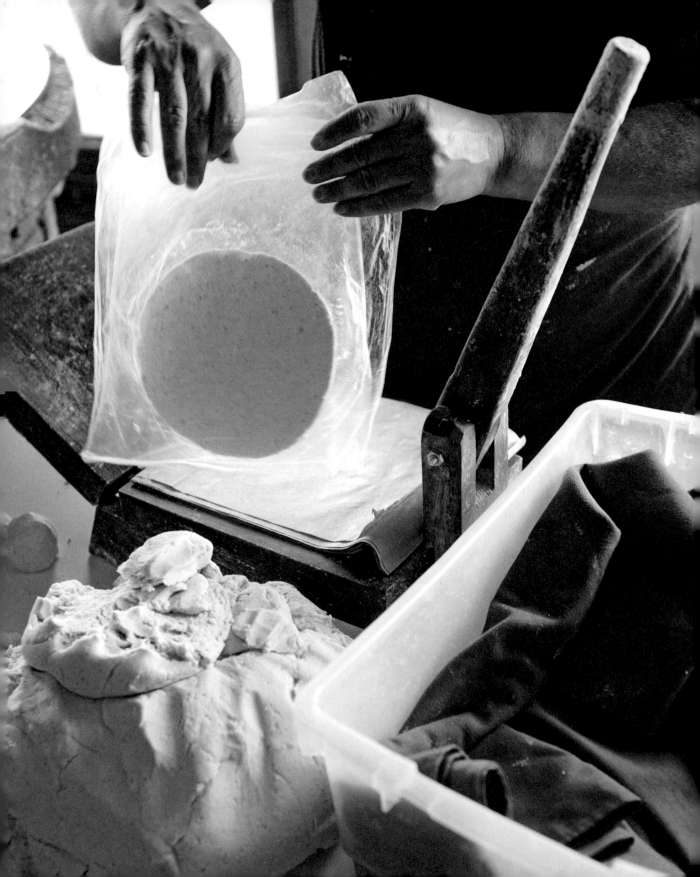

RECIPES

Corn Tortillas
(FROM DRIED CORN MASA)

Making corn *nixtamal* and *masa* dough at home is a great way to understand the ancient roots of Mexican food. The process is strung out over a number of hours, requires little but your occasional attention.

Makes 24 (5-inch) tortillas

Nixtamal (see below)
½–1 cup water

1. Grind the nixtamal with a mechanical masa mill or pulse in a food processor. The masa should have a fine texture like coarse sand. Place in a large bowl.
2. Add ½ cup water to the ground corn and stir with a fork or with your hand, tossing and turning and squooshing with your hand to mix thoroughly. Add as much of the remaining water as necessary, a tablespoon at a time, to make a very moist, soft dough that holds its shape. To test, make a small ball of dough and press flat with your fingers. If the edges crack, add water by dipping your hand in water and mixing the masa with the wet hand. Proceed with forming and cooking the tortillas (see page 241).

Nixtamal

Important: The lime used in making nixtamal is an edible variety of calcium oxide, a naturally occurring chemical compound that usually comes as a white powder. *Do not* use the lime sold at hardware stores; it is important to buy only the food-safe grade. When handling lime, do not get it on your skin or in your eyes.

　　When making the nixtamal, do not use an aluminum pot. Aluminum reacts with the lime.

4 cups dried maíz or hominy corn
8 cups water
2 tablespoons edible lime (cal or calcium oxide; see note above)

1. Carefully pick over the maíz for foreign matter, place in a colander, and wash under cold running water. Drain.
2. Place the water in a large nonreactive pot. Stir the lime into the water.
3. Bring the water to a rolling boil. Stir in the dried corn; it will immediately turn yellow. Return to a rolling boil and boil for 5 minutes. Turn off the heat, cover, and let stand for 24 hours.
4. Drain the corn into a colander. You will see that the skins have dissolved into a yellow coating on each kernel. Rinse the corn well with cold running water until most of the yellow color is gone. Then rub the corn with your hands under the water until every trace of the skins is washed away and the corn is clean. For an exceptionally fine masa, remove the small, hard nubbin at the base of each kernel.
5. The corn is now ready to be ground into dough for tortillas (*masa para tortillas*).

MASA FOR TAMALES: Clean the dried kernels for nixtamal and prepare the lime water. Boil the corn in the lime water until softened, about 2 hours, adding more water as needed. Remove the skins under running water as directed and remove the small, hard nubbin at the base of each kernel. Grind immediately and add water, as if making tortillas.

MAÍZ
(DRIED CORN)

■ ■ ■

Corn is the heart of Mexican cooking: the underpinning flavor of Mexico and the scent that lingers in the air on every street and in every kitchen. There is no substitute for it. Mexico is truly the genetic treasure house for this ancient, valuable basic food, jealously guarding its many varieties of corn from outside influences.

Dried or fire-parched corn is known in the United States as dried hominy, flint corn, or dent corn. It has very large kernels with full pointed tips and sometimes a dent in the sides. Excellent varieties of dried corn in an assortment of colors are available: the commonest are white, red, and blue. White corn is used for the finest corn tortillas, though the different colors can be used interchangeably. Red corn makes an interesting lavender *masa*, while blue corn *masa* comes out the color of fresh concrete with a really fabulous flavor.

Dried corn varies greatly in quality. Look for corn that is very clean, with few broken pieces and little foreign material. Pour the corn onto a rimmed cookie sheet and pick it over carefully for twigs, stones, or discolored kernels. I pop my purchased corn into the freezer for 48 hours to kill any stray bugs. Rinse well before using. *Maíz* can be purchased at Latin markets, bulk food stores, and health food stores and by mail or from Internet Mexican food sites.

MASA

Masa means dough. In the old days, masa was ground daily from dried corn soaked with lime, known as *nixtamal*. Then came *masa harina*—masa dehydrated and ground into a flour, rather like instant mashed potatoes. Factory mechanization of this process followed. In urban areas, corn tortillas are seldom made at home, because there's always a neighborhood *tortillería* pumping out stacks of warm, fresh, fragrant corn tortillas. However *sopes*, *gorditas*, and *empanadas* (see page 120) are still made by hand.

In the United States, dry masa (*masa harina*) for both tortillas and tamales can be purchased at Latin markets and many urban supermarkets. Fresh masa can be purchased from tortillerías and occasionally in Latin markets. Around Christmas, fresh masa for tamales (*masa preparada para tamales*) makes an appearance in markets.

CORN DEFINITIONS

ELOTE fresh corn

MAÍZ dried corn kernels

NIXTAMAL dried corn that has been soaked with edible lime and water until soft

MASA wet, heavy dough made from ground nixtamal; used to make tortillas and tamales

MASA HARINA instant masa; just add water

HOJAS (*TOTOMOSTL*) dried or fresh corn husks for wrapping tamales

Corn Tortillas 2
(FROM MASA HARINA)

Most home cooks use *masa harina* (dry *masa* flour) to make fresh tortillas, with perfectly acceptable results for considerably less effort and planning.

Makes 16 (5-inch) corn tortillas

2 cups Maseca brand masa for tortillas (*masa instantanea de maíz*)
1 cup plus 3 tablespoons water, plus more as needed

1. Combine the masa and water, first with a fork and then with your hands, working the dough into a uniformly damp mass. The dough should stick together and form a tacky ball that sticks a little to the bowl.
2. To test the dough, form a small ball and press it between thumb and finger. If it crumbles or cracks around the edges, dip one hand in water and work a little more moisture into the dough.
3. Proceed with forming and cooking the tortillas (see the opposite page).

FORMING AND COOKING CORN TORTILLAS

Tortillas may be patted out by hand or formed into balls and flattened in a tortilla press.

Patting out tortillas by hand looks easy, but take it from me, it isn't. When Melinda Perez taught me to make tortillas, she could barely stop herself from laughing as the balky dough stuck, crumbled, and balled up in my hands—while her deft fingers slapped and whirled the tender masa into perfect circles in a few seconds. My advice: Buy a tortilla press or use a rolling pin.

The other essential piece of equipment is a *comal*, or griddle, for cooking the tortillas. A thin blue-steel comal is common but tricky to use. I prefer to use a *nonstick* pan set over medium to medium-high heat. The pan must be absolutely dry; do not spray or grease the cooking surface. Wipe with paper towels between batches.

- Form the dough into balls slightly smaller than golf balls (about 2 tablespoons), being careful to make them nice and round.
- Set up a tortilla warmer lined with a clean cloth or make a "basket" out of two layers of aluminum foil.
- Heat a *comal*, griddle, or nonstick pan over medium-high heat until a drop of water sprinkled in "dances" on the surface. (Smoking hot is too hot.)
- Slit a heavy 1-quart plastic freezer bag along the sides to make two plastic squares. Position a dough ball in the center of one sheet and top with the second.
- If you are using a tortilla press, set the ball slightly toward the hinge side. Close the press, pressing gently and evenly. Don't oversquish the tortilla. It should be 4 to 5 inches across and between $1/16$ and $1/8$ inch thick.
- If you are using a rolling pin, roll out between the two sheets of plastic. (Note: If the tortilla sticks or messes up at any point, just scrape off the masa and reroll. Masa contains no gluten and can be worked indefinitely.)
- Carefully peel off the top sheet of plastic. Turn the tortilla upside down into your hand, gently peel off the other layer of plastic, and turn the tortilla directly onto the hot *comal*.
- Cook the tortilla for 1 minute on the first side; turn and cook on the other side until cooked through, pressing down lightly with a metal spatula. (Don't brown the tortillas; they're cooked when they appear dry and set.)
- Stack the finished tortillas in the prepared tortilla warmer or foil. The tortillas will seem a bit stiff when they come out of the pan, but they will steam themselves soft and flexible in the warmer. Fresh corn tortillas should be eaten within a few minutes. If you do have to reheat them, toss them back on the comal for a few seconds on each side and replace in the warmer.

Flour Tortillas

I learned the technique of making flour tortillas from one of the cooks at a lobster restaurant in Puerto Nuevo. She made huge batches of dough by hand in a gray dish pan, then rolled and cooked them one at a time — while keeping up with the demands of the whole restaurant! What tortillas they were, too . . . warm, chewy, soft, and delicious.

Many of the settlers of Baja California emigrated from the state of Sonora to the east, which is well known throughout Mexico for its fine flour tortillas. And while corn tortillas are food for the soul, flour tortillas are sometimes considered more refined.

They are dead easy to make, even if you've never handled a rolling pin. Start making the dough an hour or two before you want fresh tortillas. The dough is very quick to make by hand, but the food processor is easier still. The tortilla dough will be soft, stretchy, and resilient. Rolling a little thicker will give you a *gordita*, or thick tortilla. Small flour tortillas can be pressed out in a tortilla press.

Makes 16 (8-inch) flour tortillas

3 cups all-purpose flour, plus more for rolling
$\frac{1}{2}$ teaspoon kosher salt
$\frac{1}{2}$ cup lard or vegetable shortening
1 cup hot tap water

1. In the bowl of a food processor, combine the flour and salt and pulse several times. Cut the lard into small pieces, add to the bowl, and pulse until very thoroughly combined; the mixture will look like sand.
2. Pour the hot water slowly through the feed tube, while pulsing the machine. Stop adding water when the dough forms a ball that rolls around the bowl.
3. Turn the dough out onto a cutting board and knead until smooth, about 1 minute. The dough will be very soft. Dust the board lightly with flour to prevent the dough from sticking.
4. Cut the dough into 16 equal pieces. Form into balls. Cover with plastic wrap and set aside for at least 1 hour before proceeding, otherwise the dough will be impossible to roll.
5. Heat a comal, griddle, or nonstick pan over medium-high heat. Dust a work surface (a wooden cutting board works best) and rolling pin with flour. (Note: For this dough, a thin straight rolling pin without handles works best.)
6. Working one piece at a time, flatten a ball of dough with your fingertips, keeping the shape as perfectly round as possible. Carefully roll out the dough into a flat disk of the desired size, working from the center out. Keep the work surface scraped clean and add as little flour as possible while rolling. When you get really good at this, you don't need to use much flour.
7. Use a dry pastry brush to remove all excess flour. Toss the tortilla onto the heated pan. In a few seconds the tortilla will start to bubble; press down with a metal spatula to flatten, then flip the tortilla over and cook a few seconds longer on the other side. The tortilla is cooked when it is no longer translucent.
8. Have ready a tortilla warmer lined with a cloth. Flip the tortilla into the warmer, wrap, and keep warm while you cook the rest.

LA TORTILLERÍA

● ● ●

The flour tortillas factory is in a low, white building on an industrial street. We walk through a screen door into searing, dry heat pressing down beneath the low ceiling. Even at the counter by the door, the heat is almost unbearable.

Casual, like most Mexican work areas, the long narrow room doesn't look much like a factory. For one thing, there is almost no machinery, just a small Japanese cash register on a table, a flour-dusted mixer, and an ancient dough-cutting machine pushed against one wall. Down the center of the room are three long "tables" framed of white-painted rough timbers with tops made of the same kind of wire screen that rabbit hutches are made of.

A crew of five is hard at work on a low-tech production line that starts with many pans of soft, white balls of dough. A tall, very thin man lifts and tosses the dough, one piece at a time, onto exactly the right spot on a dough press. The press is a heated round griddle with a stamping plate that rolls back and forth, pressing the dough into lightly cooked, paper-thin disks 10 inches in diameter. The machine never stops stamping and rolling as he peels the pressed dough off the bottom plate with one hand and tosses in another ball with the other. His timing is perfect, as if he works to a metronome (he has all his fingers, so he obviously didn't learn the hard way).

Without looking, he flips the flattened dough disk like a Frisbee onto a 6-foot-long, black iron griddle that radiates smoking heat into the tired face of a youngish, pretty woman, who is armed with a white plastic spatula. The tortillas blister and balloon up on contact, and she flips each tortilla once to cook both sides. Then she scoops and tosses it with one motion onto the screened table, where it lies in a crumpled heap like a fallen fairy until another woman picks it up and gently straightens it on the wire shelf to cool. When the tortillas cool, they are stacked in tens and bagged up. They make 6,000 a day in this way.

The whole time I am watching, the crew doesn't miss a beat. It must be incredibly hard to do this all day, yet their silent partnership is like haiku, deceptively easy. The dough press is always rolling; he is always spinning dough disks. Her griddle is always full, and she turns the tortillas in exact order, keeping perfect time and tempo with her partner, flipping once, then flicking the perfectly cooked tortillas onto the cooling table.

The tortillas are warm, tenderly chewy, speckled with brown spots from the griddle, with not a vestige of raw flour. We eat one immediately, then another. It's the essence of fresh Mexican cooking—simple, perfectly executed, and meant to be eaten immediately.

Frijoles de la Olla
(BASIC PINTO BEANS)

An *olla* is a deep, medium-sized pot or casserole used for stews, beans, and soups. This recipe makes 3 cups of cooked beans, which serves four. This recipe can be doubled or tripled.

Makes 4 servings

1 cup dried pinto beans or other beans, picked over and rinsed
6—7 cups water
1 teaspoon kosher salt

1. In a large pot, bring the beans, water, and salt to a boil. Turn off the heat and let stand, uncovered, for 30 minutes.

2. Bring the beans back to a simmer and cook for $2\frac{1}{2}$ hours, or until the beans are creamy soft. Stir occasionally and add water if necessary during cooking to keep the beans submerged and easy to stir but not soupy. The beans will continue to absorb water as they cool, so don't drain them.

Note: Beans of different ages will take more or less water and more or less time, so keep an eye on them.

BEAN BASICS

If you buy beans in bulk, shop at a market with lots of turnover. The beans should appear clean and be mostly whole with good, even color. Avoid sacks of beans that appear dusty or have many broken beans; they're old.

Pick the beans over before cooking by pouring them onto a plate or a rimmed cookie sheet. Push all the beans to the left side and then scoot a few at a time to the right, examining each one as if you were panning for gold. In a sense you are; I regularly find tooth-busting pebbles.

Watch for clumps of dirt. (Beans are earthy enough on their own.) Discard any beans that are broken, shriveled, or off-color.

Rinse the beans in a colander under cold running water. Choose a deep pot, rather than a wide one, to minimize evaporation of the water during the long simmering process.

Salt the cooking water very lightly so the beans season as they cook and use filtered or spring water.

Bring the beans to a quick boil, then pull the pot off the heat and let the beans soak for 30 minutes. This stops the skins from splitting off later and floating around in the pot. Presoaking the beans overnight doesn't speed up the cooking and can cause the beans to ferment, which is *not* the best outcome.

Frijoles Refritos

(REFRIED BEANS)

No plate is complete without refried beans. The small amount of fat in this recipe lends a little creaminess and flavor to the beans and provides needed calories to hard-working people while thriftily using up every bit of food and flavor in the *casa*.

For that down-home taste, nothing beats fresh pork lard. Don't use olive oil or beef fat; it just doesn't taste right.

To make a fat-free version, bring ½ cup water to a boil, add the onions, and cook for a moment, then start mashing the beans into the hot water.

Makes 6 servings

¼ cup lard, canola oil, or other fat (see note above)
1 tablespoon minced white onion
Frijoles de la Olla (see page 244)
Kosher salt (optional)

TO SERVE
Crumbled cotixa or Jack cheese

1. Heat the fat in a heavy 10-inch frying pan or 2-quart pot. Add the onion and cook, stirring, for 1 minute. Turn the heat to low.

2. Add a ladle of the beans and their liquid; immediately start mashing them, adding more cooking liquid as necessary to prevent the beans from drying out.

3. When the first ladleful is creamy and smooth, add another scoop of beans and liquid. Continue until all the beans are mashed and fairly smooth.

4. Add cooking liquid or water as necessary to thin out to the desired consistency. (The mixture will thicken as it cools.) Taste for seasoning and add salt if necessary. Serve with a little bit of crumbled cheese on top.

Variation: To make Frijoles with Chorizo and Crema: Make refried beans as above. Just before serving, fry up some homemade *chorizo* (see page 19) and scatter it over each serving. Finish with a drizzle of thick Mexican *crema* and sliced green onions.

SMALL BUT MIGHTY

Dried beans are an enormously important food source. Highly nutritious and easy to grow, harvest, and store, beans have been cultivated alongside corn in North America and Mexico for thousands of years, with different climate areas producing strains suited to particular growing seasons and soils.

The markets of Baja carry a wealth of different types of dried beans, each with its own distinct uses and flavor. The most popular are the mottled pinto, whose creamy texture lends itself to boiling and mashing, and black or "turtle" beans. There are many other varieties of small brown beans, as well as pale green *peruvianos*. Large beans known as *habas* are cooked and mashed as a filling for *gorditas* (thick fried tortillas). Another large bean is the purple-black *ayocote*, traditionally served with *moles*.

Frijoles Borrachos
(DRUNKEN BEANS)

These beans are thick and chunky, laced with as much beer as you can handle.

Makes 10 to 12 servings

1½ pounds dried pinto beans, picked over and rinsed
12 ounces (1 bottle) beer
Kosher salt
¼ cup lard, bacon fat, or vegetable oil
2 tablespoons very finely minced white onion

TO SERVE
Mexican crema
Crumbled cotixa cheese
Sliced green onions

1. Place the beans in a small nonreactive bowl, pour the beer on them, and refrigerate overnight. Next day, transfer to a large pot. Add 1½ teaspoons salt and enough water to cover the beans by 2 inches.
2. Simmer for 3 to 4 hours, or until very tender, adding water as needed to keep the beans just covered. There should be enough liquid in the pot so the beans are easy to stir.
3. When the beans are tender, melt the lard in a frying pan over medium heat. Sauté the onion until just translucent and turn the heat to low.
4. Add about ½ cup of the beans to the frying pan and begin to mash them with a potato masher. Repeat until all the beans are mashed (this will not be a smooth puree).
5. Add liquid from the beans as needed to keep the consistency of the beans creamy and soft. As you get toward the end, season with additional salt and more beer to taste if desired.
6. Serve right away, drizzled with crema and sprinkled with cheese and green onions.

Variation: Fry ½ cup of minced onions in the oil and add the beans, but do not mash. Serve with pieces of cooked bacon or shredded pork scattered over the top.

AN ODE TO FRIJOLES

Beans *de la olla* (boiled) or *refrito* (mashed with lard) have been a staple of the Mexican diet for thousands of years, and everyone, rich and poor, eats them—the poor just eat them more often. I once worked with a man who grew up in a poor rural area of Mexico. As he used to tell us, "Every day, we ate nothing but tortillas and beans, tortillas and beans. But on Sunday [pausing for effect] . . . on Sunday, it was *beans* and tortillas."

Fortunately for him, there are all kinds of beans available for Mexican cooks, each a little different in color, usage, or flavor. Market bins overflow with pinto and black beans, but also little yellow *peruvianos;* large, dark-purple *ayocote* that are traditional with *moles;* or buttery *habas* that are mashed and stuffed into *gorditas. Mayocoba, azufrado,* and *bayo barrento* are other varieties commonly available.

Pinto beans are common in Mexico and are perfectly acceptable in any recipe. However, if you can get them, the deliciously named little brown *flor de mayo* and *flor de junio* have slightly thicker skins and a distinctive taste.

Frijoles Negros

(BASIC BLACK BEANS WITH EPAZOTE)

Black beans, while not as common as pinto beans, are a nice change from everyday *frijoles*. They are traditionally cooked with a sprig of *epazote*, a hearty plant that will happily take over a corner of your garden and reseed itself, much like cilantro. It's hard to find fresh epazote in markets, since it's very tender, but dried works just as well. Epazote is supposed to make the beans more digestible, plus it adds an indefinable, delicious taste.

Makes 10 to 12 servings

2 cups dried black beans, picked over and rinsed
1 small onion
3 garlic cloves
8 cups water

2 tablespoons kosher salt
1 fresh epazote sprig (4 inches) or ½ teaspoon
   dried epazote

1. In a 4-quart stockpot with a heavy bottom, combine the beans, onion, garlic, water, and salt. Bring to a simmer and add the epazote. Cook until the beans are very tender, about 3 hours, adding water if necessary to keep the level just over the top of the beans.

2. Toward the end of the cooking time, fish out the onion and garlic and discard. Season as needed with salt.

3. Serve the beans whole or mashed and refried.

Variation: To make Spicy Refried Black Beans: Fry as for regular Frijoles Refritos (see page 245), adding 1 teaspoon ground cumin and 2 minced serrano chiles as you fry the beans.

Tostadas
(HOMESTYLE TORTILLA CHIPS)

The most basic *antojito* is a basket of warm, crunchy tostadas, served with a myriad of salsas and toppings to stave off hunger until the rest of the meal arrives. Call them chips if you will, but this is most people's introduction to Mexican food—so let's make them right.

    This recipe makes a large quantity, from 12 to 18 dozen—but if you're going to fire up the frying pan, you may as well make a lot.

    I fry tostadas in a combination of canola oil and lard. (Please read Safe Frying below.) This gives a light taste that still has the haunting, porky twang I love and makes them taste so authentic. If you wish to reduce the amount of fat, see the three lower-fat variations on the opposite page.

Makes 12 generous servings

36 stale corn tortillas
1 cup canola or vegetable oil (do not use olive oil)
1 cup lard
Kosher salt

TO SERVE
Salsas and toppings (see the opposite page)

1. Cut the tortillas into quarters or sixths. Turn your oven on for a few minutes to warm up, then turn it off. Line a cookie sheet with a rack or several layers of paper towel.
2. On a back burner, away from kitchen traffic, heat the oil and lard in a 10-inch frying pan over medium-high heat to a temperature of 350 degrees (a piece of tortilla dropped in will immediately form small bubbles around the edge). Fry the chips without crowding until very crisp and golden brown. Drain, place on the prepared cookie sheet, and keep warm in the oven while you finish cooking the rest of the tostadas.
3. Salt lightly and serve immediately with salsas and toppings.

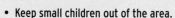

SAFE FRYING

- Keep small children out of the area.
- Have a charged fire extinguisher handy and learn how to use it.
- Never leave hot oil unattended.
- Have a tight-fitting lid for the pan nearby, in case the oil catches fire.
- Food to be fried (if it's not in a batter) should be very dry.
- Use a wide, deep pan and never fill with oil more than halfway.
- Place the pan on a back burner with the handle turned away from the edge.
- Never fry over the highest heat.
- Use a deep-fry thermometer to monitor the temperature, which should generally be between 350 and 365 degrees.
- Cook food in batches and be careful when adding the food so the oil does not splash.
- Discard oil that is smoking or has lots of burned particles.

Lower-Fat Tostadas

These tend to be a little harder in texture than fried tostadas and don't keep as well. So eat them fast.

Makes 12 generous servings

36 stale corn tortillas
¼ cup vegetable oil (do not use olive oil)
Kosher salt

1. Preheat the oven to 350 degrees.
2. Use a pastry brush to lightly brush the tortillas with oil on both sides. Stack and cut into triangles.
3. Spread in a single layer on ungreased cookie sheets and bake for 15 minutes or until crisp, turning once. Sprinkle with salt and serve warm.

Variations: To make Even-Lower-Fat Tostadas: Preheat the oven to 350 degrees. Fill a spray bottle with vegetable oil. Cut stale tortillas into triangles and place in a large mixing bowl. Lightly spray the triangles with the oil while stirring and tossing with your other hand. Spray cookie sheets very lightly, arrange the triangles in a single layer, and bake for 15 minutes, or until crisp and browned, turning once. Salt and serve immediately.

To make Completely Virtuous Tostadas: Preheat the oven to 350 degrees. In a spray bottle, combine 1 cup hot water and 1 tablespoon kosher salt. Shake until the salt is dissolved. Cut stale corn tortillas into triangles and place in a large mixing bowl. Spray the tortillas lightly with the salt water while stirring and tossing with your other hand—they should be barely dampened. Spray cookie sheets lightly with cooking spray, arrange the triangles in a single layer, and bake for 15 minutes, or until dried out and hard. Eat these right away.

SALSAS AND TOPPINGS FOR TOSTADAS

Pico de Gallo (see page 30)

Roasted Tomato Salsa (see page 32)

Raw Tomatillo Salsa (see page 44)

Naked Guacamole (see page 34)

Mexican *crema* or sour cream

Shredded chicken, shredded beef, or pork carnitas (see page 18)

Fried chorizo (see page 19), *crema*, and green onions

Frijoles Refritos (see page 245)

Spicy Refried Black Beans (see page 247)

Diced white or red onions

Shredded lettuce

Cotixa cheese, crumbled

Amparo's Spanish Rice

Amparo worked with me for only a year, but she was the perfect cook: quick, neat, and quiet. She also had a terrific palate and knew how to make simple food taste great. Her rice was always a hit with everyone.

Makes 6 servings

1½ tablespoons very finely minced white onion
1 garlic clove, minced
2 tablespoons vegetable oil
2 cups uncooked converted rice

2 cups water
2 cups tomato juice
Pinch of kosher salt

1. In a heavy saucepan with a tight-fitting lid, sauté the onion and garlic in the oil over medium heat until soft, but not browned.
2. Add the rice and cook until the rice has absorbed all of the oil and is beginning to turn golden. Pour on the water and tomato juice, add the salt, and stir to combine.
3. Turn the heat to low, cover, and cook slowly for 15 minutes, or until the rice has absorbed all of the liquid. Fluff with a fork before serving.

Fresh Tomato Rice

When your garden bursts with fresh tomatoes, try this variation.

Makes 6 servings

1½ cups water
1 ripe Roma tomato
1 large garlic clove
½ teaspoon kosher salt
1 tablespoon vegetable oil
1 cup uncooked converted white rice

1. In a blender, puree the water, tomato, garlic, and salt. Measure out 2 cups.
2. In a heavy 2-quart saucepan with a tight-fitting lid, heat the oil over medium heat and sauté the rice until it begins to toast and turn golden. Pour in the liquid, stir, cover, and turn the heat to low. Cook for about 15 minutes, or until the rice has absorbed all of the liquid. Turn off the heat and let stand for 10 minutes. Fluff with a fork before serving.

Beef Stock

Use the shredded beef in enchiladas, *chilaquiles*, or *taquitos* or simply shred and serve right in the broth. The *caldo* is an excellent, nourishing soup.

Makes 1½ quarts stock and 2 cups shredded beef

STOCK

5 cups water
1 dried ancho or guajillo chile
1 teaspoon black peppercorns
¼ white onion
2 garlic cloves
1 bay leaf
2 pounds boneless beef chuck, rump, or shoulder, cut into 2-inch chunks

SHREDDED BEEF

2 tablespoons vegetable oil
2 tablespoons minced white onion
1 garlic clove, chopped
1 Roma tomato, finely chopped

1. For the stock: Combine the ingredients in a 4-quart pot. Bring to a simmer over medium heat, then reduce the heat to low. Simmer for 3 hours, or until the meat falls apart when poked.
2. Cool for 30 minutes in the cooking liquid. Remove the meat and shred; use immediately or refrigerate.
3. Strain the stock and discard the solids. Chill quickly and remove the fat from the surface. Refrigerate and use within 2 days or freeze.
4. For shredded beef: Just before serving, heat the oil in a frying pan over medium heat. Add the onion and garlic and sauté briefly. Add the shredded meat and fry, stirring occasionally, until it starts to crisp and stick to the pan. Add the tomato and cook, stirring, a minute longer.

Chicken Stock

Save backs, wings, and trimmings to make this excellent stock. Cures what ails you, in every country.

Makes 4 quarts

4–5 pounds chicken backs, necks, and wing tips, fat removed
½ white onion
½ head of garlic
1 celery rib, cut into 4 pieces
1 small carrot, cut into 4 pieces

2 tomatoes, cut in half
10 black peppercorns
2 teaspoons kosher salt
16 cups cold water

1. Rinse the chicken pieces. Place in a large stockpot and add the remaining ingredients. Bring to a bare simmer and cook without boiling for 1½ hours.
2. Strain the stock and discard the solids. Chill quickly and remove the fat from the surface. Refrigerate and use within 2 days or freeze.

GLOSSARY

ABALÓN: abalone

ACEITE: oil

ACEITE DE OLIVO: olive oil

ACHIOTE PASTE: ground annato seeds mixed with spices, vinegar, and garlic to make a brick-red paste; from the Yucatán but used throughout Mexico

ADOBO: a marinade or spice paste

AGAVE: a succulent desert plant

AGRIA: sour

AGUA: water

AGUACATE: avocado

AGUA FRESCA: a drink made of mashed fresh fruit, water, sugar, and lime, served over ice

AHUMADO: smoked

AJO: garlic

AJONJOLÍ: sesame

A LA PLANCHA: cooked on a flat griddle

AL GUSTO: literally, "to taste"; specifically, made to *your* taste

AL MOJO DE AJO: cooked with garlic

AL PASTOR: country style or shepherd style

ALMEJA: clam

ANCHO: literally, "wide"; refers to dry chiles that are wide and short, rather than long and slender

AÑEJO: aged

ANGELITO: the Baja term for a small shark

ANÍS: fennel

ANTOJITO: a little bite of something; a snack or appetizer

ARROZ: rice. Always use long-grain white rice, except where noted.

ASADERO: the grill cook; also refers to a portable grill

ASADO: grilled over fire

ATE: a thick guava paste, served with cheese or as a sweet

ATOLE: a hot beverage of spices, thickened with corn *masa*. *Atole champurrado* is made with chocolate.

ATÚN: tuna

AVOCADO: Hass and Fuerte varieties are recommended.

AZAFRÁN: saffron

BAJA: literally, "lower." Baja California is Lower California.

BAJACALIFORNIANO: a native of Baja

BARRANCA: cliff; scrub coastal wilderness of low bushes and plants

BERRO: watercress

BIEN: good

BIRRIA: a soup of goat or mutton cooked with chiles and tomatoes

BIZCOCHO: a hard, anise-flavored cookie

BODEGA: warehouse, winery

BOLILLO: a crusty white roll, pointed at both ends

BORRACHO: drunk

BORREGO: lamb

BOTANA: a little bite of something, such as a tapa; smaller than an antojito

BOTÁNICA: a shop selling herbal remedies

BUENO: good

BURRITO: In the United States, a large flour tortilla rolled and wrapped around a variety of fillings. In Mexico, a corn tortilla squished into a doughy roll and sprinkled with sugar.

CABBAGE: Use green cabbage.

CABEZA: head

CACAHUATE: peanut

CAFÉ: coffee

CAJETA: caramelized sweetened goat's milk

CAL: edible lime, used to soften corn

CALABAZA: squash

CALAFIA: legendary queen of a tribe of Amazons. California was named in her honor, no doubt by wistful sailors.

CALAMAR: squid

CALDO: clear broth made from beef, chicken, or seafood; also refers to the hearty soups based on broth

CAMARÓN: shrimp

CAMOTE: sweet potato

CAMPECHANA: means "some of everything"

CAPIROTADA: bread pudding

CAPSAICIN: a chemical present in chiles that causes the sensation of heat

CARACOL: periwinkle or sea snail

CARNE: meat (as in *carne asada*)

CARNITAS: pork meat simmered to shreds

CAZÓN: shark (also known as *tiburón*)

CAZUELA: a cooking pot, usually made of earthenware

CEBOLLA: white, red, or yellow onion

CEBOLLITA: green onion (scallion) or spring onion

CERVEZA: beer

CEVICHE: raw seafood mixed with citrus juice and salsa

CHAMOYA: a hot-pink sauce made of salted plums, garlic, and vinegar

CHAMPIÑONES: cooked mushrooms

CHAMPURRADO: spiced hot chocolate thickened with corn *masa* (*atole champurrado*)

CHAPULINES: edible dried grasshoppers, from Oaxaca

CHARRO: cowboy

CHEESES, MEXICAN: See page 192 for a list of common cheeses and substitutions.

CHICHARRONES: fried pork rinds

CHILES: See page 36 for a list of commonly dried and fresh chiles.

CHILES DE ARBOL: long, thin dried peppers; very hot

CHIPOTLE: dried, smoked jalapeño

CHOCOLATE OR CHOCOLATL: drinking chocolate

CHORIZO: a fresh sausage of pork or beef (or in Baja, seafood) seasoned with chiles, garlic, and vinegar

CHORO: a black mussel

CHUBASCO: a furious storm in the Gulf of California

CHURRO: a long stick of dough fried in hot oil and dusted with cinnamon and sugar; eaten warm and fresh from the fryer. Served alongside hot chocolate or *champurrado*.

CILANTRO: a tender green herb, also known as fresh coriander. In Mexico, only the leaves are used.

COCADA: coconut "fudge"

COCINA: kitchen

COCINA DE AUTOR: original cuisine

COCINERAO: cook

COCO: coconut

COCKTEL: The *cocktel de mariscos* is pieces of cooked seafood (usually a combination of shrimp, octopus, clams, and squid) combined with tomato sauce or ketchup, the cooking liquid from the seafood, diced cucumber, and *pico de gallo*. Topped with hot sauce and diced avocado and eaten with crackers.

COLORADO: red

COMAL: a flat griddle of steel or earthenware

COMIDA: food

COMIDA CORRIDA: a small home-style restaurant serving pre-made food

CON: with

COPA: cup

COPA DE FRUTAS: a cup of mixed ripe fruit sprinkled with lime juice and ground chile

CODORNIZ: quail

COTIXA OR COTIJA: a type of salty, crumbly cow's-milk cheese

CREMA: thick cream, similar to crème fraîche. When slightly soured, it's called *crema agria*.

CREPAS: crepes

CRIOLLO: of the New World (Creole), a mixture of European and native

CUCARACHA: cockroach

CURANDERO: a practitioner of folk and herbal medicine

DAMIANA: a wild herb; also a liqueur by the same name flavored with the herb

DÁTIL: date

DÍA DE LOS MUERTOS: Day of the Dead; observed November 1 and 2

DIABLA (A LA DIABLA): spicy tomato sauce

DISCA: a large pan with a wide rim and a shallow center well for frying

DULCE: sweet

DULCE DE LECHE: sweetened caramelized milk

DULCERÍA: a shop selling candies and other sweets

ELOTE: fresh corn

EMPANADA: a small half-moon pie, with a variety of fillings; fried or baked on a griddle

EMPANIZADA (MILANESA): breaded with crumbs

ENCHILADA: literally, "with chiles"; *tortillas* dipped in red or green chile sauce, rolled around a filling

EPAZOTE: the herb *Chenopodium ambrosioides*; has slight taste of mint

ESPINA: thorn

ESPINAZO: marrow or spinal cord

ESTOFADO: stew

FIESTA: a party, large or small

FLAN: a firm egg custard, baked in a dish coated with caramel; turned upside down for serving

FLOR: flower

FLOR DE CALABAZA: squash flower

FONDA: a small sit-down restaurant serving home-style foods

FONDO: little bits of caramelized meat juices that stick to the bottom of the sauté pan

FRIJOLES: dried beans, such as pinto or black beans

FRIJOLES REFRITOS: literally, "refried beans"; cooked beans mashed to a thick paste with lard or oil and a small amount of onions

FRUTERÍA: a shop that sells prepared fresh fruit and juices: *copas de frutas*, *paletas*, fresh juices, salads

FUNDIDO: melted cheese

GALLETA: a wafer or thin cookie

GORDITA: a small, thick corn tortilla, stuffed with mashed beans (*habas*)

GORDO: fat

GUADALUPE: the Virgin Mary, patron saint of Mexico

GUAJILLO CHILE: a shiny, dark-red dried chile with a distinctive flavor (the taste of enchilada sauce) but little heat; commonly used in sauces

GUAJOLOTE: turkey, also called *pavo*

GÜERO: literally, "blond" or "light-skinned." Also used to refer to Americans, blond or not. The *güero chile* is pale yellow green, the size and shape of a jalapeño.

GULF OF CALIFORNIA: the body of water that separates Baja California from mainland Mexico; formerly known as the Sea of Cortés

HABAS: dried broad beans, similar to dried fava beans. They're boiled and mashed into a puree and used to stuff *gorditas*.

HARINA: flour. *Masa harina* is dried and ground *masa*, for tortillas. *Harina de arroz* is rice flour; *harina de trigo* is wheat flour. *Integral* is whole-wheat flour.

HASS AVOCADO: a black, pebble-skinned avocado; preferred for Mexican cuisine

HELADO: a frozen sweet

HIERBAS: herbs, also spelled *yerbas*

HIGO: fig

HOJAS: dry corn husks used for wrapping tamales; also refers to any kind of leaf

HONGOS: mushrooms in their natural state

HORCHATA: a beverage made of rice "milk"; sometimes thickened with ground almonds

HUACHINANGO: true red snapper

HUEVO: egg

HUITLACOCHE: a mushroom-like corn fungus, considered a delicacy

JAIBA OR XAIBA: long-legged spider crabs

JAMAICA: dried hibiscus flowers

JAMÓN: ham

JITOMATE: red tomato

JUGO: juice

LANGOSTA: lobster

LAUREL: bay leaf

LECHE: milk

LECHE QUEMADA: caramelized milk fudge topped with nuts

LEMON (LIMA OR LIMÓN AMARILLO): Lemons are used occasionally, but they're not a substitute for limes!

LENGUA: tongue

LICUADO: a drink made from fruit, ice, and milk pureed in a blender

LIMÓN: thin-skinned Mexican lime (see page 30)

LONCHERÍA: similar to a *fonda*, serving *tortas* and quesadillas

LUCAS: slang term for "crazy"; also refers to a popular seasoning mix of ground *guajillo chiles*, citric acid, and salt

MACHACA: air-dried shredded beef. In Baja, a form of *machaca* is made from skate (ray) wings.

MAGUEY: a type of *agave* used to make *mezcal*, among other things

MAÍZ: dried corn

MALECÓN: boardwalk or promenade

MANCHEGO: aged Spanish sheep's-milk cheese

MANO: literally, "hand"

MANTARRAYA: bay ray, manta ray, or skate

MANTECA: lard

MANTEQUILLA: butter

MARGARITA: a drink made from tequila, freshly squeezed lime juice, and a drop of Cointreau

MARISCOS: shellfish, such as oysters, shrimp, clams, mussels, squid, periwinkles

MASA: dough, especially dough for making tortillas or *tamales*

MASA HARINA: dehydrated, finely ground *masa*. Add water to make *masa* for tortillas or *tamales*.

MAYONESA: mayonnaise, often spiked with lime juice

MEMBRILLO: a dark amber paste, made from quince

MENUDO: the ultimate hangover cure–a spicy soup made from the lining of cow's stomach (tripe)

MERCADO: market. The Mercado Negro is Ensenada's seafood market.

MESOAMÉRICA: the term used by anthropologists to describe the pre-Conquest world of Mexico and Central America

MESQUITE: a large shrub that grows prolifically in dry areas. The wood is used for grilling and smoking; the seeds were an important native food source.

MEZCAL OR MESCAL: a distilled beverage made from the hearts of various types of *agave*. Similar to tequila.

MIEL: honey

MILANESA: lightly breaded and fried

MOLCAJETE: a traditional cooking tool of Mexico. It's a shallow bowl carved of lava rock, which stands on three legs (see page 45); used with a pestle called a *tejolote*.

MOLINILLO: a carved wooden stick, spun between the palms of the hands to whip hot chocolate into a froth

MOLINO: the mill used to grind *nixtamal* into *masa*

MORENO: dark

NARANJA: an orange

NEGRO: black

NICKNAMES: Mexicans frequently refer to each other with less-than-flattering terms: for example, *el pelon* (the bald guy), *la flaca* (the skinny woman), *el gordo* (the fat guy), and *el chapparito* (shorty).

NIEVE: literally, "snow"; used to refer to frozen desserts such as ice creams, sorbets, and gelatos

NIXTAMAL: dried corn that has been soaked with edible lime (*cal*) until swollen and soft. *Nixtamal* is ground into *masa* dough for tortillas and *tamales*.

NOPALES OR NOPALITOS: young paddles of the *nopal* (beaver-tail) cactus

NUEVA COCINA: modern Mexican cooking

NUEVO: new

OILS AND FATS: Use a light-flavored vegetable oil, such as canola or corn oil, unless olive oil is specifically called for. For baking, use solid shortening or butter, according to the recipe. In most cases, margarine may be substituted. Good-quality pork lard (*manteca*; best if you render it yourself) will give a distinctive, delicious flavor to flour tortillas and pork *tamales*. Solid vegetable shortening may be substituted.

OLIVES: Use either the mild, Mission-type green olives in brine or the black Greek or Italian varieties in brine. But dried or salt-cured olives, California pitted (mild) black olives, and stuffed olives are not suitable for Baja recipes.

OLIVO: olive

OLLA: a large pot

ONIONS: For general use, white onions are preferred; they are milder and sweeter than common yellow onions. Red onions, shallots, green onions (scallions), and so-called spring onions (with a baby onion on the end of a green stalk) may be called for in certain recipes. Onions should be cut just before use. Their bite may be "tamed" by rinsing under cold running water and draining thoroughly.

OSTIÓN: oyster

PAELLA: rice cooked in a wide, shallow pan with various sea-sonings, meats, and seafood. It's traditionally made over a wood fire.

PAELLERA: the pan used for making *paella*. It's round, comes in various sizes, and is shallow, with a sloping rim.

PAELLERO: one who makes *paella*

PALETA: frozen fruit juice on a stick

PALETERÍA: the place where *paletas* are made and sold

PAN: bread

PANADERÍA: bakery

PANELA: basket; also a type of fresh cheese that is molded in a basket

PANGA: an open wooden fishing boat with high sides, powered by an outboard motor

PAPALOTL: a native herb that tastes like very strong cilantro. The name means "butterfly" in the Aztec language.

PARILLA: a grill, set over charcoal, wood, or gas

PASILLA: a type of dried *ancho chile*

PATA DE MULA: a kind of small scallop

PATO: duck

PATRÓN/PATRONA: the owner or boss

PEPINO: cucumber

PEPITA: pumpkin or squash seed

PESCADO: a fish that has been caught

PICADILLO: literally, "finely chopped." *Picadillo* is always ground meat cooked with raisins and olives.

PICANTE: spicy

PICO DE GALLO: fresh raw salsa made with chopped tomatoes, onion, cilantro, and jalapeños or serranos

PILONCILLO: unrefined sugar; cane syrup boiled until dark brown and poured into cone-shaped molds

PIÑA: pineapple; also refers to the pineapple-shaped heart of the *agave* plant that is used to make tequila

PIÑATA: a hollow papier-mâché figure filled with candies and toys

PISMO CLAM: a very large clam, up to 5 inches across. Eaten raw in *cocktels* or stuffed and roasted.

PITAYA OR PITAHAYA: a deep-maroon cactus fruit with many tiny seeds; good eating

PLANCHA: a large, heavy steel griddle

PLAYA: beach

POBLANO: a widely used fresh *chile*; dark green, large, and wide, with shiny skin. It's used for *rajas* and *chile relleno*.

POLLO: chicken

PUESTO: a food stall or cart, usually serving only one thing. No chairs or tables.

PULPO: octopus

PULQUE: a mildly alcoholic beverage fermented from the sap of the *agave*

PUNTA: coastal point or headland

QUELITE: See *papalotl*.

QUESADILLA: a *masa* disk folded over a simple filling such as cheese or beans, cooked on a *comal*

QUESO: cheese (see page 192)

RAJAS: *poblano chiles* that are charred, peeled, torn into strips (literally, "rags"), and sautéed with onions and garlic

RASPADO: shaved ice topped with flavored syrup, like a Hawaiian shaved ice

RELLENO: stuffed

REQUESÓN: soft fresh cheese, similar to ricotta

SABOR: taste, flavor

SALSA: sauce

SAL: Salt. No, all salts are not the same! Salts come in a wide variety of textures and flavors. I prefer to use kosher salt for cooking. Made without additives, it has a clean light flavor. If you use regular table salt, reduce recipe amounts by one-third and adjust to your taste from there. Sea salt: Depending on its origin, its taste may range from extremely salty to bitter, "minerally," earth-flavored, or almost sweet. I use sea salt *on* things, not for cooking; for example, I might sprinkle sea salt on tomatoes for a crunchy, salty hit of flavor.

SANDÍA: watermelon

SANGRÍA: a wine punch with fresh fruit

SANGRITA: a drink sipped alongside tequila; usually made of tomato juice, hot *chile*, citrus, and salt.

SEA OF CORTÉS OR SEA OF CORTEZ: the old name for the Gulf of California

SESOS: brains

SHRIMP: Shell-on wild Mexican shrimp are preferred. Farmed shrimp (such as most Asian imports) are recommended but with reservations (For more information on sustainable seafood choices, see page 52.).

SOFRITO: a combination of flavoring ingredients (usually onion, garlic, and tomato) cooked in the pan before adding other ingredients. *Paella* always begins with a *sofrito*.

SOPA: soup

SOPE: similar to an open-faced sandwich. *Sopes* are thick disks of corn *masa* that are toasted, then fried and topped with any combination of meat, salsa, cheese, lettuce, and onions.

SUSTAINABLE FISHERIES: fisheries that are monitored to prevent overfishing and environmental problems (For more information on sustainable seafood choices, see page 52.)

TACO: a soft corn tortilla with any combination of fillings, *salsas*, and garnishes

TAMALES: made from coarse corn *masa* that's smeared on corn husks, topped with a highly flavored filling, folded to enclose the filling, and steamed for several hours

TAMARINDO: a tiny fruit with a powerful sweet-tart flavor; available as whole seed or in paste form

TAPENADE: a thick paste of olives and other flavorings

TAQUERÍA: a taco stand

TAQUERO: the cook at a taco stand

TEJOLOTE: a lava-rock pestle used with a *molcajete* for grinding

TELERA: an oval-shaped, soft white roll, also known as a *bolillo*

TEQUILA: liquor distilled from the heart of the blue *agave*; can be called tequila only if made in the state of Jalisco

TOMATILLO: Always available fresh from Latin markets. Looks like a small green tomato in a papery husk but is not related to the tomato. Has hard flesh with an acidic flavor. Remove the husk and rinse under warm water before using. Used for green salsas.

TORITO: a stuffed jalapeño or *güero* pepper

TORTA: sandwich

TORTILLA: a round disk of corn or flour *masa*, thinly rolled and cooked on both sides on a hot griddle

TOSTADAS OR TOSTADITAS: stale corn tortillas cut into pieces and fried until crisp; served with *salsa* or guacamole as a *botana*

TOTOPOS: See *tostadas*.

TRIPA: tripe

TUNA: a red ripe cactus fruit (called *joconoiste* when green)

UVA: a grape

VALLE: valley

VANILLA: Use vanilla beans infused in liquid or real vanilla extract, according to the recipe directions. Imitation vanilla is not recommended.

VEGAN: a stringent vegetarian style of cooking, using no animal products of any kind

VENDIMIA: the grape harvest

VERDE: green

VERDOLAGAS: soft leafy greens with small leaves, called purslane in the United States

VINEGAR: Use Heinz distilled white vinegar, unless another type is specifically called for. Rice and cider vinegars are too sweet.

VINO: wine

YERBABUENA: mint

INDEX

Underscored page references indicate boxed text. **Boldfaced** page references indicate photographs.